About the author

Julian Agyeman is a professor [illegible]on-mental policy and planning at Tu[illegible]ersity. He is an environmental social scientist whose expertise and current research interests are in the complex and embedded relationships between humans and the environment, whether mediated by institutions or by social movement organizations, and the effects of this on public policy and planning processes and outcomes, particularly in relation to notions of justice and equity. He is co-founder and editor of the international journal *Local Environment: The International Journal of Justice and Sustainability* and his books include *Just Sustainabilities: Development in an Unequal World* (with co-editors Robert D. Bullard and Bob Evans, 2003), *Sustainable Communities and the Challenge of Environmental Justice* (2005) and *Cultivating Food Justice: Race, Class and Sustainability* (with Alison Hope Alkon, 2011). He is series editor of *Just Sustainabilities: Policy, Planning and Practice* (Zed Books).

INTRODUCING JUST SUSTAINABILITIES

POLICY, PLANNING, AND PRACTICE

Julian Agyeman

Zed Books
LONDON | NEW YORK

Introducing Just Sustainabilities: Policy, Planning, and Practice was first published in 2013 by Zed Books Ltd, 7 Cynthia Street, London N1 9JF, UK and Room 400, 175 Fifth Avenue, New York, NY 10010, USA

www.zedbooks.co.uk

Set in Monotype Plantin and FFKievit by Ewan Smith, London NW5
Index: ed.emery@thefreeuniversity.net
Cover design: www.roguefour.co.uk
Printed and bound in Great Britain by CPI Group (UK) Ltd, Croydon, CRO 4YY

Distributed in the USA exclusively by Palgrave Macmillan, a division of St Martin's Press, LLC, 175 Fifth Avenue, New York, NY 10010, USA

A catalogue record for this book is available from the British Library
Library of Congress Cataloging in Publication Data available

ISBN 978 1 78032 408 1 hb
ISBN 978 1 78032 409 8 pb

CONTENTS

FIGURES AND TABLES

Figures

Tables

ACKNOWLEDGMENTS

Over the past two years, a number of people have had a role in helping me conceptualize this book, research it and write sections of it. I'm hugely grateful to all of you. Specifically, I'd like to mention Duncan McLaren for his invaluable input into researching and writing many parts of Chapter 1, 'Introducing just sustainabilities' and Chapter 5, 'Conclusions.' Similarly, the research and writing of my former students Ben Simons, on 'the local,' and Molly McCullagh, on food policy councils, with help from Jaclyn DeVore gave shape to Chapter 2, 'Food.' To former students Molly Cooney-Mesker, who researched and wrote on public space, place and place-making in parts of Chapter 3, 'Space and place,' Julia Prange, who wrote on Bogotá, and Cameron Petersen, who researched and wrote parts of the section on streets and streetscapes, I thank you for your enthusiasm and time. I thank Jennifer Sien Erickson, Alison LeFlore and Molly McCullagh, all former students, for your insights, research, and writing in Chapter 4, 'Culture.' My sincere thanks also to Bob Evans whose intellect and friendship over the past twenty-five years have supported my work.

This book is dedicated to my mother, Margaret, who nurtured my interests, encouraged my curiosity and pushed me to ask the right questions rather than only seeking answers.

INTRODUCTION

It is now ten years since the publication of *Just Sustainabilities: Development in an Unequal World*, edited by myself, Bob Bullard, and Bob Evans. In that book we broke new ground by embarking on a sustainability and sustainable development-based discourse, but one that focused explicitly on equity and justice – on the links between environmental quality and human equality. In this book, *Introducing Just Sustainabilities: Policy, Planning, and Practice*, the first in a series from Zed Books, I want to move the conversation on by doing two things. First, in Chapter 1, I want to acknowledge the origins of the concept of *just sustainabilities*, and then I want to develop it further, reflecting on the new and related thinking that has, over the past ten years, helped to strengthen the concept theoretically, policy-wise, and practically as a basis for developing more just and sustainable communities. Second, using Chapter 1 as the theoretical base of the book, I want to explore and develop three of the more significant themes within just sustainabilities: food, space and place, and culture.

Food, space and place, and culture may seem like odd, selective, even eclectic choices for a book about sustainability, but I chose them for three reasons. First, they are of growing interest but are under-researched and under-theorized in terms of their contribution to achieving just sustainabilities. Second, as I show in subsequent chapters, their consideration necessitates what Europeans call joined-up thinking, thinking across policy domains, as there are significant linkages and overlaps between them in relation to policy and planning for equity, justice, and inclusion. Third, each has a growing literature that may not be known by, but has implications for, policy-makers, planners, practitioners, and activists alike.

In terms of food, Chapter 2 looks specifically at two areas of interest to just sustainabilities. One area is a *locus of action*, 'the local,' which is dominant in food movement discourse but where there is a notable absence of an explicit recognition of just sustainabilities concerns involving the ability of minority, immigrant, refugee, and low-income populations to produce, access, and consume healthy and culturally appropriate foods. The other area is a case study of an *organizational form*, North American food policy councils (FPCs), which theoretically are representative and collaborative committees that help coordinate food-related activities that foster the local (or state or provincial) economy, protect the environment, and strengthen the community via the food system. The case study looks at FPCs' attempts to include diverse community voices and the tools they use to do this.

Next, in Chapter 3, I look at space and place, and argue that as spaces of recreation and resistance, spaces of relaxation and reflection, or as spaces of security and surveillance, public spaces offer unlimited possibilities in relation to achieving just sustainabilities. I look at the growing discourse in planning and policy-making around *place-making*, using examples from Dudley Street, Boston MA, and Bogotá, Colombia, to show how equity and justice can be a focus. I also look at place-making as, among other things, the contestation of historical narratives, where some narratives are privileged above others. In the second part of the chapter, I look at the *democratization* of streets; that is, the growing success in reclaiming space for people in streets that had previously been allocated almost exclusively to private cars. The US narratives of 'complete streets' and 'livable streets' frame the message that streets are ultimately public spaces, and that they should be spatially just – everyone in the community should have equal rights to space within them. I will also look at contestations of the complete streets narrative: some low-income neighborhoods and neighborhoods of color argue that changes such as bicycle lane additions and street accessibility improvements will foster gentrification, thus further diminishing their rights and roles in the community.

In terms of culture, Chapter 4 will look again at public space and place but this time through the concepts of *difference* and *interculturalism*. As difference increases in cities worldwide, how do we think about, plan, design, maintain, and ultimately mainstream *culturally inclusive spaces and places*, and, equally importantly, how do we develop *culturally inclusive practices*? In addition, however, I ask how we can do this in a way that inculcates and then mainstreams culturally inclusive practice. This has implications for the difference, diversity, and cultural make-up of urban design, planning, and policy-based professions, and for the cultural competency of those professionals and elected officials.

Finally, in Chapter 5, I will attempt to close by teasing out some significant themes emanating from the earlier chapters and by looking at the implications of reformist change or system transformation on the likelihood of achieving just sustainabilities.

1 | INTRODUCING JUST SUSTAINABILITIES

Why just sustainabilities?

The ideas of 'sustainability' and 'sustainable development' began to achieve prominence in the 1980s among local, national, and international policy-makers and politicians, together with policy entrepreneurs in non-governmental organizations (NGOs). A significant contributing factor was the 1987 World Commission on Environment and Development's report *Our Common Future*, or more commonly, the Brundtland Report. Following the 1992 United Nations (UN) Conference on Environment and Development (the so-called Rio Summit or Earth Summit), there has been a massive increase in published and online material dealing with 'sustainability' and 'sustainable development.' This has led to competing and conflicting views over what the terms mean, what is to be sustained, by whom, for whom, and what is the most desirable means of achieving this goal. To some, the sustainability discourse is too all-encompassing to be of any use. To others, the words are often unthinkingly prefaced by 'environmental' and 'environmentally,' as in 'environmental sustainability' or 'environmentally sustainable development.'

Beginning as a critique of what I eventually called the 'equity deficit' (Agyeman 2005, 44) that still pervades most 'green' and 'environmental' sustainability theory, rhetoric, and practice, the *just sustainabilities* concept began to take shape in the early 2000s, when I, Bob Bullard, and Bob Evans wrote:

> Sustainability cannot be simply a 'green', or 'environmental' concern, important though 'environmental' aspects of sustainability are. A truly sustainable society is one where wider questions of social needs and welfare, and economic opportunity are integrally related to environmental limits imposed by supporting ecosystems. (Agyeman et al. 2002, 78)

Integrating social needs and welfare, we argued, offers us a more 'just,' rounded, and equity-focused definition of sustainability and sustainable development, while not negating the very real environmental threats. A 'just' sustainability, we argued, is therefore:

> The need to ensure a better quality of life for all, now and into the future, in a just and equitable manner, whilst living within the limits of supporting ecosystems. (Agyeman et al. 2003, 5)

While defining 'just sustainability,' we used the term 'just sustainabilities' because we acknowledged that the singular form suggests that there is one prescription for sustainability that can be universalized. The plural, however, acknowledges the relative, culturally and place-bound nature of the concept. For instance, a piece in the *New York Times* (9 October 2011), 'When the uprooted put down roots,' highlighted the growth across the US of 'refugee agriculture' among, for example, Somalis, Cambodians, Liberians, Congolese, Bhutanese, and Burundians. This story gave me pause to think about the potential of new agricultures to help us reimagine what constitutes 'local foods.' Is it, for example, what our increasingly diverse populations want to grow and buy locally as culturally appropriate foods, or is it what should be grown locally according to the predominantly ecologically focused local food movement? A just sustainabilities approach would suggest the former.

Similarly, the environmental movement with its dominant 'green' or environmental sustainability discourse does not include strategies for dealing with current or intra-generational inequalities and injustice issues within its analysis or theory of change. While researching a BBC TV program in the early 1990s, I asked a Greenpeace UK staffer if she felt that her organization's employees reflected the diversity of multicultural Britain. She replied calmly: 'Equality? That's not an issue for us. We're here to save the world.' I can understand what she means. She thinks, as do a lot of environmental organizations, that as her organization is saving the world, the environment, for *everyone*, an inherently equitable act, there's no need to look at, for instance, who's at the Greenpeace table in terms of the workforce, the board of directors, and, in short, who's setting the agenda.

Twenty years on, however, British researchers Wilkinson and Pickett (2009) have changed the debate. Now equality is an issue, and a big one. In *The Spirit Level: Why equality is better for everyone*, they revealed what many of us had suspected. Based on 30 years' research, the book convincingly demonstrates that societies that are more unequal are bad for most everyone – rich as well as poor. The data and the comparison measures Wilkinson and Pickett use in their book allow global comparisons. The differences are striking, even among the supposedly 'rich' countries. Virtually every contemporary social and environmental problem – violence, obesity, drugs, physical and mental illness, life expectancy, carbon footprint, community life and social relations, long working hours, teen birthrates, educational performance, prison populations, you name it – is more likely to be worse in less equal societies.

In terms of moving toward just sustainabilities, and especially combating climate change, Wilkinson, Pickett, and De Vogli (2010) argued that there are three reasons why greater equality is necessary. First, inequality drives competitive consumption, or the desire for materialistic satisfaction ('keeping up with the Joneses'). People with materialistic values exhibit fewer pro-environmental behaviors and have more negative attitudes toward the environment. This drive toward materialism, to consume, pushes up carbon footprints. Second, cohesion and levels of trust are higher in more equal societies, leading to more public-spirited actions toward the common good. Evidence they cite includes smaller ecological footprints, higher levels of recycling, fewer air miles, lower levels of consumption of water and meat, and less waste production. Finally, developing sustainable communities needs high levels of adaptability, innovation, and creativity. They cite that more equal societies show higher levels of patents granted per capita, positing that this is because people are more socially mobile and possess higher qualifications.

Educational attainment requires investment in human capital and potential. As a geography teacher in the UK in the early 1980s, I was confronted by a student of mine called David, who said: 'Sir, what do thickies [dumb kids] like me do now we've finished our exams?' Nothing in my education had prepared me for this. David was not dumb. He was an average kid who felt he'd failed himself and us, his teachers. He hadn't. We'd failed him in our inability to help him flourish and find out what he was good at. We were, of course, far too quick to tell him what he wasn't good at and he'd internalized this, probably to this day. Twenty-five years later I was traveling in Ghana and was stopped by a young woman selling hot peppers. She asked me if I wanted to buy her peppers, and quickly assured me that I shouldn't think of her only as a seller of peppers – she was trying to make money to pay for her education.

Two instances, thousands of miles and 25 years apart, made me fully realize the need for a just sustainabilities approach to development. People around the world are simply trying to flourish, to develop their capabilities, and to realize their potential. In the environmental movement, the loss of environmental potential is rightly lamented: 'Every acre of rainforest we lose might have held a cure for cancer.' To me, however, David in the UK, the Ghanaian hot pepper seller, and African American men generally, more of whom are in prison than in college,[1] comprise the tip of the iceberg of global inequality. They represent a desperate planetary waste of human potential and denial of capability. These could be the future researchers discovering those cures for cancer.

This loss of potential is every bit as profound as the loss of environmental potential as we destroy the rainforest and other ecosystems. Of course, a focus on increasing both human potential and environmental potential is necessary if the spirit level is to balance. So what's the message? From global to local, human inequality (the loss of human potential) is as detrimental to our future as the loss of environmental potential, and only a just sustainabilities approach to policy, planning, and practice has an analysis and theory of change with strategies to transform the way in which we treat each other and the planet.

Toward just sustainabilities

The definition of just sustainabilities above focuses *equally* on four essential conditions for just and sustainable communities of any scale. These conditions are:

- improving our quality of life and wellbeing;
- meeting the needs of both present and future generations (intragenerational and intergenerational equity);
- justice and equity in terms of recognition (Schlosberg 1999), process, procedure, and outcome; and
- living within ecosystem limits (also called 'one planet living') (Agyeman 2005, 92).

I will take each of these four conditions in turn and expand on them. Of course, in reality, just sustainabilities can only be fully interpreted as an integrated whole, and these conditions are deeply interconnected (and thus their separation here is somewhat arbitrary).

Improving our quality of life and wellbeing In this section I will explore why improvement in wellbeing is essential for both justice and sustainability, and why economic growth cannot be relied upon to deliver just sustainabilities. I will also ask whether wellbeing can be delivered without continued economic growth. I will consider better yardsticks for progress that are based on wellbeing and will begin to consider the sort of economic models that might enable social wellbeing and flourishing.

There are several reasons why the achievement of just sustainabilities requires improvement in wellbeing and quality of life. For the vast majority of the world's people – in poorer developing economies – there are patent shortcomings in health and wellbeing. Some of these can be overcome through conventional economic growth and increased material consumption. But even in wealthy societies it is arguable that the majority of people are not able to experience a good quality of life, as a result of various sources of stress. However, justice implies that all people should have the capability to flourish (Sen 2009), and flourishing must mean more than simply survival. Moreover, it is also fairly obvious that, in a democratic system, winning public support for policies inspired by just sustainabilities would require the delivery of some sort of improvement in quality of life.

Growth and wellbeing Conventional economic growth cannot be relied upon to deliver wellbeing and quality of life for a number of reasons. First, there is serious doubt over the ability of the economy to continue to generate rates of growth adequate to allow for population growth and consumption increases (Harvey 2011). Second, there are potentially serious limits to the growth model arising from environmental factors (notably climate change). Finally, there is little evidence of a sustained relationship between growth and wellbeing, especially at higher levels of income and consumption.

Setting aside for a moment the underlying challenge of environmental sustainability, the capacity of the economy to generate continued growth has been cast into question by the crises of recent years, which were predicted by economists such as Stiglitz (2002). Neo-Marxists such as Harvey also suggest that the last phase of growth was achieved

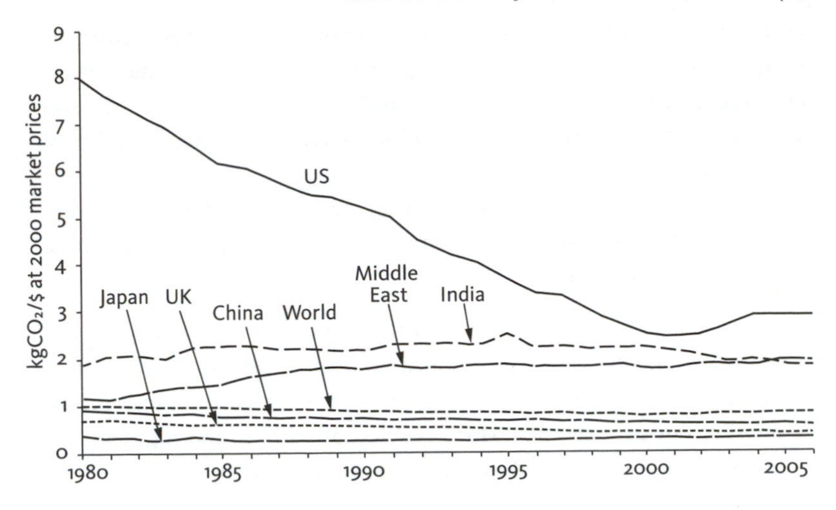

1.1 Carbon dioxide intensity of GDP across nations: 1980–2006 (*source*: Jackson 2009, 70)

through an unsustainable credit boom, which saw long-term increase in indebtedness, finally running aground on the economic impossibility of making secure loans to the unemployed and insecure in society (Harvey 2011). Harvey suggests that following the financial sector boom and bust, further bubbles might arise in 'green technology' or healthcare, especially on the frontiers of nanotechnology. However, future cycles of boom and bust in these areas seem unlikely to provide the levels of global growth required to provide increased wellbeing in conventional economic models.

In terms of environmental sustainability, while there is clearly still further scope to sidestep problems such as peak oil by paying ever more to obtain it, achieving continued compound growth, while at the same time successfully limiting carbon emissions to a sustainable level, is a technological challenge beyond anything previously achieved. Jackson (2009) reports that the carbon intensity of every dollar came down by a third in the last three decades, but total carbon emissions have still increased by 40 percent since 1990 (see Figure 1.1).

For everyone to have a chance of having a standard of living equivalent to those in Western Europe by 2050, Jackson calculates that we would have to increase our technological efficiency 130-fold, ten times faster than anything that has happened in the past. While authors such as von Weizsäcker et al. (1997) have offered convincing models for achieving a decoupling of economic activity from environmental consumption at up to four times the current level, and others have identified targets between 20 and 50 times the current level (Reijnders 1998), a factor of 130 would seem to lie in the realm of science fiction.

Sarkar (2011, 165) also argues that technological solutions are impractical. He suggests that our unpaid debts to nature are a source of our present prosperity:

> Exhausted deposits of non-renewable resources ... cannot be refilled. Since the future generations will most certainly have to live in an environment degraded by us, we can say that the impoverishment of our descendants, which we accept without the slightest qualm, is also a source of our huge present-day surplus.

Even if high rates of growth could be sustained, past evidence suggests that this would not deliver increased wellbeing for all. The failure of growth to trickle down to benefit poorer groups in all societies is well documented, and can be seen most dramatically in India, where income inequality has widened rapidly alongside high growth rates. Nair (2011) argues that the Chinese experience, despite creating a massive middle class, is little different. His conclusion is that in the face of resource and environmental constraints, Asia as a whole must seek new models of consumption, which he terms 'consumptionomics.'

At the other end of the scale, Wilkinson and Pickett's (2009) work on the corrosiveness of inequality has strongly confirmed previous claims that continued growth in rich societies adds little if anything to wellbeing (see Figure 1.2). In wealthy societies they find much stronger relationships between income distribution and health and wellbeing. In other words, above a certain threshold, greater equality makes far more difference to real lives than greater income. In particular, the relationship between the material standard of living and rising life expectancy observed in 'developing' countries breaks down, and is partly replaced by a positive correlation between greater equality and longer lives (see Figure 1.3).

All this could be taken to suggest that economic depression or recession should be welcomed as a positive trend for just sustainabilities. However, without a guided transition to a different economic system, this is not so. Jackson (2009) notes one real dilemma arising from the role of growth as a 'stabilizer' for the economy (mopping

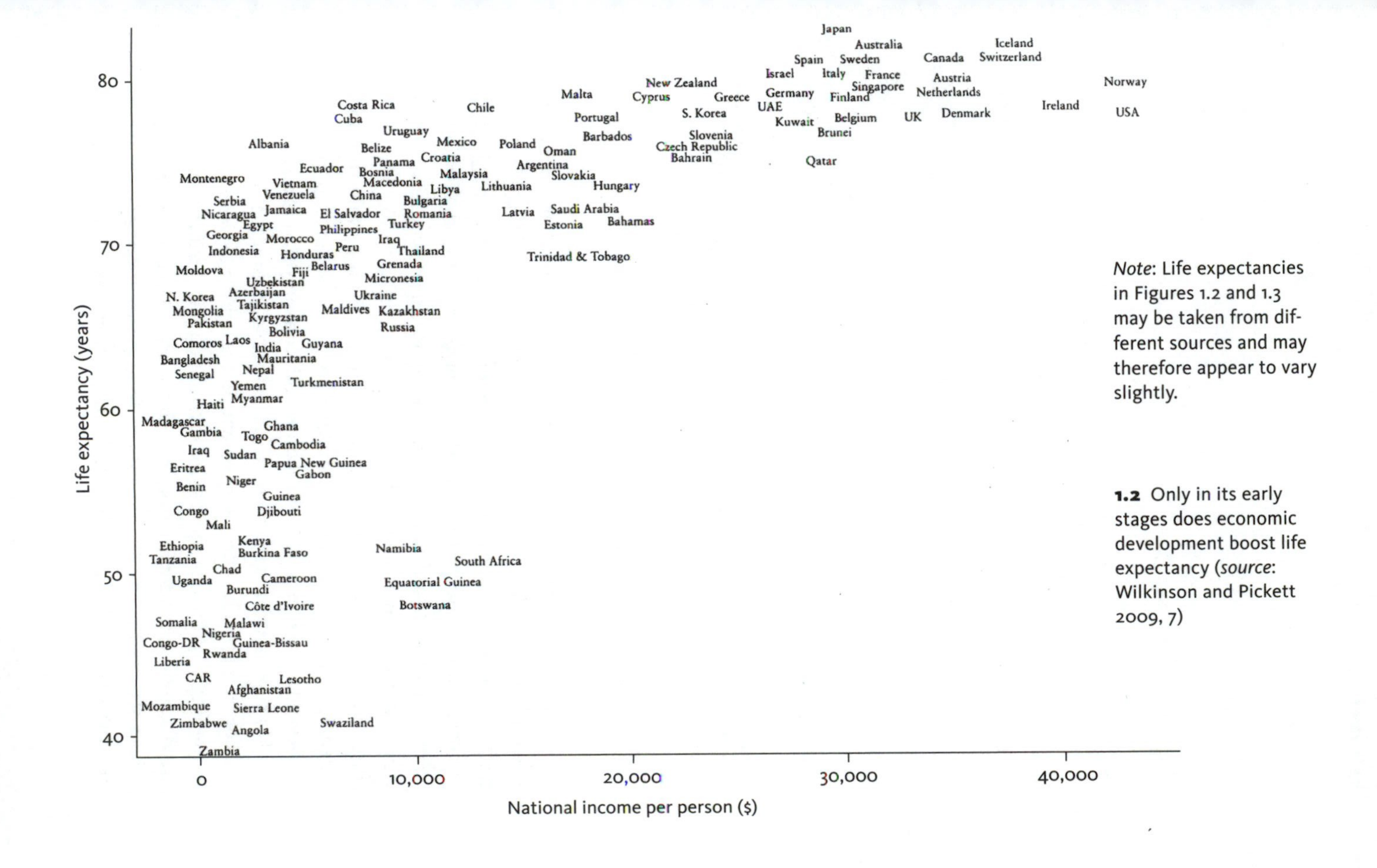

Note: Life expectancies in Figures 1.2 and 1.3 may be taken from different sources and may therefore appear to vary slightly.

1.2 Only in its early stages does economic development boost life expectancy (*source*: Wilkinson and Pickett 2009, 7)

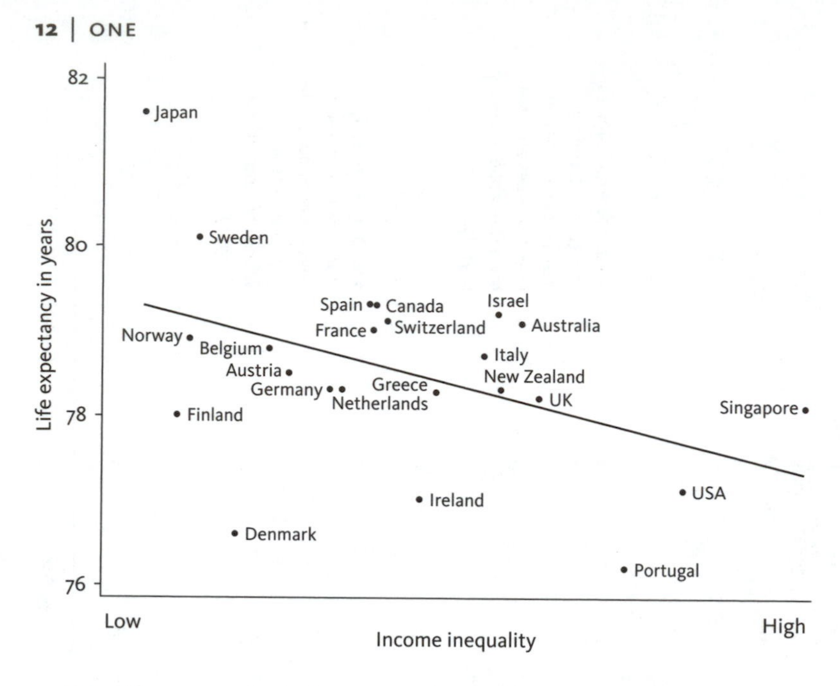

Note: Life expectancies in Figures 1.2 and 1.3, and income inequality in Figures 1.3 and 1.8, may be taken from different sources and may therefore appear to vary slightly.

1.3 Life expectancy is related to income inequality in rich countries (*source*: Wilkinson and Pickett 2009, 82)

up productivity increases). He sees 'no clear model for achieving economic stability without consumption growth' (ibid., 10) but suggests that sharing out work and increasing leisure time might help stabilize output, and that with higher savings rates the challenge may be more manageable (both permitting higher investment in sustainability infrastructure, and reducing current consumption rates). In other words, he appears to propose a transfer from private to public consumption. Jackson also notes the positive relationship between growth and wellbeing at low income and consumption levels.

This suggests that growth remains desirable in much of the world. Moreover, if growth simply stalled within the current system, it would do nothing to reduce inequality, and could equally well trigger further retrenchment and domination by elites. Finally, current economic infrastructures for energy generation, food production, and transport are environmentally intensive, and unless they are replaced, even a low- or no-growth economy will still be likely to exceed environmental constraints within a few decades.

Intriguingly, there is also evidence that the failure of the growth model to address inequality is a fatal internal shortcoming in that, far from the economy requiring inequality to function, inequality is a source of economic instability and thus detrimental to wellbeing.[2] Authors from a range of economic traditions, including Harvey, as noted previously, have suggested that growing inequality lay at the heart of the global financial crisis. We can conclude not only that growth per se does not necessarily deliver wellbeing, but that greater equality could both enhance wellbeing and stabilize economies. One consequence of such an analysis is that relying on economic measures as indicators of wellbeing is undesirable.

Measuring wellbeing The foregoing is clearly much more than just a critique of the use of gross domestic product (GDP) as an indicator of wellbeing. But the fetishism of GDP is a serious part of the problem, and one that was brought starkly to US attention in a 1995 *Atlantic Monthly* article by Clifford Cobb, Ted Halstead, and Jonathan Rowe: 'If the GDP is up, why is America down?' Institutions respond to the indicators they measure: politicians routinely promise GDP growth, call it 'progress,' and seek to deliver it regardless of the consequences. A wide range of alternative indicators have been suggested that attempt to measure what matters. Typically, they either adjust economic measures such as the Index of Sustainable Economic Welfare (ISEW) (Jackson et al. 1997) or the Genuine Progress Indicator (Cobb et al. 1999), or combine economic indicators with others, such as health and education, to create a composite indicator such as the Human Development Index (HDI) (Klugman 2010).

For example, the ISEW adjusts GDP to take account of defensive expenditures on environmental protection and healthcare, and to value leisure and unpaid work (primarily carried out by women in the home). From this it can be seen that even simply adjusted economic indicators can be much more just. The ISEW also confirms an apparent divergence between wellbeing, which is stagnating, and growth, which has continued in 'developed' economies since the 1970s (see Figure 1.4).

In 2010, the HDI was adjusted to account for inequality in all three of its components, recognizing that 'significant aggregate progress in health, education and income is qualified by high and persistent

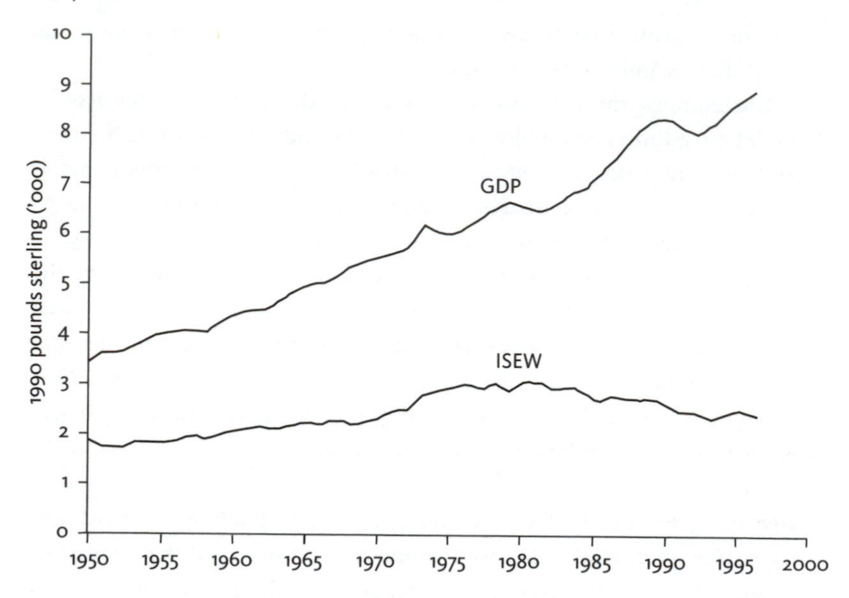

1.4 UK Index of Sustainable Economic Welfare (ISEW) contrasted with GDP per capita, 1950–96 (*source*: www.parliament.the-stationery-office.co.uk/pa/cm199798/cmselect/cmenvaud/517-iv/8042116.htm)

inequality, unsustainable production patterns and disempowerment of large groups of people around the world' (ibid., 85). The report estimates that global aggregate HDI is reduced by almost a quarter as a result of inequalities.

The innovative Happy Planet Index (HPI) (Abdallah et al. 2009) takes life expectancy, self-reported life satisfaction, and ecological footprint into account to create a measure of the ecological efficiency of delivering long and happy lives. Costa Rica is top of the table in this respect. While the HPI does not take equality directly into account, the work of Wilkinson and Pickett (2009) suggests that equality can be expected to correlate strongly with both life expectancy and life satisfaction.

Stiglitz et al. (2011), in a report commissioned by former President Sarkozy of France, also call for a shift to measuring what matters – from measuring economic production to measuring people's wellbeing. The report distinguishes between an assessment of current wellbeing and an assessment of sustainability. Wellbeing arises from both economic resources, such as income, and from non-economic aspects of people's lives. Whether this wellbeing can be sustained over time depends on whether stocks of capital that matter for our lives (natural, physical, human, and social) are passed on to future generations.

Among other things, Stiglitz et al. call for indicators that broaden income measures to include non-market activities and give more prominence to the distribution, not only of income, consumption, and wealth, but also of non-economic 'quality of life' factors. Quality of life depends on both people's objective conditions and their capabilities. Stiglitz et al. call for steps to improve measures of people's health, education, personal activities, and environmental conditions, including robust and reliable measures of social connections, political voice, and insecurity that can be shown to predict life satisfaction.

Stiglitz et al. also recognize the pitfalls of single measures such as ecological footprint. They conclude that sustainability assessment requires a dashboard of indicators that represent variations of some underlying 'stocks' (of natural, physical, human, social, and economic capital). In addition, they find a need for a clear indicator of our proximity to dangerous levels of environmental damage (such as that associated with climate change or the depletion of fishing stocks).

These alternative indicators typically have common features: direct measures of wellbeing, attention to inequality, and a recognition that conventional economic measures can be misleading. Importantly, it is not only nations that are beginning to think this way. In 2009, the US state of Maryland formed 'an inter-agency workgroup to explore how government could measure social wellbeing and develop an alternative metric to traditional economic indicators' (Maryland Genuine Progress Indicators). In 2011, the city of Seattle, WA, made a Happiness Proclamation[3] and the city of Somerville, MA, in its local census asked: 'On a scale of 1 to 10, how happy do you feel right now?'[4]

There are profound implications for the economic models that might be designed if more politicians and decision-makers pursued an agenda based on just sustainabilities, maximizing and optimizing such alternative indicators of happiness and wellbeing. It is no coincidence that the state of Maryland and the cities of Seattle and Somerville are also creatively looking at issues of food, space, and culture, the focus of the chapters of this book.

Alternative economic models An alternative model must address the shortcomings of the conventional model in delivering wellbeing and an overall improvement in people's quality of life. These shortcomings include, crucially, the phenomenon of jobless growth (Rifkin 1995). One of the main mechanisms by which economic prosperity can be turned into wellbeing is through the provision of fulfilling employment (helping to meet a range of personal and social needs, not just income). If growth does not generate additional jobs, then it does little to meet needs and increase wellbeing. Rifkin (ibid.), while identifying the trend of jobless growth early, saw it as largely a product of technology, to which we should adapt. He describes the coming challenge as redefining the role of the individual in a near workerless society, with new models for informal work and for income distribution. As we will see below, new models offer scope for more than informal work, but Rifkin (ibid.) usefully highlights the importance of the distribution of work, as well as the distribution of income.

Similarly, to increase wellbeing, an alternative model will need to redistribute consumption between private and public forms. Increased private consumption is closely related to the inequalities and related social problems identified by Wilkinson and Pickett (2009), and by Schor (1999a). A larger share of public consumption, providing more shared resources, and a revived public realm or sphere and public spaces, especially in cities, is a key tool for improving quality of life and wellbeing, as I will demonstrate in Chapter 3.

Indeed, Low and Smith (2006, 6) argue that 'an understanding of public space is an imperative for understanding the public sphere' and that 'investigating the means of making and remaking public space provides a unique window on the politics of the public sphere, suggesting an even more powerful imperative to the focus on public space' (ibid., 7). People around the world continue to fight for, create, and re-create public spaces in light of the 'neoliberal onslaught,' which brought a 'trenchant reregulation and redaction of public space' (ibid., 1). From pocket parks to PARK(ing) Day, they are carved from the commerce of urban centers, the abandoned industrial structures of yesteryear, and even the automobile-lined streets. These spaces are used for everything from people-watching to Occupy movements, and other political (r)evolutions.

In the US a national alliance called the Right to the City (RTTC) emerged in 2007 as a unified response to gentrification, with a call to halt the displacement of low-income people, lesbian, gay, bisexual, and transgendered (LGBT) individuals, and youths of color from their historic urban neighborhoods. Harvey (2008, 23) casts the net wider: 'The freedom to make and remake our cities and ourselves is ... one of the most precious yet most neglected of our human rights.' He highlights the common impacts and causes of slum clearances in Seoul and Mumbai, and the privatization of public spaces in US cities.

One of the environmental implications of such privatization is increased environmental consumption resulting from the loss of shared resources. However, one of the more hopeful of recent trends is the re-emergence of resource-sharing and collaborative consumption in many major cities. Typical is Shareable.net:

> The online magazine that tells the story of sharing. We cover the people and projects bringing a shareable world to life. And share how-tos so you can make sharing real in your life. In a shareable world, things like car sharing, clothing swaps, childcare coops, potlucks, and cohousing make life more fun, green, and affordable. When we share, not only is a better life possible, but so is a better world. The remarkable successes of sharing projects like Zipcar, Wikipedia, Freecycle, Kiva, and Creative Commons show this. They tell a hopeful story about human nature and our future, one we don't hear enough in the mainstream media.

Clearly, delivering wellbeing justly and sustainably requires a change in market structures, not just in the content of what we purchase (Holt 1999; Frank 1999). This takes us far beyond the current fad of green consumerism or its food equivalent, 'voting with your fork' (see Chapter 2), and even beyond the clearly growing ability of consumers to influence companies' social responsibility throughout their supply chains through the use of social media (Hertz 2009; Mainwaring 2011).

But even changing the content of consumption to reflect justice or sustainability has been slow. Consumption, as Schor (1999b) points out, is defended as a personal choice and a matter of liberty. As a result, green consumerism is seen as a voluntary, choice-based policy – choice-editing[5] – which, despite the strong advocacy of bodies such as the former Sustainable Development Commission in the UK, has made little headway in terms of delivering change. Witness also the media and corporate outcry when unlimited choice to travel by air is challenged, and the way in which policy options such as personal carbon allowances or other forms of rationing are seen as extreme options. It might be argued, especially in the US, that personal liberty to consume is part of the freedoms that constitute justice. But this would be an extreme interpretation. Sen (2009) reminds us that justice is measured in more than consumption or even wellbeing. It is measured in capabilities and freedoms, too. He also points out that with freedoms come accountabilities – in this case justifying state intervention.

Insofar as consumption is a signal of status, it is also likely to have an impact on health through the same psychosocial mechanisms that create a relationship between hierarchy and health. Research (primarily in workplaces) shows that poor health is correlated with subordinate positions and lack of autonomy (Wilkinson and Pickett 2009). Improving quality of life therefore not only requires changes in consumption, but also in production, particularly to provide more autonomy. Wilkinson and Pickett (ibid.) speculate that much could be achieved with the wider deployment of organizational models such as cooperatives and other mutuals.

At a fundamental level, any potential economic model based around just sustainabilities will need to recognize the dependency of the economy on a diverse, healthy society. Such a society would have a healthy public sphere, a healthy public space, and a healthy environment, rather than assuming that a larger economy can in some way compensate humans for damage to society, places, and the wider environment. As we shall see, both social and environmental health are dependent, to a large extent, on greater justice and equality.

Co-production One suggestion is that the concept of just sustainabilities lends itself to the idea of co-production as a possible alternative economic model. In its broadest sense, reflecting the capabilities approach of Sen (2009), it sees people as assets rather than burdens, invests in their capacities, and uses peer-support networks in addition to professionals to transfer knowledge and capabilities. In narrower, economic terms, co-production refers to the involvement of the user or consumer in the design, manufacture, and delivery of the goods and services they consume, thereby blurring the distinction between the producer and the user/consumer.

Co-production is already emerging in several diverse arenas. While some of the trends (an increase in self-assembly of furniture) offer little benefit, others (domestic energy generation, timebanking/time-dollar schemes, self-build co-housing, open source software) exhibit key benefits in that people are reclaiming and reinventing work, refusing to be directed by the logic of capital, engaging their individual and collective capacities to invent, create, shape, and cooperate without monetary incentive.

The New Economics Foundation (NEF 2008, 11–12) notes:

> The past three decades have produced many successful examples of co-production in action around the world. People living in the squatter camps of Orangi in Karachi successfully provided themselves with drainage and mains water faster and at a far lower cost than the more accepted top-down method. Habitat for Humanity has made houses more affordable by including work building other people's homes into the mortgage payments. Some programmes – notably the Bolsa Escuela scheme in Brazil that pays mothers to make sure their children attend school – have made direct payments to clients or their families to recognise the efforts they are making.

One can contrast the co-production model with labor specialization in the capitalist model, which leads to excess 'leisure' for some – that is, the unemployed – and all the lack of purpose and stigma the label brings. This model also leads to overwork for those who are employed, with the stress-related health effects that can bring. These extremes, together with the commodification of leisure itself, mean there is even less potential for self-fulfillment. Co-production differs from the Scandinavian and Dutch social contract models of capitalism. It would theoretically deliver some of the same outcomes in terms of sharing costs and responsibilities between employer, employees, and state, but through mechanisms that in many respects pool or aggregate individual freedoms into collective freedoms on a much smaller scale than that of the nation state. The results are impressive:

> If you are discharged from the Lehigh hospital outside Philadelphia, you will be told that someone will visit you at home, make sure you're OK, if you have heating and food in the house. You are also told that the person who will visit you is a former patient, not a professional, and that – when you are well – you will be asked if you could do the same for someone else. The result is a dramatically cut re-admission rate, and all by using the human skills of patients and their own needs to feel useful. (ibid., 18)

In the UK, the charity Nesta,[6] working in partnership with NEF, sees:

> Co-production [as] a new vision for public services which offers a better way to respond to the challenges we face – based on recognising the resources that citizens already have, and delivering services *with* rather than *for* service users, their families and their neighbours. Early evidence suggests that this is an effective way to deliver better outcomes, often for less money.

Through a series of groundbreaking reports such as *The Challenge of Co-production*, *Public Services Inside Out* and *Right Here, Right Now*, Nesta deepens our understanding and puts forward a convincing argument and evidence base for co-production across a range of public services, and recommends a radical reimagining of policy to support the diffusion of co-production (see Figure 1.5). With widespread, contagious uptake (and co-production is reliant in many ways on the existence of social networks), no longer could waged jobs be assumed to define people, and no longer could they be a key basis for politics. Further, nor could consumerism hold such powerful sway over politics if greater levels of wellbeing were generated by such participatory activity, rather than by consumption of the end products.

		Responsibility for design of services		
		Professionals as sole service planner	Professionals and user/community as co-planners	No professional input into service planning
Responsibility for delivery of services	Professionals as sole service deliverers	Traditional professional service provision	Professional service provision but user/community involved in planning and design	Professionals as sole service deliverers
	Professionals and users/communities as co-deliverers	User co-delivery of professionally designed services	Full co-production	User/community delivery of services with little formal/professional input
	Users/communities as sole deliverers	User/community delivery of professionally planned services	User/community delivery of co-planned or co-designed services	Self-organized community provision

1.5 User and professional roles in the design and delivery of services (*source*: adapted from Tony Bovaird 2006)

In *Wikinomics*, Tapscott and Williams (2006) see co-production as a function enabled by new technology (especially participatory web-based networks – the eponymous 'wiki'), emerging first in fields such as software and cultural products, and extending with the development of modular design and decentralized fabrication technologies (3D 'printers') to many other sectors, including industrial products. The growth of small-scale (domestic and community) renewable energy schemes and, similarly, of local food production and distribution schemes offers an insight into how co-production can build capacities and increase freedoms (in terms of providing security from unstable and insecure global markets for food and energy).

Other emerging emanations of co-production may involve the commoditization of leisure, which could be a dangerous development in that it could bring even more of life into market spheres. Here, the mechanisms and institutions will be critical if play and innovation are to become a foundation for co-production and sustainability (Kane 2011a), rather than co-opted into a new cycle of conventional economic development. Kane suggests that:

> play can help redirect our passions from consumption to craft, from lifestyle narcissism to joyful participation, and thus live lighter (though just as richly) on the planet.

Kane also highlights:

> the importance of craft – the personal construction of objects and services, as a route to meaning, mastery and autonomy … [and] the power of festivity and carnival – forms of collective, organised behaviour whose end is experiential pleasure, and whose means is participatory involvement.

He concludes:

> Communication and game platforms can amplify and coordinate this new, joyful activism. But the aim is to re-channel our playful natures from serving an isolated, subjective escapism, to supporting a civic, inter-subjective engagement.

It is the potential of co-production to meet needs. These needs include not only the desire for novelty, entertainment, and freedom, but also the need for security, community, solidarity, and identity. Further, that these needs will be met while transforming economic models away from the treadmill of growth and consumption is what makes the potential of co-production so exciting. Next, I turn to a deeper consideration of needs.

Meeting the needs of both present and future generations In this section I explore further the relationship between material consumption and needs. In particular, I consider the extent to which justice and equity are needs, and how inequality damages our capabilities for flourishing and our ability to meet our needs. More specifically, I examine health, the need for social identity, and how the current role of consumption in defining social identity could be supplanted in a more just and sustainable manner. I then turn to issues of international and intergenerational justice arising from the uneven distribution of natural resources.

The concept of sustainable development, while contested (see, for example, Jacobs 1999; Gunder 2006), embodies a process in which reasonable material needs are met. Despite legitimate critiques regarding various and culturally specific definitions of 'development,'[7] Larrain et al. (2002) helpfully describe from a global south perspective the concept of the 'dignity line' – a culturally specific minimum level of material consumption needed to allow a life lived with dignity. Dignity, however, is not simply a matter of overcoming material scarcity. For instance, as Sen (1999) has convincingly argued, famines typically occur in the presence of plenty, but in the absence of democracy. At the global scale, too, we produce more than enough food to feed everyone well, but too much is wasted – that is, dumped to maintain prices – and too much is consumed by individuals whose health is threatened by overconsumption. A policy focus on trade liberalization without protections for those with fewer capabilities to benefit from markets has exacerbated the situation, especially in the absence of land reform to allow fair distribution of productive resources (Shiva 2002). Justice is clearly the missing element (see box).

Inequality and ill-health Equality and justice are not only important in terms of material needs. As Wilkinson and Pickett (2009) have shown, material inequality harms mental and physical health and wellbeing with consequences including shorter life expectancy, greater incidence of obesity, and lower overall health. For example, Americans generally

Food justice

In recent years, food has become one of the key arenas in which conflicts around justice and sustainability have played out, particularly as a result of the opposing trends of globalization and localization of food production. In the US especially, as Chapter 2 shows, the interplay of race[8] and class has had a profound effect on food policy, politics, production, distribution, and consumption (Alkon and Agyeman 2011). Globally, as with other key environmental resources, absolute scarcity has not been the principal driver of conflict, although it may yet prove to be so (Godfray et al. 2010). Rather, the issues have been about distribution and the sustainability of production methods.

Controversy over genetic modification (GM) of food crops has encompassed potential concerns for health, environmental impact, and control over the food chain. In India, serious opposition to GM has mainly reflected concerns regarding the food chain and the efforts of agri-businesses to patent and control crop varieties. This is only an extreme example of the debates over food security in developing countries as their markets have reoriented toward exporting foodstuffs to the richer world. This has typically improved food security for those involved in formal agriculture, but has often undermined it for those on the margins, whose access to land and other resources has been reduced. Across the developing world, justice movements have begun to talk not of food security but of 'food sovereignty'[9] (Holt-Giménez 2011). The food sovereignty paradigm treats access to food as a human right and seeks to reorient production to prioritize self-sufficiency.

The challenges raised by global markets have been further highlighted by the impacts of biofuel production. Conceived as a means of helping mitigate climate change, demands for biofuel feedstocks have grown rapidly, and have been widely blamed as a contribution to rising food prices and scarcity. The control of productive land for biofuel production, especially in Africa, has been one element bringing the practice of 'land-grabbing' by European companies to public attention.

> At the other end of the food chain, in rich countries we have seen continued intensification of production and monopolization of food retailing by a handful of supermarkets. We have, however, also seen emerging forms of co-production in food systems, driven by largely niche preferences for local and organic food, and to some extent by demands for fair trade food. These have led to popularization of farmers' markets, box delivery schemes, and growing demand for urban agricultural spaces or allotments (in the UK). On one hand, on a global scale, the International Assessment of Agricultural Knowledge, Science and Technology for Development (2009) has called for 'sustainable intensification' but has recognized that, for example, GM is not required to feed the world. On the other hand, lower meat consumption may be a necessity in the rich world if equity is to be achieved in food systems.

are healthier and living longer, but there are sectors of the population who are in poor health, defined principally by race/ethnicity, socio-economic status, geography, gender, age, disability status, and risk status related to sex and gender. The 'health disparities' agenda (often called 'health inequalities' outside the US) aims at eliminating health disparities for these vulnerable populations. This agenda could be yet another area where a co-production model might work. Betancourt et al. (2003, 299) note: 'Given the strong evidence for socio-cultural barriers to care at multiple levels of the [US] health care system, culturally competent care is a key cornerstone in efforts to eliminate racial/ethnic disparities in health and health care.' A co-production approach would prioritize culturally competent care.

In their comparative studies of the Organisation for Economic Co-operation and Development (OECD) nations and US states, Wilkinson and Pickett (2009) demonstrate that benefits from greater equality would arise across all income deciles, even the wealthiest. In other words, everyone suffers from the stresses of competition, or what Wilkinson and Pickett (ibid.) call 'evaluative anxiety.' The data is, however, not of a fine enough grain to tell whether the true elites in the modern world, the wealthiest 1.0 or 0.1 percent, also experience worse mental and physical health. What is true, clearly, is that in more unequal societies even the richest elites incur additional defensive costs (high security and insurance costs, for example).

Wilkinson and Pickett (ibid.) stress that different mechanisms operate in developed and developing countries. In the rich world, inequality does damage via status and psychosocial effects, while in the poor world, the impacts of absolute poverty also come into play, impairing the health and capabilities for flourishing of the poorest. In the rich world, the psychosocial impacts they identified reinforce the effects of competitive consumption (Frank 1999; Schor 1999b), which means that large segments of even the middle classes in rich nations such as the UK and US report 'difficulty getting by' on their incomes.[10]

Evaluative anxiety has also increased as a result of social and technological changes resulting in the disintegration of settled communities (as we will see below, this factor is potentially a key trigger in changes in the basis of social identity) and what Bauman (2005) describes as 'liquid life.' For Bauman, liquid life is a state in which life circumstances change more quickly than our actions can be consolidated into habits or norms. Thus it is a 'precarious life, lived under … constant uncertainty' (ibid., 2).

In this situation, increasing inequality would seem likely to have more severe psychosocial impacts, and thereby dramatically impair capabilities – thus undermining justice, in Sen's (1999) sense. As Wilkinson and Pickett (2009, 42) put it: 'People's sense of identity … [has been] cast adrift in the anonymity of mass society … As a result, who we are, identity itself, is endlessly open to question.' In such circumstances, combined with the power of marketing highlighted by McIntosh (2008), vulnerability to the pursuit of identity through consumption is high. McIntosh suggests we have fallen prey to a numbing culture of violence. Combined with the motivational manipulation of marketing, McIntosh argues that this numbing culture of violence has established an addictive consumer mentality. In such a fractured and uncertain culture, vulnerability to divisive group identity creation is also high.

Reimagining needs At this point, it is essential to consider what we mean by 'needs.' Neoclassical economics uses the term interchangeably with 'wants' or 'desires,' but there is a substantial and critical literature examining the nature and definition of needs. Maslow's (1954) hierarchy of human needs offers a solid foundation. He sets out the case that, as immediate (and fairly obvious) physiological and safety needs for things such as food and shelter are met, humans are motivated, sequentially, by needs for belonging, esteem, and finally self-actualization. As we will see later, in a capability-based approach to justice, one can also consider rights and liberties as needs (Sen 2009).

Max-Neef (1991) and Schwartz (2006) have sought to develop universal approaches to human needs and values, respectively. These authors both recognize the complexity of needs and values, and the potential contradictions that arise between them and as a result of different ways of satisfying them (Max-Neef calls these various ways 'satisfiers'). Max-Neef rejects the proposition that 'human needs tend to be infinite, that they change all the time, that they are different in each culture or environment and that they are different in each historical period' (1991, 17). He also rejects the idea of a hierarchy, such as the one proposed by Maslow, while recognizing the overriding effect of unsatisfied subsistence needs. Needs may have evolved through a hierarchy in evolutionary time, but for modern humans the idea of a hierarchy is potentially unjust. Of course, it would be unfair to suggest that it would be acceptable to seek to meet only the basic needs of poor people or people in poorer countries, but a hierarchical conception of needs can be interpreted in such a way. Not all people will express the same needs in the same ways, so a hierarchy may therefore appear to exist. In the context of justice, this implies that all people are entitled to the same capabilities and recognition of their needs (and values), which is in line with the thinking of Sen (1999), Schlosberg (2007), and Schlosberg and Carruthers (2010), as outlined below.

Max-Neef (1991, 32–3) organizes human needs on two interacting axes: 1) the existential needs of being, having, doing, and interacting; and 2) the axiological needs of subsistence, protection, affection, understanding, participation, idleness (leisure), creation, identity, and freedom (see Table 1.1). Each combination of existential and axiological can have multiple satisfiers that may change over time. For example, food and shelter are merely one form of satisfiers for the having and doing needs of subsistence. He distinguishes carefully between 'destructive' satisfiers that may fulfill one need but damage another (consumerism comes to mind) and those – education for example – that are *synergistic* and fulfill multiple needs.

Schwartz (2006, 2–3) has constructed a circle or spectrum of values

TABLE 1.1 Needs and satisfiers in Max-Neef's model of human-scale development

Fundamental human needs	Being (qualities)	Having (things)	Doing (actions)	Interacting (settings)
subsistence	physical and mental health	food, shelter, work	feed, clothe, rest, work	living environment, social setting
protection	care, adaptability, autonomy	social security, health systems, work	cooperate, plan, take care of, help	social environment, dwelling
affection	respect, sense of humour, generosity, sensuality	friendships, family, relationships with nature	share, take care of, make love, express emotions	privacy, intimate spaces of togetherness
understanding	critical capacity, curiosity, intuition	literature, teachers, educational policies	analyse, study, meditate, investigate	schools, families, universities, communities
participation	receptiveness, dedication, sense of humour	responsibilities, duties, work, rights	cooperate, dissent, express opinions	associations, parties, churches, neighbourhoods
leisure	imagination, tranquillity, spontaneity	games, parties, peace of mind	daydream, remember, relax, have fun	landscapes, intimate spaces, places to be alone
creation	imagination, boldness, inventiveness, curiosity	abilities, skills, work, techniques	invent, build, design, work, compose, interpret	spaces for expression, workshops, audiences
identity	sense of belonging, self-esteem, consistency	language, religions, work, customs, values, norms	get to know oneself, grow, commit oneself	places one belongs to, everyday settings
freedom	autonomy, passion, self-esteem, open-mindedness	equal rights	dissent, choose, run risks, develop awareness	anywhere

Source: www.rainforestinfo.org.au/background/maxneef.htm

that has profound similarities to Max-Neef's system. These are listed in Figure 1.6 below along with the related motivations (or needs):

1 *Self-direction*: independent thought and action; choosing, creating, and exploring.
2 *Stimulation*: excitement, novelty, and challenge in life.
3 *Hedonism*: pleasure and sensuous gratification for oneself.
4 *Achievement*: personal success through demonstrating competence according to social standards.
5 *Power*: social status and prestige, control, or dominance over people and resources.
6 *Security*: safety, harmony, and stability of society, of relationships, and of self.
7 *Conformity*: restraint of actions, inclinations, and impulses likely to upset or harm others and violate social expectations or norms.

1.6 Theoretical model of relations among ten motivational types of values (*source*: Schwartz 2006; http://segr-did2.fmag.unict.it/Allegati/convegno%207-8-10-05/Schwartzpaper.pdf)

8 *Tradition*: respect, commitment, and acceptance of the customs and ideas that traditional culture or religion provide the self.
9 *Benevolence*: preserving and enhancing the welfare of those with whom one is in frequent personal contact (the 'in-group').
10 *Universalism*: understanding, appreciation, tolerance, and protection for the welfare of all people, and for nature.

Schwartz (ibid., 4) notes that his:

> structure can be summarized with two orthogonal dimensions. *Self-enhancement vs. self-transcendence*: On this dimension, power and achievement values oppose universalism and benevolence values. Both of the former emphasize pursuit of self-interests, whereas both of the latter involve concern for the welfare and interests of others. *Openness to change vs. conservation*: On this dimension, self-direction and stimulation values oppose security, conformity and tradition values. Both of the former emphasize independent action, thought and feeling and readiness for new experience, whereas all of the latter emphasize self-restriction, order and resistance to change. Hedonism shares elements of both openness and self-enhancement.

Even these dimensions are not wholly mutually exclusive, although most people hold these various values to greater or lesser degrees, and are more likely to jointly hold values that are adjacent in the circle than those that are more distant. Rose (2010) has adopted a similar values analysis to identify three broad groups in society: *settlers* (sustenance driven, with values dominated by Schwartz's 'conservation' group); *prospectors* (outer-directed, with values dominated by self-enhancement, and openness to change); and *pioneers* (inner-directed, with values of self-transcendence). Rose argues that these groups are fairly exclusive and, implicitly, that there may be a (slow) progression between them (following Maslow).

From a just sustainabilities point of view, it is important to recognize that people hold different and fairly robust non-material values. While conflicts may arise if their consequent needs are met in particular ways, those needs can be met through different satisfiers, which thus at least theoretically raises the prospect of there being both socially just and environmentally sustainable ways of fulfilling them. I also want to emphasize the importance of a secure self-identity as universal among people's non-material needs. Even identity is not a simple concept, as it typically involves a balance between two needs, for assimilation or conformity, and differentiation. The combination of these has been described as 'optimal distinctiveness theory' (Brewer 2003). For Brewer, distinctiveness is the motive determining the selection and strength of social identities. Optimal distinctiveness theory states that distinctiveness within an in-group must be equalized by assimilation, which is an independent yet opposing motive for group identification.

As I outline below, both these motives can be clearly seen in the construction of modern social identities through consumption, with damaging consequences for justice and sustainability.

Consumption and identity Schor (1999b) argues that our sense of social standing and belonging comes from what we consume and, moreover, that consumption habits and patterns are central to the reproduction of class inequality, alienation, and power. This is particularly true in contemporary consumerism, with its emphasis on 'bling': luxury, expensiveness, exclusivity, rarity, uniqueness, and distinction. Schor sees modern consumption as a comparative or competitive process in which individuals try to keep up with the consumptive practices of the social group with which they identify. She suggests that in the modern consumer society, our reference points are no longer neighbors or workmates, but rather a wealthy elite.

Several authors (see, for example, Lamont and Molnár 1999) have offered a (multi)cultural critique of Schor, arguing that she focuses too narrowly on conventional white, middle-class consumption patterns (in the rich world). Schor's model, they argue, is 'that of a single individual entering a shopping mall and *choosing* among goods to maximize the investment of his or her resources, with the primary goal of accumulating goods to gain status,' whereas 'an alternative, more cultural, model would frame consumption as a social act – shopping, for example, is often done with a friend or family member and with someone else's needs in mind.'

In another paper, Lamont and Molnár (2001, 42) stress the use of consumption practices to define positive ethnic and racial identities in the face of discrimination:

> Consumption is uniquely important for blacks in gaining social membership. Their experience with racism makes the issue of

membership particularly salient, and consuming is a democratically available way of affirming insertion in mainstream society.

Is there a way of creating positive individual and collective identities that is not consumer-driven? McIntosh (2008, 143) suggests that it may be pointless to seek a positive model of consumerism:

> Violence hollows out the capacity to have an inner life. It does so by desensitising the ability to feel and to relate to others … it opens up the gnawing emptiness of in-authenticity in human relations … this is the chasm into which the retail therapy of consumerism pours, and here are the roots of nihilism.

Marketing and advertising designed to create new addictive and self-destructive 'needs' flood through the 'chasm.'

Taken as a whole, these analyses lead to three conclusions: 1) that excessive consumption must be curbed, perhaps through some form of progressive consumption tax mechanism; 2) that the operations of the advertising industry must be more strictly regulated; and 3) following from Lamont and Molnár (2001), that we must redouble our efforts to end racism and discrimination, since we know that, in addition to their moral repugnance, they are also drivers of identity-based consumption.

The role of consumption in the global economy is equally pivotal. In the face of contemporary Western calls for China to accelerate consumption rates to create a consumer-led boom to rescue the faltering global economy, Nair (2011) suggests that Asia as a whole should instead reject Western models of consumer economics. He argues that if Asians were to achieve consumption levels taken for granted in the West, the results would be environmentally catastrophic and geopolitically destabilizing as nations scrambled for diminishing resources. He calls for new models of capitalism with strong states, greater equality, and high investment in sustainable resource management, especially sustainable land use. Clearly any such model would have to retain or incorporate tools to constrain competitive status consumption.

Jackson (2009) also recognizes the importance of moving away from consumerist economies. He describes the need as one for 'alternative hedonism' – sources of identity, creativity, and meaning that lie outside the realm of the market. Both Nair and Jackson are echoing the concept

Consumerist riots?

In summer 2011, several UK cities experienced rioting and looting. Initially triggered by a police shooting in Tottenham, London, these events occurred largely with no obvious political cause. Looting of fashionable clothes, sports shoes, and gadgets was typical. While many stores in London's Clapham Junction were looted, Waterstone's bookstore was left untouched! Many commentators have subsequently made connections with inequality and with consumerist values and identities, combining the sense of loss of other forms of value and identity with the dominance of consumerist values.

A range of other factors, of course, contributed. Some examples of such factors include government cuts in services, and loss of trust in unjust institutions and individual actors in politics and the media (notably arising from recent scandals of Members of Parliament abusing expense allowances, and the Murdoch-owned *News of the World* hacking mobile phone voicemail accounts). Further factors included failings in policy measures designed to support multiculturalism (especially from the mistrust exhibited by security forces in the misplaced 'war

of 'sufficiency,' as elaborated by McLaren et al. (1998), which seeks to combine understandings of the environmental and of the personal implications of consumption. This paradigm of sufficiency suggests that there might be an optimal level of consumption. An optimal level of sufficiency refers to one that meets both material and non-material needs associated with consumption, but does not damage other needs, such as environmental quality, social equality, or individual health. McLaren et al. (ibid.) also propose that policy measures to promote sufficiency would increase the wellbeing achieved for every unit of consumption, acting as a multiplier with 'efficiency' measures that reduce the environmental impact of each unit of production.

Given the importance of consumption to identity, and the importance of reducing consumption (at least in wealthy societies), a key question arises: can we envisage a way to square the circle? Is there any opportunity to establish different sources of identity? Social identity theory (for example Turner et al. 1987) suggests that a significant on terror'), and the increasing loss of a shared public realm as public spaces in our cities are privatized and consumerized. But the role of inequality, consumerism, and specific reference groups, in particular, is well summed up by one blogger:

> These kids aren't rioting for the right to a job in traditional sectors threatened by neo-liberalism … No, this generation is cursed with semiotic plenitude. They have been super-conditioned by all kinds of powerful media and branding to think they live in a world sprinkled with stardust. A world where self-expression and recognition, not just through the medium of art (*X-Factor*), but via the basic interactions of their lives (*Big Brother*), is what essentially matters. If you don't have the talent … then you have to buy into the lifestyle that at least evokes such stardom. When you realise you are always going to fall far short of the spending power to live that lifestyle, that's a recipe for permanent, corrosive dissatisfaction. What's different compared to the seventies is the explosion of media – meaning the explosion of ways to get a tantalising, frustrating taste of the consumer identity you know you'll never quite possess. (Kane 2011b)

part of individual identity is established through the way in which people identify themselves as part of specific groups (in-groups) in terms of factors such as race, ethnicity, class, occupation, and education, and consumption patterns clearly signal such self-identification. The social identity literature suggests, however, that individuals can undergo identity shifts as part of significant life transitions such as career changes, or enforced external events such as the return of Hong Kong to China (Brewer 2003). Schwartz (2006) notes three systematic sources of value change in adulthood: historical events that impact on specific age cohorts (e.g. war, recession), physical aging, and life stage (e.g. family formation).

Experience with state-building in Eastern Europe offers an interesting perspective here. Kuzio (2002) highlights not only the contradictions between democratization and marketization in post-Communist states, but also the incompatibility of state institution-building and civic nation-building with democratization and marketization. In particular,

Socio-economic system	Peasant societies	Industrial societies	Consumer societies	Post-material/ post-capitalist societies
Dominant values modes	*Settlers (security, belonging)*	*Settlers/ prospectors (security, esteem)*	*Prospectors (esteem/ novelty)*	*Pioneers (novelty/ personal growth)*
Source of identity	Land/place	Work/union	Wealth/ possessions	Co-production community?
Key trends	Political and economic freedoms increasing			
	Resource use/consumption increasing ...			... **de**creasing
	Equality increasing ...	... **de**creasing		... **in**creasing

1.7 The identity transition (*source*: McLaren PowerPoint slide)

he emphasizes the importance of national identity within the former processes, but bemoans the failure of the actors involved to even recognize the task of national identity-building as a process that can be guided. Of course, Smith (1981), who foresaw an ethnic revival in the USSR, might argue that the survival of national and ethnic identities underlay the collapse of the Soviet Union, but still Kuzio has identified a real missed opportunity. Rifkin (2010) picks up a similar thread in his book *The Empathic Civilization*, in which he argues that national identity is a progressive step forward from religious and blood-kin identity, but one that needs to be supplanted by the extension of empathy from our countrymen (and -women) to the global population and indeed to other species.

These examples suggest that deliberate and large-scale intervention in identity formation may be possible. McLaren (2011a; pers. comm.) has also speculated that, over time, the dimensions on which in-group and out-group categorizations (and thus social identities) are primarily determined have changed in the past, sequentially from place, to job, to consumption patterns (see Figure 1.7).

Social identities may have become more fluid (indeed, in Bauman's 'liquid life,' it might even be suggested that they are temporary and multi-layered, if they have time to form at all). However, the work of

Schor, Jackson, and Lamont and Molnár, cited above, confirms that consumption habits are critical – perhaps increasingly so, at present – in establishing identity in modern society. The idea of a transition allows us to consider what might replace consumption as the central source of identity in a society based around just sustainabilities.

Castells (2010) suggests a model for the transformation of identity that involves identifying three basic forms: 1) *legitimating identity*, 2) *resistance identity*, and 3) *project identity*. The third is a deliberate collective effort by social actors to reshape identity, potentially following the definition of resistance identities that are rooted in factors such as ethnicity and locality, but that are used to resist the stigmatizing effect of being defined in terms of a dominant or legitimating identity. On a global scale, he suggests that both feminism and environmentalism have been largely successful project identity transformations.

It might be argued that the very definition of in-groups and out-groups is inimical to justice, and that just sustainabilities should be about eliminating such constructions (in the way Rifkin implies). However, the psychological and sociological literature suggests convincing reasons why humans make such constructions as a consequence of evolutionary interactions (Ridley 1996). To even change the basis of social identity would constitute a major transformation, and that is what is suggested here.[11] My proposition is that a shift to an economic model of co-production would allow (and perhaps even demand) such an identity transition, with much more dominant roles in identity formation being found in creativity and within the multiple and overlapping in-groups of co-productive activities.

Needs and resource scarcity I cannot leave the issue of meeting present and future needs without considering the implications of the scarcity of material and environmental resources, for both international and intergenerational distribution. Both renewable and non-renewable resources can be the objects of scarcity. Overexploitation of renewable resources, such as forests, runs down our natural capital stocks, thereby reducing future productivity. The use of finite, non-renewable resources leaves fewer – and typically lower-grade – resources for future generations.

The conventional response to resource shortages has been colonization of new territories, with neocolonial land-grabbing and resource-grabbing going on to this day, concentrating resources and capabilities in the hands of the relatively rich and powerful. Conventional theories of justice such as Rawls (1971) find it difficult to address international justice questions, as they rely on the shared democratic institutions of the nation state to deliver justice, while weak and unelected international institutions cannot play the same role.

In some respects it should not be surprising that there are no international agreements regarding the distribution of material resources, and that even agreement over common property resources such as fisheries, oceans, and the atmosphere is the subject of fraught negotiation. Nonetheless, principles of equity, vulnerability, and capability are frequently cited and often incorporated to some degree in international relations. But the dominant international institutions – that is, the World Trade Organization (WTO), International Monetary Fund (IMF), and World Bank – are dominated by neoclassical economic ideologies of distribution, thus leaving consideration of justice at the margins.

In considering intergenerational distribution, Rawls (ibid.) suggests that each generation should put itself in the place of the next and ask what it could reasonably expect to receive. He presents this thought experiment so as to identify 'just savings.' Sustainability theorists have suggested that sustainable or fair rates of use of finite resources could be calculated in relation to the rate at which alternative ways of meeting the same needs are created. For example, it might be sustainable and just for one generation to use fossil fuels in the creation of a renewable energy infrastructure able to meet the needs of following generations.

This example, of course, is made more complex by the implications of fossil fuel use on climate change, and it is here that consideration of large-scale environmental justice has been developed most. Here, consideration of justice and distributional issues has led to the development of a number of proposals for climate justice, such as Meyer's (2000) *Contraction and Convergence*, which is the idea that emissions should not only gradually contract to an overall sustainable level, but also eventually converge upon equal per capita levels in all countries. Despite its apparent simplicity, this concept has yet to win widespread support even from poorer nations, perhaps because it effectively postpones equity to a future date and does not include any compensation for past inequality. Some, such as McLaren (2003), have termed these past inequalities 'climatic' or 'ecological debt.'

Alternative schemes such as Greenhouse Development Rights (Baer et al. 2008) seek not only to take account of these critiques, but also to take account of intra-national equity. Intra-national equity refers to attributing to each country a degree of responsibility (based on cumulative emissions) and capability (based on income available to those living above a relevant poverty line), and suggests that rich developed nations must shoulder more of the burden of emissions reduction than contraction and convergence would suggest.

The conventional economic approach to climate change is to see it as an externality, and thus seek to include it in market prices through the creation of carbon markets. This carries a real risk of establishing a new financial bubble and further economic instability, rather than actually reducing emissions. The challenge of climate change is also revealing new finite resources such as geological carbon storage capacity, which is also unevenly distributed (with apparently much more capacity in Europe, for example, than in India). The implications of the use and allocation of storage between countries and over time have only just begun to be considered (McLaren 2011b). The distributional implications of both climate vulnerability and adaptation and emerging geo-engineering proposals are also significant. Adaptation to higher temperatures and lower rainfall in tropical climates will be far more difficult than in temperate climes, while the countries affected also typically have fewer capabilities to adapt, and more pressing poverty alleviation demands. The distributional implications of geo-engineering methods of lowering global temperatures are also poorly understood as yet. It does appear, however, that the widely touted option of stratospheric sulfur injection could have dramatic negative impacts on the behavior of the monsoon across the Indian sub-continent.

Walker (2011) provides a summary of three key dimensions of distribution in addition to the distribution of environmental goods or burdens: 1) vulnerability, 2) need, and 3) responsibility. All these might be considered in establishing justice. Further, he argues that these distributive aspects must be supplemented by both procedural justice and recognition. Such considerations suggest an urgent need for the development of assessment methodologies and appropriate governance mechanisms and institutions if future societies are to enjoy any prospect of meeting the needs of future generations. Next, I turn to the characteristics and principles of justice that must underlie appropriate governance, institutions, and objectives.

Justice and equity in terms of recognition, process, procedure, and outcome In this section I consider the theoretical conception of justice appropriate to our understanding of just sustainabilities. Following Sen (1999; 2009) and Schlosberg (1999; 2004; 2007), I take a multidimensional approach. I then consider implications in practice, including the role of political and economic freedoms in just sustainabilities, and the procedural mechanisms – from human rights to corporate accountability – that might be deployed to enable justice in a sustainable society. I also reflect on the role of democracy in just sustainabilities.

Understanding justice Justice is not a simple concept. Different ideological foundations can lead to very different conclusions and outcomes. For example, utilitarian (justice as the most beneficial outcome for wider society), egalitarian (justice as meeting individuals' needs), and libertarian (justice as fulfilling merit) perspectives can differ radically. Sen (2009) takes this as reason to argue for a goal of reducing manifest injustice, rather than seeking perfect justice. Sen also, and wisely, emphasizes the significance of actual outcomes in practice and the behaviors of individuals, as well as the nature and processes of institutions in moving toward justice. He criticizes much of modern philosophy for its focus on the design of perfect institutions.

Instead of striving for perfect institutions, both Sen (ibid.) and Nussbaum (2000) suggest that the notion of capabilities for flourishing plays a central role. Nussbaum's full capability list includes: life, bodily health, bodily integrity, senses, imagination, thought, emotions, practical reason, affiliation, other species, play, and control over one's environment. Sen, on the other hand, suggests that communities must be involved in listing their own set of capabilities. He recommends this approach more because control over the conditions of life is necessary for justice than because capabilities may be culturally specific. This latter factor, however, should not be ignored.

This central positioning of capabilities within justice should not be confused with the modern political compromise of the left that argues for 'equality of opportunity' in a quasi-libertarian fashion. Sen does not disregard outcomes, and the capabilities approach still recognizes that justice requires institutions, resources, social and physical environments, and behaviors that permit individuals to flourish. Basic freedoms are indeed a critical part of this, but so is recognition of individual character and capacities within society (Schlosberg 2007). Recognition goes beyond non-discrimination. Moreover, for Sen, greater freedom does not imply impunity but, on the contrary, establishes responsibility and accountability for our actions.

Schlosberg concurs with Sen that justice is not only about securing a fair distribution of material goods or consumption. Indeed, neither gives primacy to material wellbeing, but rather to social factors. Schlosberg (2004; 2007) argues that just treatment involves recognizing people's membership of the moral and political community, as well as providing for the capabilities needed for their functioning and flourishing, and ensuring their inclusion in political decision-making. Schlosberg (2007) further argues that distribution, recognition, capabilities, and participation are interrelated and interdependent.

Recognition is a critically important dimension of justice in multicultural and intercultural societies, where other dimensions of justice might be culturally distorted. This is discussed more fully in Chapter 2, 'Food,' Chapter 3, 'Space and place,' and Chapter 4, 'Culture.' Recognition of the rights of those with sexual and gender differences (including LGBT individuals), among other forms of difference, is an area where much progress can be identified in the last few decades, at least taking Sen's maxim of seeking to mitigate manifest injustice (an ideal form of justice is clearly still lacking for LGBT people, as it also is for women). Urban planning's traditional focus on distributive and procedural justice is challenged by Milroy (2004, 48), among others: 'Planning-related literature of the last decade or so illustrates that resource distribution is just one fundamental dimension of the politics of urban life. The other is recognition.'

Our understanding of justice and equity also includes material outcomes, which in turn further determine capabilities. Material income and wealth provide very real capabilities to meet needs for shelter and security, and thus to avoid the stresses and insecurities of life without sound financial resources. Material inequality, measured in terms of income or the standard of living, is also harmful to physical and mental health (Wilkinson and Pickett 2009) and a fairer distribution of material consumption would improve health and reduce other social ills (as noted previously; see also Figure 1.8).

Here it should be noted that Wilkinson and Pickett (ibid.) identify psychosocial mechanisms – specifically social networks, social status, and stress in early childhood – that have an impact on health as a

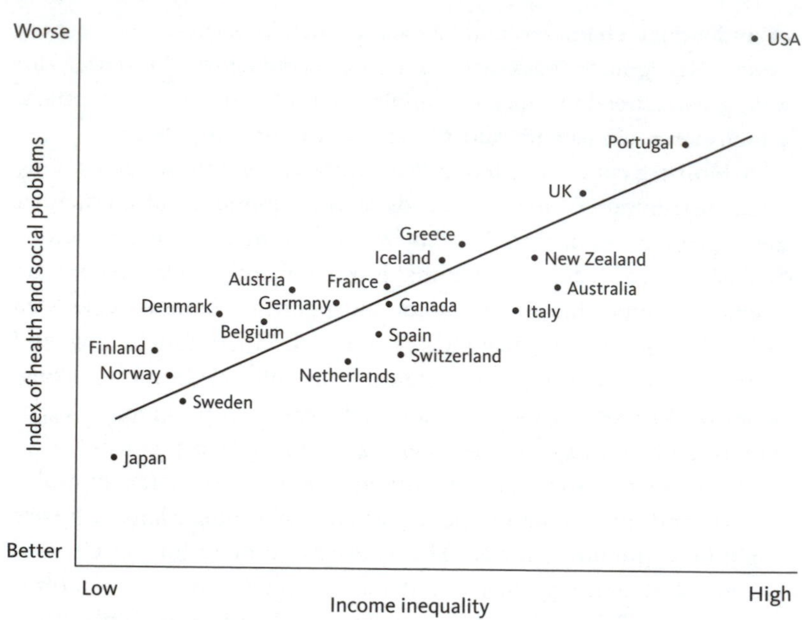

Note: Income inequality in Figures 1.3 and 1.8 may be taken from different sources and may therefore appear to vary slightly.

1.8 Health and social problems are closely related to inequality in rich countries (*source*: Wilkinson and Pickett 2009, 20)

result of material inequality. There is every reason to expect that injustice measured in other dimensions, such as racism, discrimination, or lack of recognition, could equally powerfully trigger such psychosocial mechanisms.

Justice and human rights From the foregoing, it should be clear that a key potential tool for just sustainabilities is the recognition and exercise of human rights. Despite significant experience in defending individual social freedoms, some groundbreaking cases in the US, and in Europe using the European Convention on Human Rights, there is little evidence that human rights legislation as yet provides an effective tool for defending environmental rights. There are at least three reasons why this is so. First, human rights legislation typically does not directly recognize rights to a clean and healthy environment. In places where such rights are constitutionally recognized, rights in general are often poorly defended in the law. Second, human rights legislation focuses on the rights of individuals rather than those of groups. Schlosberg (2007) argues more broadly for an ecological justice where concern is not solely for individuals but for social groups and ecological systems as well. A focus on individuals, and specifically present rather than future individuals, creates additional difficulties for a legal defense of environmental rights. Third, procedural rights of access to information, participation, and justice are patchy even where governments have adopted measures designed to provide such rights.

There are signs of progress in all three of these areas. The UN recently recognized a right to clean water and sanitation, which provides a strong foundation to press for the recognition of wider environmental rights. In 2007, the UN adopted a Declaration on the Rights of Indigenous Peoples, embodying important justice principles such as free prior informed consent. The declaration provides a framework in which we can consider the rights of other collectivities. The Aarhus Convention, adopted in 1998, has led to European Union (EU) directives on freedom of information and, in a limited form, environmental participation. While implementation of the convention's third pillar – access to justice – has been especially patchy, there were moves afoot to ratify the globalization of the convention – currently a UN Economic Commission for Europe (UNECE) instrument – as part of the agenda for Rio+20: the 2012 Earth Summit. This did not materialize. However, at Rio, Ireland bought the number of Parties to the Convention to 46 and the Parties to the Amendment on GMOs (genetically modified organisms) to 27.

Justice and property rights A further reason why legal approaches to just sustainabilities have been limited lies in the implications of other rights that are robustly defended by legal systems worldwide: property rights. Property rights are applied to land, physical, and intellectual property, all of which exhibit highly inequitable distribution. Land rights, as Wightman (2010) demonstrates for Scotland, are in many ways a fabrication to defend the past acquisition of land by force. Even where ownership is demonstrably legal, a host of measures, including rules of inheritance, follow the interests of the already wealthy. For example, Wightman highlights the injustice of primogeniture on Scottish landed estates where the law leaves widows and younger children disinherited.

Whether considering the land or intellectual property, there are dramatic implications for justice defined in terms of capabilities and control. Access to land, resources, and technologies are basic capabilities for development and poverty alleviation, all of which can be denied to billions of people in the modern world insofar as it suits the financial interests of already wealthy elites and corporations.

Directly contrary to conventional economic approaches to environmental problems, which seek to privatize currently common property resources – by creating carbon markets, for example – a just sustainabilities approach would look to create new forms of common property through land reform, and to develop 'open-source' solutions that do not rely on proprietary technologies or intellectual property rights. Harvey (2011, 233) calls for 'a wholly new conception of property – of common rather than private property rights' to underpin 'radical egalitarianism.' The work of the late Nobel Prize-winner Elinor Ostrom suggests that this might be compatible with a 'polycentric' nested series of democratic structures to provide more flexible governance (Ostrom 2009).

Justice, democracy, and freedom There are both moral and instrumental reasons for treating just sustainabilities issues as issues that concern rights. Sustainability concerns rarely take center stage in political conflicts, but struggles for increased freedoms and rights for groups or peoples can dominate them. In my understanding, such campaigns constitute no less of a demand for just sustainabilities than would explicitly environmental activism:

> [Just] sustainability is, at its very heart, a political construct rather than a technical or scientifically objective notion. The policy goal of [just] sustainability can be usefully understood as what might be termed an 'over-arching societal value'. In this sense, it is more akin to notions like 'freedom', 'justice' or 'democracy' than to specific policy commitment. (Agyeman and Evans 1995, 36)

Such struggles also illustrate that social change typically has a non-linear nature. From the emancipation of women and slaves to current struggles to globalize sexual freedoms, and the 'Arab Spring' revolutions, tipping points have been surpassed, usually as the result of targeted campaigning and mobilization, reinforced by evolving social change, and subsequently enforced through the emergence of new norms. The rate of such social change is arguably increasing together with the power of new communication technologies, reinforcing the enabling effects of previous generations of technologies that have played a role in earlier social transformations.[12]

In the Arab Spring revolutions, as in previous struggles in Eastern Europe and South Africa, progressive struggles for social, cultural, or political rights have spread contagiously. It is important to recognize that in all these cases economic freedoms have been a significant part of the agenda. People have actively sought to participate in free(r) markets for labor or goods and services, and to enjoy the benefits of consumerism. The consequences of such transformations are likely to include increased resource consumption and environmental impacts.

Efforts to prevent such examples of progressive struggles because of their short-term environmental outcomes would be misplaced for at least three reasons. First, there are overriding benefits to be obtained from the reduction of manifest injustice. Second, a reasoned approach to environmental sustainability will require recognition of all those who have a stake in the earth's resources, present and future generations alike. If injustice and discrimination persist against particular groups or populations, solutions to global environmental problems are likely to remain remote. Third, democracy is arguably a minimum requirement for justice. Sen (2009) sets out how democratic participation is a necessary capability. Democracy is also a minimal requirement for a system of public reasoning, and is necessary to determine what is just in a given society.

Environmental overconsumption and degradation prevent many people from enjoying a decent quality of life. As Sen or Schlosberg might say, without a clean environment and a fair share in the earth's resources, our capabilities to flourish are constrained. But for the majority in the world, environmental issues and constraints are not a pressing matter of rights, freedoms, or liberties. Exceptions are severe, such as communities displaced by land-grabbing, or those who have had their health damaged by living close to dirty industry, but these are by no means the normal experience for the majority of people.

Few would conceive of environmental issues as a matter of rights, and even those who would like to are apt to see them as less pressing than rights issues arising from discrimination and poverty. Even progressive organizations such as Amnesty International struggle to frame environmental concerns as matters of rights, despite real willingness to do so (see, for example, Sachs 1995). But by properly integrating environmental issues and rights into the framework of just sustainabilities, the two become inseparable.

Rights, responsibilities, and accountability The connection must also be made in respect of the flipside of rights: responsibilities. Like Sen, I recognize that freedoms come with accountabilities, and rights with responsibilities, but in this context the issue is more about the responsibilities that arise not for individuals but for states and for non-state actors such as companies as a result of the definition of individual and collective human rights.

States are clearly responsible for establishing and enforcing a framework of law, and for complying with international treaties that they have ratified. However, like environmental treaties, rights conventions also typically lack strong compliance mechanisms. For example, the Aarhus Convention compliance committee may rule that a state is in breach, but it can do nothing more than make recommendations as to how it might establish compliance. Worse, where there is an apparent conflict between responsibilities under such conventions and economic obligations enforced by the WTO or the international financial institutions, there is a massive imbalance. The latter enjoy effective sanctions, whether formal (as under the WTO, which can authorize the use of punitive trade sanctions) or more informal (such as those enjoyed by the IMF and World Bank with their discretion to make and withdraw financial backing).

The responsibilities of corporations are an even greyer area. Increasingly multinational in nature, corporations enjoy many powers and privileges, and their decisions – on anything from mining to advertising – have a daily impact on human rights and the capabilities of individuals and communities to flourish. Even if there appear to be grounds for a legal challenge to a corporation, it is often debatable in which jurisdiction a company should be challenged. So far, there has been only a handful of successful cases brought against the most egregious impacts, such as Shell's widely discussed involvement in the execution of Ogoni activist Ken Saro-Wiwa. Typically, even 'successful' cases are settled out of court with a fairly token monetary settlement.

However, the recent report by John Ruggie, Special Representative of the UN Secretary-General on business and human rights, opens the door to a fuller and more consistent approach to corporate accountability. Ruggie (2011) confirms that companies do bear responsibilities to respect human rights and to address human rights issues arising in the conduct of their business, regardless of liability.

In the context of just sustainabilities, corporate accountability means more than respect for human rights, and extends to the wider environmental and social impacts of corporate activities. Without controls over the activities of corporations, justice is unachievable – and inequality will continue to grow. McLaren (2004) suggests a need for regulatory frameworks for governance and investment to provide a degree of accountability.

The revised OECD guidelines for multinational enterprises are a move in the right direction, requiring due diligence on environmental, social, and human rights impacts, and effective consultation, and clearly apply to the whole supply chain and to financial industry activities too. But the guidelines still fall well short of genuine stakeholder participation and lack an effective enforcement mechanism (Wilde-Ramsing et al. 2011).

It remains open to question whether even with substantial reforms, such as strict liability for environmental and social impacts to balance the fiduciary duty to shareholders, the public, stock market-listed corporation can be made into a just institution.[13] If not, then an alternative economic model for just sustainabilities can no longer include such organizations. In this case, many of their roles may be taken on by mutual and cooperative companies, or by public bodies.

A just transition? The implication of public, stock market-listed corporations being incompatible with just sustainabilities is that the economic transition faced by workers may be even more dramatic than foreseen by the 'just transition' literature (such as TUC 2008; Lee and Carlaw 2010), which considers how workers' rights can be protected in the transition to a low-carbon economy. This transition will involve the replacement of many major firms and sources of employment with different and more sustainable ones.

The just transition approach, however, is critical to managing changes in employment patterns fairly, without a decline in working conditions. It also seeks to ensure fair implementation of other environmental policies (such as green taxes, which could otherwise exacerbate existing income inequality). Just transition typically also demands high levels of employee representation and involvement in decision-making.

While the challenges faced by workers as a result of the need to change the content and nature of economic activity are severe, it is not only workers who need just treatment. The challenges faced in preventing further reproduction of unemployed and undereducated underclasses of the sort that have persisted for more than a generation in deprived urban areas in the US and UK (at least) are even greater.

Processes of just transition are needed to eliminate the structures and institutions that reproduce injustice. Our economic alternative must involve the co-production of justice. But such alternatives cannot be unconstrained in their use of environmental resources. The need to live within ecosystem limits is a hard reality if collapse is to be avoided, and it is to this that I turn next.

Living within ecosystem limits In this section, I begin with a short discussion of the concept of environmental limits, explaining the nature of such limits and discussing their implications for distribution and equity. I make the case that environmental limits result in unfair distribution of environmental 'goods,' thus exacerbating the effects of unfair distribution of environmental 'bads.' I also call for an environmental politics of redistribution, as well as a practical root and branch redesign of economic practices and institutions.

Environmental limits Despite several decades of research, the very concept of environmental limits remains controversial, especially in the US. The Club of Rome report (Meadows et al. 1972) framed the debate in terms of 'limits to growth,' a concept that stimulated very powerful and well-funded counterarguments and rebuttals. By the 1990s, in public and political discourse in the US especially, the very idea of 'limits' had been discredited both by its challenge to the invincibility of the American Dream, and by the apparent failure of predicted shortages of natural resources to emerge.

Ecosystem limits, however, are very real. Whether they constitute a fundamental limit to economic growth probably depends more on the nature of the economy than on the economy of nature. What is clear is that, as constraints on natural resources have emerged, the capitalist economy has sidestepped them by shifting the crisis in space, in time, or between domains. For example, shortages of material resources have been overcome by exploitation of lower-grade ores, requiring more energy to extract and process them. The approach of peak oil has triggered the cry of 'Drill, baby, drill!' exhorting us to exploit oil in yet more remote locations, and to develop unconventional gas and oil sources through fracking and tar sands extraction. Both of these methods involve significantly higher carbon emissions than conventional fossil fuels. As a result, apparent limits in resource availability have been translated into still greater pressure on the climate system.

It is important to note that limits are not entirely unchanging physical absolutes. The resilience of natural systems changes over time. For example, simplified ecosystems are typically far less resilient than complex ones, even if they have the same gross productivity. In considering the implications of limits we also need to consider resilience and vulnerability – including the vulnerability of affected human populations.

Environmental space In the 1990s, research at the Wuppertal Institute in Germany and elsewhere made a determined effort to measure and characterize environmental resource constraints. Following initial Dutch research (Opschoor and Weterings 1994), Spangenberg and others estimated the boundaries of 'environmental space' as defined in terms of sustainable rates of use of key resources such as fossil fuels, timber, and fresh water (Spangenberg et al. 1995; Hille 1997; McLaren et al. 1998). Sustainable rates were estimated globally in terms of per capita consumption levels. Different constraints pertain to different resources. Two examples include fossil fuel and timber use. Fossil fuel use is seen as limited by the implications of climate change. Timber use is restricted by the sustainable harvest possible without reducing biodiversity.

In most cases, the resource is treated as global, and estimates of sustainable consumption rates require some form of distributional allocation. The environmental space approach typically chooses equitable per capita allocation according to a share of forecast global population in 2050. Advocates of the environmental space approach acknowledge that this is a crude simplification that ignores any economic, cultural, or geographical variation in need, and also overlooks any past historical inequalities (or 'ecological debts').

Environmental space analyses showed clearly that human societies were not pushing up against merely local limits or facing scarcity of individual resources. Rather, these analyses showed how we were approaching, or in some cases already exceeding, global limits for a whole suite of fundamental resources. The concept of *environmental space* allows an equal right to resource consumption for all people in the world within the carrying capacity of the planet. In so doing, it provides a clear understanding that justice, equity, and rights, and environmental limits, are inseparable. It also demonstrates that consumption of environmental resources has a minimum for dignity, as well as a maximum – that is, a 'dignity floor' as well as a 'sustainability ceiling.' The Universal Declaration of Human Rights recognizes this, of course, albeit without explicit inclusion of the environmental dimension:

> Everyone, as a member of society, has the right to social security and is entitled to realization ... of the economic, social and cultural rights indispensable for his dignity. (Article 22)
>
> Everyone who works has the right to just and favourable remuneration ensuring for himself and his family an existence worthy of human dignity. (Article 23)

Since the 1970s, globalization, while in theory increasing economic efficiency and specialization, has further increased the interconnectedness of global economic systems. In the past, economies ran up against local or regional limits and devised ways to adapt, or they failed. In an era of globalization, the key strategy has been to circumvent local scarcity by drawing in resources from more distant locations. As a result, human society has claimed an ever greater share of net primary productivity, a greater share of incoming solar energy, and has approached genuinely global limits. The story of biofuels shows how encroaching limits in one area, the supply and emissions of fossil energy, have been translated into impacts on others, such as productive land, forest area, and food supply. While the economy does not care how energy to fuel vehicles is obtained, society actually needs a whole series of different environmental resources for sustainability.

Ecological footprinting At much the same time, William Rees and Mathias Wackernagel developed the ecological footprint methodology (Wackernagel and Rees 1996). This starts from much the same premise as environmental space – that sustainable supply of environmental resources is limited, and should be measured directly. However, it seeks to place all resource use on a single comparable axis, converting all consumption into units of 'productive land area.' For the products of farming and forestry, this is fairly straightforward. For fossil fuels and other minerals, it is more challenging. In the case of fossil fuels, it is achieved by estimating the area of productive land required to recapture the carbon dioxide emitted by combustion of fossil fuels.

The result is a measure that has major communication advantages, notably exploited by WWF with the development of the concept of 'one planet living,'[14] but also has major, if not fatal, epistemological and methodological flaws. To assume that environmental resources are fungible is as erroneous as assuming that the environment is not physically limited, but that it can be traded off for a larger economy. Human survival and flourishing depend not only on a minimum quantity of productive land, but also, for example, on the maintenance of a stable climate, a minimum thickness of stratospheric ozone, clean water, and much more. Sustainability can be defined only in multiple dimensions, not shrunk to a single one, whether that one is measured in dollars or acres.

Morally, too, the ecological footprint approach has weaknesses. While Wackernagel and Rees typically compared per capita ecological footprints with a global fair share of productive land, many of their followers make aggregate comparisons or compare the footprint of a particular group (for example Americans, or Londoners) with the physical area of the territory the group controls, without regard for the underlying inequality of land distribution.

This error becomes particularly significant when considering the sustainability of cities. A crude use of ecological footprints typically states that cities, especially large ones, have an ecological footprint much larger than their physical area. This is implied to be a problem. But it is simply an artifact of high population density, which pays no regard to the actual or potential per capita footprints of different urban lifestyles. In fact, high-density, walkable cities can, and typically do, have much lower per capita footprints than low-density, car-dominated cities (Newman and Kenworthy 1999), and lower per capita footprints than suburban and dispersed rural settlements (when controlled for income). In other words, footprinting tends to imply that the city is bad for sustainability, when a more sophisticated approach may find that it enables both lower per capita impact and greater political freedom.

This is partly because, as I mentioned above, one key to reducing

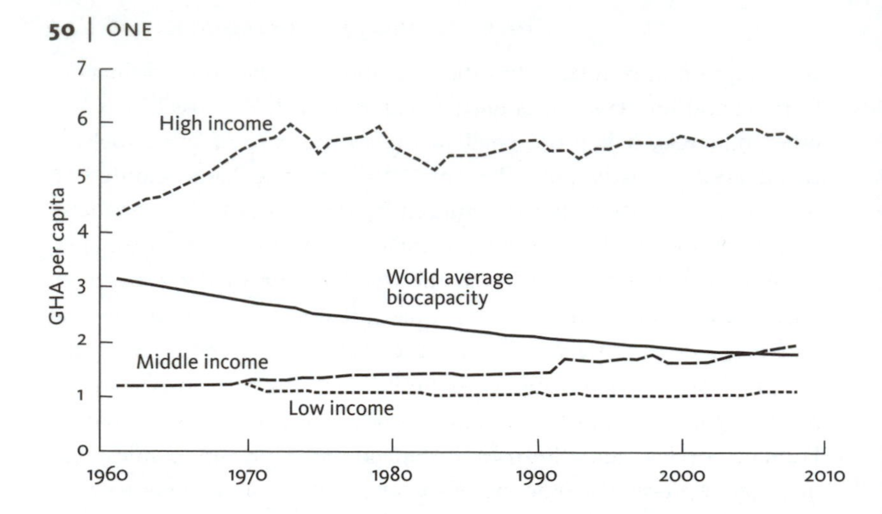

1.9 Changes in the ecological footprint per person in high-, middle- and low-income countries, 1961–2008 (*sources*: Global Footprint Network 2011; WWF *Living Planet Report 2012*, 56, http://awsassets.panda.org/downloads/1_lpr_2012_online_full_size_single_pages_final_120516.pdf)

environmental impact while enhancing capabilities is sharing resources and co-production. The private sector can do this, with leasing and rental mechanisms, but typically public services offer a much more intense level of sharing. Examples of such public services include public transport and libraries. The planning and management of cities are key tools in enabling sharing, yet in modern cities even basic shared public space is at threat, whether from insecurity or privatization. Urbanism is clearly compatible with sustainability (Sherlock 1991; Elkin et al. 1989), but, in practice, too often the potential is not met. Urban districts are redeveloped in ever less sustainable forms, with massive material consumption. Harvey (2011) argues that this is simply because capital surplus absorption needs a physical location. Urban redevelopment has kept the cycle of capitalism going. The built environment represents first an opportunity for, but before long an obstacle to, capital accumulation. Thus, redevelopment cycles are far shorter than would be environmentally or socially optimal.

Despite its shortcomings, ecological footprinting can be used to undertake valuable analysis if adequate data is available. This data needs to be properly normalized in order to compare, for example, the footprints of different income groups (see, for example, Chambers et al. 2000; White 2007).

Planetary boundaries: a safe operating space for humanity More recent research by an international team of earth system scientists has developed our understanding of global environmental thresholds and boundaries:

> Nine planetary boundaries [are] identified … the global biogeochemical cycles of nitrogen, phosphorus, carbon, and water; the major physical circulation systems of the planet (the climate, stratosphere, ocean systems); biophysical features of Earth that contribute to the underlying resilience of its self-regulatory capacity (marine and terrestrial biodiversity, land systems); and two critical features associated with anthropogenic global change (aerosol loading and chemical pollution). (Rockström et al. 2009a, 6)

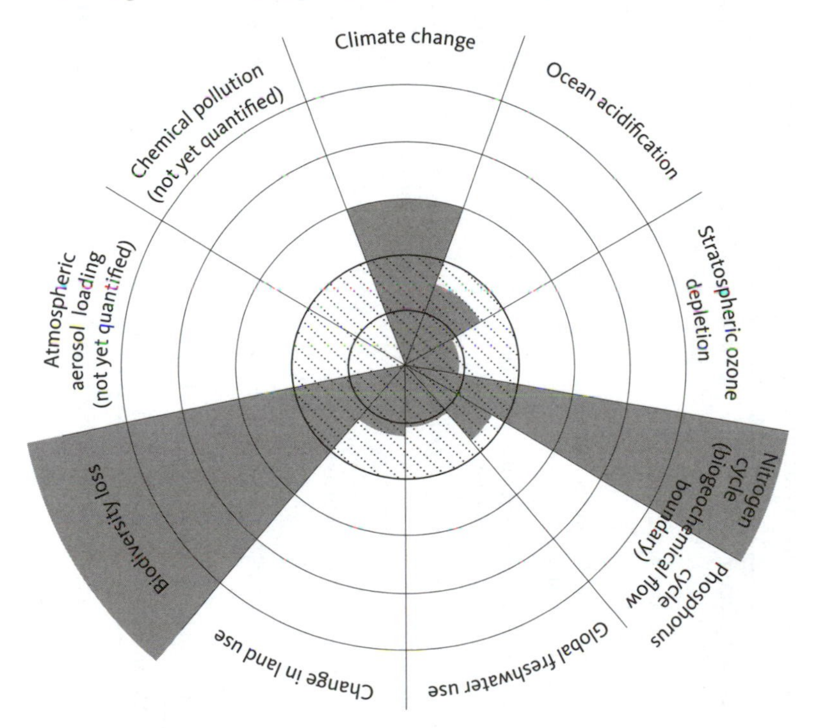

The inner dotted shading represents the proposed safe operating space for nine planetary systems. The grey wedges represent an estimate of the current position for each variable. The boundaries in three systems (rate of biodiversity loss, climate change, and human interference with the nitrogen cycle) have already been exceeded.

1.10 Beyond the boundary (*source*: Rockström et al. 2009b, 472)

TABLE 1.2 Beyond the limits: global limits and required reductions in resource consumption

Resource	Limiting factor	Sustainable level – reduction needed	Rockström et al. 2009 for comparison
Fossil energy	CO_2 emissions and climate impacts	50 to 75 percent cut	350 ppm CO_2 (would require emissions cut at the upper end of the e-space range)
Agricultural land	Impacts on soils, forests, water, and biodiversity	Up to 15 percent cut	Crop land no more than 15 percent of ice-free land surface (implies 30 percent increase sustainable)
Timber	Sustainable harvesting rates and impacts on biodiversity	Up to 30 percent cut[1]	Biodiversity less than 10 spp/million pa (currently 100 plus)
Water	Impacts on biodiversity, regional water balance	Regionally determined, 15 percent cut in the UK	Global: no more than 4,000 km^3 pa
Non-renewable resources	Impacts on human health, biodiversity, and productive land and forests	50 to 100 percent cut	Consider nitrogen and phosphorus; 75 percent reduction in nitrogen required
Chlorine	Impacts on health and ozone layer	100 percent cut	No more than 5 percent decrease in stratospheric ozone (currently within safe limit)
Cement	Material flows (and energy use)	50 percent cut	n/a
Aluminum	Material flows (and energy use)	50 percent cut	n/a

Note: 1. An increase of up to 30 percent may be possible through the development and widespread adoption of efficient sustainable harvesting techniques.

This research found that three of the system parameters are in overshoot: the climate system, biodiversity loss, and nitrogen loading (see Figure 1.10).

While rates of biodiversity loss mostly exceeded the researchers' best estimates of a sustainable level, neither biodiversity loss nor nitrogen loading are considered to experience 'global scale thresholds' that would hinder or prevent recovery.[15] The climate system, on the other hand, is known to experience such thresholds (from research into past system states).

Rockström et al. (2009a) note drily:

> The thresholds in key Earth System processes exist irrespective of peoples' preferences, values, or compromises based on political and socio-economic feasibility, such as expectations of technological breakthroughs and fluctuations in economic growth.

This can be seen as a response to the commonly held view – on both the right and left wings of politics – that societies cannot afford to bear the additional economic costs of environmental protection and that it is in some way unrealistic to expect rational economic actors to bear such costs. Rockström et al. remind us that physical realities are even less forgiving than economic ones.

Oxfam's 'doughnut': a safe and just operating space for humanity Building on the 'environmental ceiling' of Rockström et al. (2009b), by developing a 'social foundation' Kate Raworth (2012, 4) notes that:

> The social foundation forms an inner boundary, below which are many dimensions of human deprivation. The environmental ceiling forms an outer boundary, beyond which are many dimensions of environmental degradation. Between the two boundaries lies an area – shaped like a doughnut – which represents an environmentally safe and socially just space for humanity to thrive in. It is also the space in which inclusive and sustainable economic development takes place.

She also states that:

> This framework brings out a new perspective on sustainable development. Human-rights advocates have long focused on the imperative of ensuring every person's claim to life's essentials, while ecological economists have highlighted the need to situate the

economy within environmental limits. The framework brings the two approaches together in a simple, visual way, creating a closed system that is bounded by human rights on the inside and environmental sustainability on the outside (ibid., 15; see Figure 1.11).

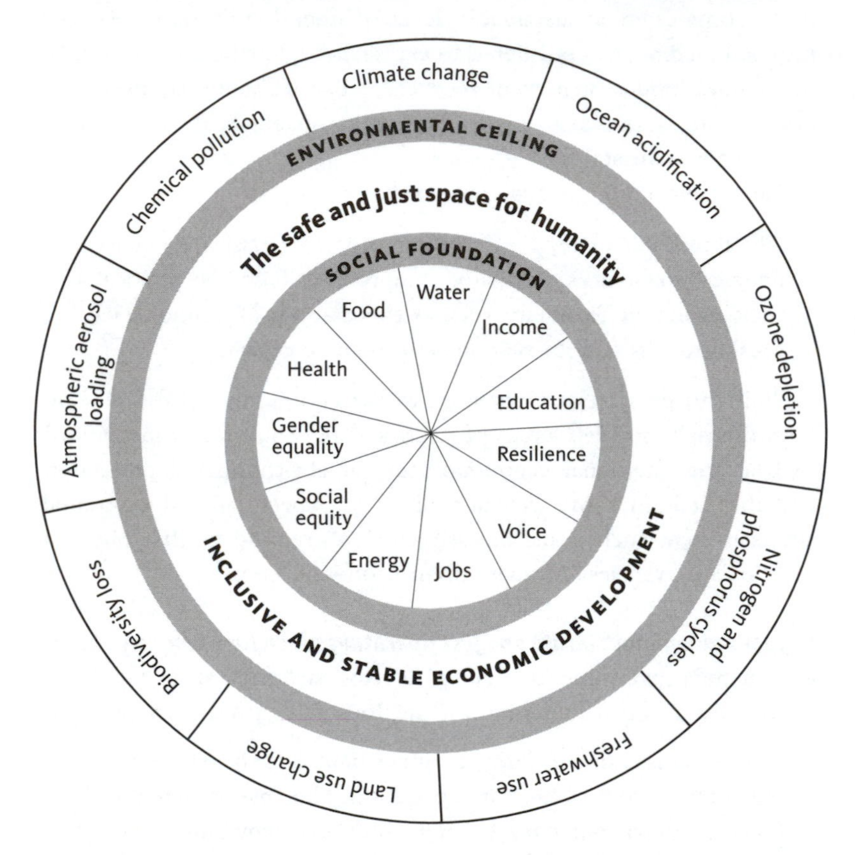

Note: The 11 dimensions of the social foundation are illustrative and are based on governments' priorities for Rio+20. The nine dimensions of the environmental ceiling are based on the planetary boundaries set out by Rockström et al. 2009b.

1.11 A safe and just space for humanity to thrive in: a first illustration (*source*: Oxfam: www.oxfam.org/sites/www.oxfam.org/files/dp-a-safe-and-just-space-for-humanity-130212-en.pdf.

Environmental overshoot and distribution Whether the yardstick is planetary boundaries, Oxfam's 'doughnut,' environmental space, or ecological footprint, there is little doubt that, overall, humanity is in a state of 'environmental overshoot,' consuming more environmental resources than the planet can continue to provide (see Table 1.2). Thus, the current generation is accumulating an 'environmental debt' to future generations. But the aggregate impact on humanity is only one aspect of the problem. From a just sustainabilities standpoint, we need to ask: what is the cause of the overshoot? For whose use of the environment, and for what purposes?

The data that is available is fairly clear-cut. Environmental resource use by poor people in poor countries is typically considerably less than that of rich people in rich countries (see Figure 1.9). Resources to meet basic needs (such as food and shelter) constitute only a small part of the total. Considered in distributional terms, it is inequalities and the consumption patterns of the so-called developed world (as discussed at length earlier) that lie at the root of the problem. Countries that want to develop, and are doing so rapidly, such as China, are having to appropriate the environmental resources of Africa because they do not have the bio-capacity in their own country.

It is worth remembering that not only do poor people cause less environmental damage as a whole, but that pollution and resource degradation disproportionately impact the poor and disadvantaged, who are both more vulnerable to widespread effects such as climate change, and less able to resist the imposition of activities or developments with localized impacts, such as waste dumps, mines, or polluting factories.

Climate justice The issue of climate change has stimulated much thinking about justice, particularly as it has become clear that excess emissions have been, and remain, mainly the fault of high-consuming populations in rich countries, while the most immediate impacts of climate change on rainfall patterns, temperatures, and sea levels will be, and are being, experienced by low-consuming populations in poor countries. Disparities in per capita emissions are dramatic (Jones and Edwards 2009), and the inequalities become even more intense when the capability to act is considered.

The concept of Greenhouse Development Rights (Baer et al. 2008) makes an allowance for emissions to meet basic needs, and takes into account the capabilities available to reduce emissions (as a function of disposable income) in attempting to determine just targets for emissions reduction. Typically, such assessment (ibid., for example) concludes that rich countries need to make greater reductions in emissions than current emissions levels. In other words, as well as reducing their own emissions to zero, they also need to take responsibility for financing additional reductions in poor countries, or develop technical means to remove carbon dioxide from the atmosphere, the so-called 'negative emissions technologies' (NETs).

The climate change issue also demonstrates clearly the critical importance of distribution in a world of limits. If growth in environmental consumption is (effectively) unlimited, it remains conceivable that inequalities in such consumption and the wellbeing which, up to a point, is derived from it could be overcome by disproportionate future growth in consumption, allowing poor groups and countries to 'catch up.' Where such consumption is globally limited at a smaller level than today, inequalities can be addressed only by redistribution.[16] But, as we saw earlier, the current response of existing global elites to scarcity (that is, to the threat of real or regulated scarcity) is to seek secure access to resources regardless of environmental or social impact, either through land grabs or by using unconventional hydrocarbons such as tar sands.

A growing literature confirms Rockström et al.'s conclusion that we are already in overshoot with respect to climate thresholds and that we face the risk of multiple positive feedbacks, such as the melting of Arctic ice, Amazon wildfires, thawing tundra, and melting methane clathrates – a class of compound that consist of a cage of molecules that can trap gases, such as methane; see Pearce (2007) for a good summary.

Fortunately, there is more inertia in the physical climate system than in the economic system affecting it. As a result, temperature increases and sea level rises lag decades, perhaps centuries, behind rising carbon dioxide concentrations. Humanity still has a window, albeit one that is rapidly closing, in which to address climate overshoot. The best efforts of climate modelers suggest that it may still be possible to avoid highly risky levels of temperature rise with fairly dramatic emissions cuts. Hansen et al. (2008) suggest that if we rapidly – that is, by 2030 – phase out unabated consumption of coal, avoid unconventional fossil fuels, and enhance natural carbon sinks such as forests, we might return carbon dioxide concentrations to a fairly safe 350 ppm by the end of the century. Translated into emissions targets, this sort of scenario suggests that net global emissions would have to fall close to zero by 2050. Any allowance of continued growth in emissions for development in poorer countries would require even more rapid emissions cuts among the major wealthy emitters in Europe and North America, with reduction rates as great as eight to 15 percent per year, as calculated by Friends of the Earth (2011), even in scenarios where newly industrialized countries, including China, are achieving absolute emissions reductions by 2015.

Even those who think such rates of reduction are politically plausible have to consider alternative or complementary strategies such as adaptation and geo-engineering. Despite the inertia in the climate system, some degree of warming and sea level rise is certain to occur. Adaptation to those changes will be necessary, whether undertaken in a planned or a responsive fashion. Necessary adaptations will include managing coastal defenses and/or managed retreat (Agyeman et al. 2009), changing cropping systems and techniques, enhancing urban cooling in many regions, improved flood management, and new approaches to weather insurance. All these could also have distinctive distributional consequences.

Similarly, if geo-engineering technologies are implemented to slow the rate of temperature change via solar radiation management (SRM) or to accelerate the removal of carbon dioxide from the atmosphere, or carbon dioxide removal (CDR) through NETs, there are also distributional issues to be considered, of which 'who pays' is only one of the questions.

Triple decoupling Achieving climate justice is clearly necessary for just sustainabilities, yet climate change is caused by the use of resources to meet real needs and sustain real wellbeing. For climate, as well as for other environmental resources, there are three broad strategies that must be combined if we are to bring aggregate impacts within planetary boundaries in a socially just manner, as suggested by the Oxfam 'doughnut' (Raworth 2012).

These can be conceived as a process of triple decoupling:

- decoupling material consumption from energy/resource use (or 'efficiency');
- decoupling the delivery of wellbeing from consumption (or 'sufficiency'); and
- decoupling the delivery of fundamental needs such as political freedom and identity from consumption.

Progress on the first can be achieved within the conventional economic system. Failure to achieve progress on the latter two, however, would most likely result in higher consumption levels and no reduction in environmental overshoot. As I have suggested above, an alternative economic model is essential, and one founded in co-production seems to offer most potential, being apparently already poised for emerging change.

Conclusions

The idea of just sustainabilities arose in the early 2000s as a conscious effort to (re)place the issues of equity and justice into the growing sustainability agenda. Too many people thought that the environmental justice movement was 'dealing with' equity and justice issues so the sustainability movement could and would focus on 'green' issues. The work of Warner (2002) and Pearsall and Pierce (2010) in the US, together with my and Bob Evans's (2004) work in the UK, showed the need for this (re)placement. Since then, the argument has been won, and, as this chapter has shown, there is a robust and growing theoretically informed literature that draws on a diverse range of academic and scholarly areas.

What also seems to be happening is that, slowly, silos are breaking down and there is increasing evidence of 'joined-up thinking.' For instance, Rockström et al. 2009a developed their 'Planetary boundaries: exploring the safe operating space for humanity,' which focused on environmental limits or boundaries. This was subsequently 'joined-up' to an essential 'social foundation' by Raworth (2012) and her colleagues at Oxfam in their report *A Safe and Just Operating Space for Humanity: Can we live within the doughnut?* What this chapter has demonstrated, I hope, is that in terms of just sustainabilities, we have a pretty clear roadmap – we know what to do, but we're simply not doing it. In the following chapters, I hope to develop the roadmap some more.

2 | FOOD

Introduction

As I mentioned in Chapter 1, food has become one of the key arenas in which conflicts around justice and sustainability have played out, particularly as a result of the opposing trends of globalization and localization of food production. Food has also long been a driver of social movements. Allen (2004) notes that conditions in American food and agriculture have been associated with a variety of resistance movements, including the populist, environmental, and food safety movements. Recently, a variety of specific causes have been included in the 'food movement': local food, sustainable agriculture, food justice, anti-hunger, food sovereignty, and community food security to name but a few. The broad goal of the food movement is to revolutionize the conventional, industrial food system, yet it includes diverse – and at times competing – organizational forms, strategies, and loci of action (Hassanein 2003).

In this chapter I want to look specifically at two areas of interest in terms of just sustainabilities. One is an *organizational form* (food policy councils or FPCs), the other a *locus of action* ('the local'). Firstly, I will look at the reification of 'the local,' where there is a notable absence in much of the popular discourse surrounding local food systems of an explicit recognition of just sustainabilities concerns relating to the ability of people of color, immigrants, and low-income populations to produce, access, and consume healthy and culturally appropriate foods. I will examine these conflicts and contradictions with the goal of forming a more robust understanding of the true potential of local food systems and the appropriateness of local food initiatives in addressing just sustainabilities issues. Secondly, and related to the first point, I want to present a case study of the role of policy as a tool to improve community food security within the current food system. In North America, one way of engaging local stakeholders around food policy is through the creation of city, state, or provincial/regional FPCs. These councils are theoretically representative, collaborative committees that help coordinate food-related activities that foster the local economy, protect the environment, and strengthen the community via the food system.

'The local'

Over the past decade, the production and consumption of locally grown food have become *the* clarion call for food movement advocates in Europe and North America especially, but also in countries such as Brazil, where the city of Belo Horizonte became 'the city that ended hunger' thanks to pioneering 'food as a right' policies and local farm-to-school programs (Moore Lappé 2009). Local food systems have emerged, virtually unproblematized as a catch-all notion for sustainability. For many proponents, local food systems provide the antithesis to the destructive tendencies of global capitalist industrial agriculture, by offering ecologically sound agricultural practices, support for small-scale family farms and local economic development, fresher and healthier food for the consumer, greater democracy and transparency in food systems decision-making, and a more holistic connection between the consumer, the farmer, and the rural landscape. In North America, the local food movement has garnered significant attention in the mainstream media and participation among certain segments of the population (see, for example, Pollan 2006; Kingsolver 2007), while celebrity chef Jamie Oliver has championed local foods in the UK and more recently in the US. Rising interest has been matched by a proliferation of farmers' markets and community-supported agriculture projects and programs (CSAs), as well as by food co-ops, groceries, restaurants, and food services of large institutions across the country sourcing more of their food locally. In 2007, 'locavore,' one who eats locally, was the Oxford English Dictionary's 'word of the year' (Prentice 2007). Local food boosters have framed their approaches from a variety of perspectives, ranging from rural development to environmentalism, from communitarianism to anti-globalization.

Absent in much of the popular discourse surrounding local food systems, however, has been an explicit recognition of just sustainabilities concerns relating to the ability of people of color, immigrants, and low-income populations to produce, access, and consume healthy and culturally appropriate foods. Popular local food narratives have largely focused on the ecologically damaging forces of corporate power in food systems as the primary site of resistance, while issues of race, racism, and justice have been given less attention (Slocum 2006a and b; Alkon and Agyeman 2011). The dominant discourse has been framed from a mostly white, middle- and upper-class perspective of food system activism concerned with environmental sustainability, the support of small-scale family farms and the local economy, and issues of health, taste, and nutrition. The bias toward 'voting with your fork' ensures that mainly middle- and upper-income populations participate in local food, and has earned it the moniker 'yuppie chow,' due to the niche market status of organic and local foods and the common focus on providing environmental sustainability and sustainable incomes for small-scale farmers rather than social justice, namely affordable healthy food for low-income populations (Guthman 2008a).

In Alkon's (2008) study of two San Francisco Bay Area farmers' markets, one located in a white, affluent neighborhood of Berkeley and the other in a low-income, predominantly African American neighborhood of West Oakland, she explores the just sustainabilities implications of localization by highlighting the disconnect that can exist between the environmental sustainability and social justice agendas operating within the local food movement. She found that the Berkeley market vendors and attendees were primarily concerned with the environmental sustainability agenda, placing emphasis on reconnecting with nature through local and organic farms, while the mostly African American West Oakland market vendors and attendees were primarily concerned with a social justice agenda that situated the local food movement as a response to racism and inequality. Alkon (ibid., 280) observed that:

> Because the North Berkeley Farmers' Market works to improve the environment, defined as beautiful, diverse, non-human nature, some of its participants need not see the harsh realities of food insecurity. This inhibits the incorporation of social justice goals.

The emphasis on either environmental sustainability or social justice reflects the racial and socio-economic complexion of the communities that the markets serve. Alkon (2012) develops her analysis further by carefully highlighting the strengths and weaknesses of these two farmers' markets and, through them, the contradictions, compromises, and exclusions inherent in the emerging green economy. She foregrounds food politics as a contested, deeply racialized, gendered, and class-based space in which meanings and messages, discourses and practices determine who participates. Only through an active cross-pollination of justice and sustainability typical of a just sustainabilities approach, she argues, can a more just, inclusive green economy emerge.

One aspect of local food system functioning that has received greater academic and activist attention has been the social justice and inequality issues in underserved urban (Wrigley 2002) and rural areas (McEntee 2011), known as 'food deserts.'[1] These are low-income communities, often of color, in North America and Europe with limited access to nutritious, affordable food, where the population is characterized by multiple deprivation and social exclusion. The concept of food justice has consequently risen to the top of the agenda for food system scholars and activists, and local food initiatives – such as urban agriculture, community gardening, farmers' markets, CSAs, and grocery co-ops – have been offered as a means to provide greater food security for underserved urban communities (Baker 2004). According to the long-established organization Just Food (2010), food justice is:

> communities exercising their right to grow, sell, and eat [food that is] fresh, nutritious, affordable, culturally appropriate, and grown locally with care for the well-being of the land, workers, and animals.

The follow-on question then becomes 'What is a just urban food system?' (Bedore 2010), and this is the focus of academic research for an increasing number of geographers and sociologists. In addition, many non-profit and other activist groups have emerged in cities across the world in recent years to address these issues, some to great effect. However, a growing body of scholarship is critically analyzing the valorization and ability of local food systems, as they are being framed and constructed currently in popular food movement discourse, to address issues of just sustainabilities: food insecurity, inequality, and insensitivity to cultural difference. For all the potential that exists in moving away from globalized capitalist industrial agriculture toward more localized production and consumption of food, there arises a whole new set of conflicts and contradictions when framing 'local' as more sustainable and socially just. For instance, Moseley (2007) argues:

> While the local food craze is all well and good, we should not be so quick to denounce organic and fair trade foods that are imported from the developing world. By shunning these products, we do

not encourage local markets to flourish in these countries, but we condemn these farmers to the ills of conventional production for the global market (the only other real alternative at this time).

There is nothing inherent about scale

When analyzing the discourse surrounding local food systems, it is clear that 'the local' has been imbued with multiple connotations, many of which are not necessarily deserved. As Born and Purcell (2006) have pointed out, scale is socially constructed and there is nothing inherent about any scale, 'the local' included. Injustices and inequality can be perpetrated at any scale, and acting on the local level does not guarantee a more sustainable or just result. A small-scale local farmer, for instance, is no more likely to use organic agriculture methods or pay a living wage to his or her field workers than a large-scale export farmer half the world away, based on the simple fact that he or she is producing for local consumption. Similarly, the Filipino immigrants in San Diego, California, interviewed by Valiente-Neighbours (2012):

> Demonstrat[e] translocalism, Filipino immigrants carry with them the idea that Filipino food is local food, which they cook at home or eat in restaurants. They also exercise this translocalism when they tend their fruit and vegetable gardens. The discourse within agrifood literature and the food localisation movement needs more reflexivity.

The framing of the local food movement in popular discourse has often confused the ends, which are a more sustainable and socially just food system, with the means: the localization of food production and consumption. In other words, the goal has become the creation of a local food system, rather than the creation of a more sustainable and just food system using localization as the means. Born and Purcell (2006, 195–6) term this 'the local trap':

> No matter what its scale, the outcomes of a food system are contextual: they depend on the actors and agendas that are empowered by the social relations in a given food system.

That being said, the localization of food does theoretically provide greater potential for transparency in farming practices and mutual responsibility between the farmer and consumer due to their geographic proximity and ability to see each other on a regular basis. It is easier, as hilariously demonstrated by *Portlandia*'s Peter and Nance,[2] in order to make sure that one's restaurant order is ethical and humane, to visit a farm 15 miles outside one's home town than it is to visit a farm on the other side of the world. What is important to determine, then, is who is being empowered by and benefitting from the localization of food, and who may be experiencing disempowerment or exclusion.

Politics and heterogeneity within 'the local'

A second, related conflict in much of the local food system discourse is a denial of the heterogeneity of 'the local.' The assumption is that the localization of food will benefit all who take part, yet those who are unable to participate, or are excluded, are simultaneously made invisible by the localization process. 'The local' is constructed as discrete, homogeneous, and static (Hinrichs 2003). As we know, diversity and deeply unequal power relations exist within any given locality, and, as noted above, certain actors and agendas may be empowered by food system localization while others may be disempowered or left out.

In her research into the development of the local food system in Iowa and the 'Iowa-grown banquet meal,' Hinrichs (ibid.) observed that localization can create the defensive, exclusionary protection of a region with the assumption of homogeneity and common interests within that region and 'otherness' outside. Yet, within any given region, there can exist unequal and contentious power relations between the elite and the marginalized, the diverse ethnic and racial groups, and the different social classes. As noted by DuPuis and Goodman (2005), localization may simply reinforce the agendas of the elite within a given region through the establishment of defensive protective territories for themselves at the expense of other local actors. Localism can serve the interests of family farms, restaurateurs, and their mostly white middle- and upper-income consumers, while denying equal access to locally grown and culturally appropriate food for minority and low-income populations in a region. As Allen et al. (2003) have demonstrated in their examination of alternative agrifood practice in California, leaders of the local food movement have expressed a clear preference for ecological sustainability over social justice in their discourses and agendas. Thus, localism can deny the 'politics of the local' and reflect the interests of a small, unrepresentative group, with potentially problematic social justice consequences (DuPuis and Goodman 2005).

Gibb and Whitman (2012) offer another perspective on the heterogeneity of the local in their study of Chinese Canadian farmers, who make up 15 percent of Metro Vancouver's farmers and farm managers. They found that:

> the new and emerging alternative food networks promoted by the local food movement are but one pathway through which food moves from Metro Vancouver farms to local consumers. The roadside farm stores and greengrocers supplied by some Chinese-Canadian farmers constitute a second alternative food network operating in the urban region.

Due to a 'history of anti-Chinese racism in Canada, together with Chinese-Canadian farmers' creative resistance and entrepreneurialism in responding to social and economic changes' (ibid., 15), they argue that there are 'parallel' networks in which 'both sets of networks are "local" in that they shorten relationships between producers, consumers, and place; however, these networks have few points of intentional connection and collaboration' (ibid., 15).

Hinrichs and Allen (2008) provide another example of 'scalar fetishism' (Bedore 2010, 5) in their exploration of exclusionary practice and selective patronage inherent in 'buy local' consumer campaigns. 'Buy local' campaigns establish ambiguous boundaries for what is encompassed by the local; these boundaries are often delineated by state lines, such as is the case with the MassGrown 'Buy Fresh, Buy Local' campaign (Massachusetts Department of Agricultural Resources). These market-based campaigns emphasize the support of local businesses and keeping consumer dollars circulating in the local economy, but often pay little or no attention to issues of social justice or food security for underserved communities within the local boundaries. There is little guarantee that the benefits of a 'buy local' campaign will be distributed to the full range of producers and consumers within an ambiguous boundary, as only select farms will be listed in the campaign materials and directories and only some consumers will have the economic means to patronize them (Hinrichs and Allen 2008).

Not only is there the danger of denying the politics *within* the local, there also exists the problematic exclusion of anything *outside* the local. The local/non-local binary can ignore the deleterious effects of localization on those who are placed outside the local boundaries. The classic example would be export farmers in developing countries who are denied access to markets in developed countries due to their local food preferences and exclusionary practices. In the research of Cross et al. (2009) into variances in farm worker health between localized and globalized food systems, they found that horticultural workers in Kenya's export-oriented farms were often healthier than the population norm in their country, due to the stringent corporate responsibility practices of the UK supermarkets that their farms supplied. Similar to Moseley's (2007) arguments about the US noted above, the growing move toward more localized food systems in the UK will diminish the export market for Kenyan farmers, and some of these farms may go out of business, resulting in a negative impact on the horticultural workers especially. The effects on those who are deemed 'outside the local,' or on those who are not granted access to 'the local,' must be taken into consideration when attempting to build a more just and sustainable food system.

Finally, even those who do participate in the localization process are not necessarily better off because of it. As Jarosz (2008, 232) found in her examination of the local food system in western Washington state:

> Increasing urban demand for seasonal and organic produce grown 'close to home' and the processes of rural restructuring which emphasise small scale sustainable family farms and its direct linkages to cities do not necessarily enable all farmers to consistently make a living from season to season.

In her case study of various small-scale family farmers in the region, she found that many could not support themselves solely from selling produce directly to customers in urban markets but often had to take second jobs or have a spouse employed in another field. The inability to earn a living was primarily due to high transportation costs and competition among farmers within farmers' markets as well as from organic and health food groceries offering similar choices that drive down the prices urban consumers are willing to pay for their produce (ibid.). Thus, those who are benefitting the most are the middle- to upper-income urban residents driving the demand for local produce who have a wide variety of choices in consumption, while some of the family farmers who are supposedly benefitting from the localization of food are having trouble making ends meet.

The local, however it may be defined, is never likely to be homogeneous and static but rather it is heterogeneous and dynamic, with its own power relations, inequalities, and idiosyncrasies, and food system localization will have varying and selective beneficiaries as well as detrimental effects and exclusions (see Allen 2008; 2010). Again, the point must be emphasized that who is empowered and who is disempowered by food system localization is the key issue. Just sustainabilities policy-making and planning would focus on allowing for inclusive and democratic processes, and those processes that are exclusive and perpetuate inequalities would be recognized and prevented.

New agricultures: race, class, culture, and 'the local'

As I have shown, the social justice and cultural concerns relating to the ability of immigrants and refugees, people of color, low-income communities, and 'new' populations to produce, access, and consume healthy and culturally appropriate foods have not been top of the 'locavore' agenda. The local food movement has constructed and foregrounded a narrative reflecting:

> like-minded people, with similar backgrounds, values and proclivities, who have come to similar conclusions about how our food system should change. Moreover, those active in the food movement tend to have the wealth necessary to participate in its dominant social change strategy – the purchase of organic food. (Alkon and Agyeman 2011, 2–3)

Similarly, in constructing (and constricting) 'the local' they have used ecological arguments in the main to tell us what should be grown, and have focused on growing native food plants, especially plants local to a given (bio)region. But this is being challenged.

In August 2011, US National Public Radio's *All Things Considered* aired a segment 'Some US farms trade tobacco for a taste of Africa,' which reported on George Bowling's 60-acre farm in southern Maryland which has started growing African crops for the region's 120,000-strong African population. On 10 October that year, an article in the *New York Times*, 'When the uprooted put down roots,' highlighted the growth across the US of 'refugee agriculture' among, for example, Somalis, Cambodians, Liberians, Congolese, Bhutanese, and Burundians.

Together, these two stories illustrate the potential of 'refugee' and 'new agricultures' to help us reimagine what constitutes both 'the local' and 'local foods.' In terms of reimagining 'the local,' these stories help disrupt the cozy elite exclusivity criticized by, among others, Hinrichs (2003), DuPuis and Goodman (2005), and Hinrichs and Allen (2008). The local becomes global and cosmopolitan as new immigrants bring new ideas and new ways. Metropolis becomes cosmopolis. In terms of what are characterized as 'local foods,' there is a similar moment of disjuncture, of rupture with ecological and agricultural 'norms,' when increasingly diverse local populations want to buy, as at George Bowling's farm, locally grown culturally appropriate foods, which are not what *should* be grown locally according to the predominantly ecologically focused local food movement.

Consider the following from the *New York Times* article:

> New Roots [San Diego], with 85 growers from 12 countries, is one of more than 50 community farms dedicated to refugee agriculture, an entrepreneurial movement spreading across the country. American agriculture has historically been forged by newcomers, like the Scandinavians who helped settle the Great Plains; today's growers are more likely to be rural subsistence farmers from Africa and Asia, resettled in and around cities from New York, Burlington, Vt., and Lowell, Mass., to Minneapolis, Phoenix and San Diego.

Many of these low-income 'new' and refugee populations live in food deserts resulting from a history of disinvestment in, and neglect of, mostly low-income urban (and rural) areas. In their most physically and spatially extreme forms, these areas have not been recognized as profitable sites for supermarket and full service grocery store locations and have therefore been left with limited and often less healthy options for food access, such as corner stores and fast food establishments (McClintock 2011). The residents of these neighborhoods, such as City Heights, San Diego, where New Roots Community Farm is located, are more vulnerable to food insecurity and have less ability to determine their access to healthy, affordable, and culturally appropriate food as a result. As the *New York Times* article notes:

> In City Heights, where half the residents live at or below the

federal poverty line, the three-year-old farmer's market was the city's first in a low-income neighborhood, a collaboration between the nonprofit International Rescue Committee and the San Diego County Farm Bureau.

But food is far more than a product that merely sustains life. Alkon and Agyeman (2011, 10) note that:

> Winson (1993) refers to food as an 'intimate commodity' that is literally taken inside the body and imbued with heightened significance. Not only is it a physiological necessity, but food practices – what scholars often call foodways – are manifestations and symbols of cultural histories and proclivities. As individuals participate in culturally defined proper ways of eating, they perform their own identities and memberships in particular groups (Douglass 1996). Food informs individuals' identities, including their racial identities, in ways that other environmental justice and sustainability issues – energy, water, garbage and so on – do not.

Food, food production, and food access are not the solely ecological concerns foregrounded by the dominant food movement narrative, reducible to questions of environmental sustainability, vitally important though this is. Food and 'foodways' are fundamental to peoples' individual and collective identities, and these are even more to the fore in 'new' populations and other marginalized groups who are made invisible by, and in, the dominant culture. Furthermore, while foodways are manifestations and performances of cultural history, their spatial or place-based manifestations are of equal importance. Mares and Peña (2011) use two predominantly Latino/a urban community garden projects – the now defunct South Central Farm (SCF) in Los Angeles and Puget Sound Urban Farmers (now the Seattle Urban Farm Company) – to analyze how food and farming can connect growers to local and extra-local landscapes, creating an 'autotopography' that links their life experiences to a deep sense of place. In effect, they are writing their cultural stories on the land- or cityscape. This is a type of cultural place-making (see Chapter 3) through the growth and celebration of culturally appropriate foods. Mares and Peña (ibid., 209) note:

> One gardener at the SCF, a thirty year old Zapotec woman, described her involvement at the farm in the following way: 'I planted

> this garden because it is a little space like home. I grow the same plants that I had back in my garden in Oaxaca. We can eat like we ate at home and this makes us feel like ourselves. It allows us to keep a part of who we are after coming to the United States.'

As we move toward a more intercultural world, the local food movement should recognize, embrace, and celebrate the possibilities and opportunities of translocalism, of *cultural diversity* as much as it currently celebrates *biodiversity*.

The urban farm as 'plantation'?

Due to the dominant framing of the discourse from a white, middle-class perspective, much of the community food security work that is being done also reflects white cultures of food and white histories that may be culturally insensitive to those being served (Guthman 2008a). Guthman has observed how many of the food justice initiatives targeted at underserved minority communities are met with less enthusiastic responses and participation rates than the organizers had anticipated. These initiatives often involve the establishment of urban farms or community gardens and encourage community residents to grow their own produce and provide food security for themselves.

Yet, sometimes, those being targeted have specific cultural histories that can see farming and growing food as reminders of past oppression. This can be the case especially with African American communities whose ancestors have had a tormented past of slavery and share-cropping in the United States and whose residents may want little to do with growing their own food. An act seen as positive and empowering from a local food perspective reflecting white cultural histories can be perceived as an unwanted reminder of past injustices from a black cultural perspective.

With virtually no consultation, in November 2011, Boston's Zoning Commission unanimously approved a zoning change to turn two vacant city-owned lots in the Dorchester neighborhood, with one-third of its population African American, into urban farms. The local elected representative invoked notions of the mayor imposing a 'plantation,' and stated that the heavily polluted soil would 'poison' people. As Guthman (ibid.) noted, some of the residents in the African American communities she observed would rather have had a Safeway locate in their neighborhood than an urban farm. Many of these residents simply wanted the same privilege that most middle-class Americans enjoy – that is, convenient access to grocery stores – and were uninterested in more alternative forms of food production and consumption.

Initial community opposition to the Dorchester farms demonstrates how, especially given a sensitive issue and a history of tension between city and community, a lack of consultation and participatory planning can negatively affect community responses to zoning decisions, even when the proposed land use change had generated considerable popular attention. There are clear lessons for urban planners and city officials in making assumptions that the benefits of urban agriculture are so compelling that everyone will want it in their neighborhood.

Thinking beyond the local

As I have shown in the examples and reasoning in this chapter so far, the mantra of the popular local food discourse does not resonate equally among all communities. Implicit in the popular discourse is the dominance of white cultural histories, and white privilege directs much of the local food agenda. For the local food movement to become truly transformative in social and food justice issues, institutionalized racism and cultural insensitivity must be recognized and confronted. As long as race, culture, and justice concerns are overshadowed by an emphasis on environmental sustainability, then the potential exists for certain racial and cultural groups to be marginalized or excluded. Furthermore, some academics believe that not only do popular notions of local food activism create the potential for exclusion, they also reinforce the hegemonic economic and political paradigms that have fostered the dominant food system that the local food movement is supposedly attempting to counter in the first place.

The question remains: when, if ever, is the localization of food production and consumption an appropriate means for achieving social justice within food systems? While it is beyond this chapter's scope to address this question fully, there are significant insights from those who have analyzed the local food movement that should be considered when advocating local food systems.

First, localization should be recognized as a means, not an end. Producing and consuming locally does not guarantee any greater concern for social justice or more ecologically sustainable practices, unless those principles are internalized into the movement. Localization does have the potential to help make democratic decision-making more understandable and achievable by decentralizing decision-making processes and involving greater numbers of stakeholders who experience the effects of their decisions in a more tangible manner. Localization can also provide greater transparency in food system processes due to the physical and relational proximity between producers and consumers. Furthermore, as Anderson (2008, 603) notes: 'Localization allows greater food system diversity because each locale can support unique foodways and a unique set of relationships between producers and buyers.' Yet none of these enabling processes of food system localization guarantees a more socially just result. Social justice and cultural sensitivity must be intentional and explicit goals, rather than implicit aims, for this to be possible.

Second, in striving for social justice in food system advocacy, we must recognize that food is heavily culturally situated. Different ethnicities and different cultures have different takes on (trans)localism and food(ways), and experience them differently. This may seem challenging and 'non-conforming' to a movement predicated around white cultures of food and white narratives and histories (Guthman 2008b). Each group has its own unique cultural understandings, practices, performances, and autotopographies of food. Thus, any attempt to foster social justice in food system activism must take a multi-lens approach that recognizes the diversity of the cultural experiences and histories involved. Food system activists must acknowledge the hegemonic white cultural framing of the popular food system activism and the existence of white positionalities and privilege within the movement, and attempt to reconcile these inequalities through cultural sensitivity and anti-racist framings. Food system activism must also be socially inclusive and democratic, involving the greatest possible participation of stakeholders. By taking a reflexive, translocal, multi-lens approach, the heterogeneity and context of the local can be accounted for.

Finally, recognition of human rights, or of a shared responsibility to ensure good food provisioning for all, in terms of production, distribution, and consumption, must be the ultimate goal if we are to develop a more socially just food system, *and* a more inclusive food movement. Alkon and Agyeman's (2011) concept of the 'food movement as polyculture' offers a promising framework for moving forward, as it turns our gaze toward the crossroads of the sustainable agriculture and justice-oriented food security movements by embodying both ideals of environmental sustainability *and* the ability of underserved, marginalized, and diverse communities to produce, access, and consume healthy and culturally appropriate food. Only by recognizing the diversity of histories, cultures, and objectives at play, and through establishing a dialogue between the range of interests in order to negotiate the polyculture, can a truly inclusive and representative solution be imagined. One place we might look to see if this is happening would be in the FPCs.

Case study: food policy councils

Introduction Many organizations involved in community food security work around North America understand the importance of policy to their ability to increase healthy food access for residents. Such groups have advocated for cities (and states or Canadian provinces, in some cases) to adopt 'food policy councils' (FPCs) – collaborative committees that help to coordinate regional food-related activities that strengthen the local economy, the environment, and the community. FPCs bring together diverse players in the food system to promote the concept that nutritious food is a basic right of all citizens and to bring 'democratic principles' to the food system by increasing the voice of the community in food system policies (Allen 2008).

Since their inception in the 1980s, FPCs have identified and addressed various policy and programing gaps in their local food systems. Some examples of these gaps include: food deserts, where supply does not meet demand; the desire to produce cottage foods; inappropriately scaled regulations; and the availability of vacant plots but no zoning allowance for urban agriculture. Bellows and Hamm (2002) discuss how many FPCs developed in relation to the emergence of the 'community food security' framework. Community food security describes a community-wide approach to the lack of food security, which is defined by the United States Department of Agriculture (USDA) as 'the ready availability of nutritionally adequate and safe foods, acquired in socially acceptable ways' (USDA Economic Research Service 2009). Proponents take on system-wide issues, such as land use planning, transportation, urban food production, economic development, food assistance, and public health (Gottlieb and Fisher 1995; Allen 1999). Leaving aside critiques of 'the local,' it is claimed that FPCs have supported the creation of markets for locally produced foods and improved food security for low-income people, the preservation of farm land, the alteration of zoning laws to allow food production in cities, and the adoption of tools that encourage more informed and healthy food choices.

The multi-sectoral composition of FPCs contributes to their potential to create 'innovative programs, policy and planning approaches that might not have been created' without such synergistic efforts (Schiff 2007, 8). Nearly 150 FPCs are operating in various capacities in American and Canadian cities, regions, and states/provinces, and they can be established by state, provincial, or local governments or by grassroots initiatives. Each council is different and generally has broadly defined missions, which allow them to tackle a variety of the most pressing local needs (ibid.). Some predict that FPCs will 'become the fastest-growing institutional innovation in food governance over the next 25 years and will become as commonplace as city departments of public health or recreation' (Roberts 2010, 173).

Clearly, FPCs have the potential to create far-reaching change to address just sustainabilities because, as Harper et al. (2009, 6) argue, 'the failings of our current food system are largely suffered in neighborhoods and constituencies with little political or economic voice.' FPCs, which are usually situated between a government and a community, can increase the voice of low-income, minority, refugee, and 'new' populations in relation to food system policies and outcomes. As I argued above in relation to the local, the leadership of local food system organizations is often not reflective of those they represent (Guthman 2008a; Winne 2008; Slocum 2006a and b). My question is therefore: are the voices of those typically marginalized in the food system (including low-income, minority, refugee, and 'new' populations, food service workers, farm workers, youth, and seniors, for example) adequately incorporated into FPC policies and programs aimed at improving their access to safe, affordable, culturally appropriate, and healthy food; as Winne (2008, 191) notes, 'who is affected most by the food gap and who participates in the efforts to narrow that gap are critical questions.'

Without meaningful inclusion of the food insecure in crafting the alternative food system:

> the priorities and actions of local food projects are unlikely to advance social equity … we need to be creative about finding ways

> to incorporate vulnerable people into a deliberative democratic process that can be used to improve both individual and structural equity. (Allen 2010, 304)

In the process of documenting creative practices that FPCs are currently using to be more inclusive, the research below touched on some fundamental just sustainabilities concerns relating to justice, equity, and democracy in the food movement. The emphasis of community food security on locally based decisions means that community food security projects 'provide people with an opportunity to participate in projects in which they feel they can make a difference' (Allen 1999, 120). Hassanein (2003, 78) argues that food system actors seeking sustainable solutions cannot rely on experts alone to make decisions about the food system because 'those decisions involve choosing among values.' To make value-based decisions, we need to involve those who Cabbil (2010) says have the 'lived experience.' FPCs, then, have a real opportunity and imperative to both embody justice and improve their effectiveness by meaningfully including those who have previously been left out of discussions about policy solutions. This is a necessary element in creating just sustainabilities within the food system, so that 'power and material resources are shared equitably so that people and communities can meet their needs, and live with security and dignity, now and into the future' (Allen 2010, 297).

Echoing Guthman (2008b), the objective of the foregoing research is not to condemn FPCs outright for not doing enough, but to raise questions of why the inclusion of diverse community voices must go beyond simply 'inviting others to the table,' which she points out is 'an increasingly common phrase in considering ways to address diversity in alternative food movements,' when the critical corollary is 'who sets the table?' (Guthman 2008b, 388). The research also addresses what tools FPCs can use to engage citizens in creating a more just and sustainable food system.

To see who was 'setting the table,' graduate student researchers Molly McCullagh, Jaclyn DeVore, and myself, reviewed existing FPC literature, undertook an online survey distributed directly to FPC directors, and used semi-structured interviews with key people selected according to their responses to the online survey.[3] Contact information for the survey distribution was derived from a list on the Community Food Security Coalition's website together with an internet search for

TABLE 2.1 Projects and policies for community food security

Category	Specific examples given by survey respondents
Food retail and food access	Promote initiative for healthy corner stores
	Establish farmers' markets in low-income areas
	Enable farmers' market vendors to use Electronic Benefits Transfer (EBT) machines and accept Women Infant and Children (WIC) and Senior Farmer's Market Nutrition Program (SFMNP) coupons[1]
	Improve access to fresh foods through: grocery delivery at libraries, new grocery stores in food deserts, produce stands at transit centers, mobile markets, and community kitchens
	Develop local food guide that provides information about nutrition and which farmers' markets accept EBT, WIC, and Senior FMNP vouchers
	Work with public transportation department to prioritize bus routes that improve access from low-income neighborhoods to grocery stores
Community food assessments	Community-based mapping project focused on low-income neighborhoods and 'food desert' areas
	Publish report that identifies and discusses the different interventions to address rural and urban food gaps
	Support a photovoice project targeted to specific cultural or immigrant groups: young Hispanic males, low-income parents, students, the Guatemalan community, elderly residents
Transportation	Link public transportation with healthy food outlets and emergency food providers
Urban agriculture	Establish or advocate for gardens in low-income or food desert areas
	Challenge high fees for zoning variances or vendor permits for small-scale urban agriculture

Emergency food programs	Support emergency food program efforts to procure and supply more healthy food choices
Workshops/education	Nutrition education in low-income neighborhoods or to food bank populations
School meal programs	Establish or advocate for school gardens, farm-to-school initiatives, healthy vending machines
	Change state law to remove competitive foods from schools
	Advocate for the federal Farm to School grant program in the Child Nutrition Reauthorization Bill
Local food purchasing	Recommend that their city/county/region adopt an institutional food purchasing policy for government agencies, schools, and prisons

Note: 1. EBT is an electronic system in the United States that allows government's states benefits departments to issue money, accessible via a plastic debit card. WIC is a federally funded health and nutrition program for women, infants, and children. WIC helps families by providing checks for buying healthy supplemental foods from WIC-authorized vendors. SFMNP awards grants to States, United States Territories, and federally recognized Indian tribal governments to provide low-income seniors with coupons that can be exchanged for eligible foods (fruits, vegetables, honey, and fresh-cut herbs) at farmers' markets, roadside stands, and community-supported agriculture programs.

additional groups. Of the 155 FPCs found, 87 were 'accessible' (with accurate and functional email addresses). A total of 53 responses to the survey were received, which represented 43 distinct FPCs (49 percent of all accessible FPCs). The survey addressed background information about the FPC itself and requested examples of policies and programs the council undertook that impacted diverse community residents. It included short-answer and multiple-choice questions, some of which were required and others optional. Interviews were with FPC leaders (mainly directors or chairs, although some were regular steering committee members). In all, a range of FPCs was represented operating on different scales (interviewees represented thirteen local, four county, one regional, and one state) and in different geographical areas of North America (three Northeastern, eight Midwestern, two Southern, three West Coast, one Western Range, and two Canadian).

Projects and policies that address food security and diverse community residents The survey and interviews found that FPCs are directly involved in many projects and policies that are aimed at improving community food security measures for diverse community residents, as shown in Table 2.1.

Some indicated that improving food security was a central goal that is supported through specific policies and programs or through an informal directive that engenders their council's mission and decisions, especially because FPCs deal with locally relevant issues: for example, 'All ten of our recommendations are about increasing access to healthy food for people living in underserved areas or who have poor access to healthy food overall,' and 'In a city like [ours] it has to be!'

Methods of inclusion FPCs are involved in activities that impact diverse community residents in many ways. These are detailed below and divided into two groups: council-based techniques and project-based techniques.

1. Council-based techniques Council-based techniques are opportunities that FPCs take to change their structure, membership, and meetings to accommodate diverse community residents.

a. Inclusive language written into the mission statements or terms of reference Many FPCs show interest in improving the racial, economic, age, or gender diversity of representatives on their councils, but most set this only as a vague goal that they keep in mind when considering new members. One FPC explicitly addresses the council's diversity in its founding document, stating: 'The [council's] membership should reflect [the region's] diverse population, including, but not limited to, race, rural/urban residency, gender, and socioeconomic status.' However, despite this clear directive, the FPC has not treated this policy with high priority and their council members do not yet reflect the community's full diversity. This deliberate prioritization of inclusion is important to maintaining diverse participation (as members retire, drop out, or are term-limited), but language alone can only go so far in ensuring diversity.

b. Diverse representation on the council Of the FPCs surveyed, 16 percent set aside specific seats for particular food system sectors. Some of these designations related to diverse community residents, including 'person working in the area of food security,' 'at large members,' 'consumption,' 'youth,' and 'anti-hunger advocates.' In some cases, food-insecure and low-income residents fill the designated seats themselves. More commonly, however, FPCs engage professionals to act as indirect representatives of diverse community residents. These indirect representatives include food bank staff members, community organizers, Women, Infants, and Children (WIC)[4] nutrition educators, and soup kitchen directors. Although some interviewees feel that direct representation of 'low-income voices would really help,' others express the view that advocates can also play an important role in bridging one person's experience with broader systemic issues. Indirect representation may be a way to avoid making a food-insecure person feel stigmatized or asking a presumably time-stressed person for an additional time commitment.

> I think that it's important to have people directly from the community, not just advocates from the social service agency. I will say that people who work on the front lines, who work directly with clients … do get a real breadth of information and can represent a large population and integrate multiple stories whereas one individual represents themselves. I think there are advantages to having both, especially people who work directly on providing services at an agency on behalf of clients.

Some indirect representatives may once have been low-income or homeless, and are still grounded in the community. One FPC that does not have any members who are currently using Supplemental Nutrition Assistance Program (SNAP)[5] or WIC does have a member who was previously homeless. Now, that member runs a soup kitchen, and 'so she's very in touch with issues regarding emergency food.'

Six of the FPCs surveyed either currently include youth on their council or are a youth-only council. In general, FPCs define 'youth' to mean high-school age to age 30. Councils working with youth may set aside youth-only seats and choose youth-centered topics such as farm internships, school food, and cooking competitions, or other topics suggested by the youth members or focus groups. FPCs interviewed collaborate with existing youth programs, such as youth agriculture groups or high school food training classes, to recruit youth members. FPCs also invite youth groups to give presentations about their work at the FPC in the hope that they will continue to be involved with the council's work or will become council members.

At times, engagement of youth on the FPC requires some participation from their adult leaders or teachers to transport youth or prepare them for the upcoming council meeting by going over the agenda and talking points. Adult council members also require some training to know how to engage positively with youth in a way that does not perpetuate 'adultism.' One FPC that holds separate youth meetings felt that the separation between the youth and adult council was important because young people who attended the adult meetings felt intimidated by the presence of the veteran food system actors who populated the council. Interestingly, high school students attending the 'youth-only' FPC also expressed the view that they felt intimidated by the presence of members in their twenties, many of whom had completed college or graduate school. To counteract this, the council changed part of its meeting structure to be more welcoming to people without academic credentials: it used icebreakers to allow attendees to interact without the pressure of impressing others with food system knowledge. Despite the changes to accommodate high school students, the conflict of dinnertime and FPC meetings and students' eventual departure to colleges in other communities remain major barriers to youth participation.

c. Use of 'official attendees' Some FPCs struggle to balance the relatively small number of council seats available with the number of dedicated food system actors whose experiences and voices they wanted to include. One FPC creates a list of 'official attendees' at each meeting, which allows interested parties who are not currently members of the FPC to be more engaged in the council's work. Other examples of non-voting roles for community members include inviting members of the general public with food system expertise to address a specific topic. These examples generally include community members who are professionals in the food system. In both these examples, the attendees lack voting rights.

d. Use of working groups and committees Many interviewees recognize the time stress that many people feel in their daily lives but suggest that there might be other ways to involve people who 'want to hop in there for a short-term project' rather than attend monthly meetings. Committees are often used to organize the large general council into more manageable groups, and being part of a committee carries less responsibility than full council membership. These smaller groups ensure that people's 'time is well spent' on projects that are directly relevant to members' experiences and interests.

e. Strategic meeting or event location, time, and structure Many FPCs struggle with finding a meeting time that works for all of their diverse stakeholders, including community residents, both for their council meetings and for public events. In some cases, the FPCs hold separate meetings for each stakeholder group, such as during a campaign relating to school food. Another FPC found that their film night attracted many young people, which they attributed to the location – a centrally located coffee shop. However, the meeting location alone will not attract diverse participants. Despite moving their meetings to an African American community, the demographics of one council's meeting attendees did not change initially.

Some FPCs have also altered their meeting structures to allow for more public participation. These alterations might include a standard public comment section after each topic of discussion, but may go further toward ensuring that people feel that their views are being respected. One interviewee describes the importance of smaller group discussions in allowing everyone's voice to be heard, especially community residents who 'haven't been given a voice in the past,' as well as integrating time to share personal stories, which they feel is important to the functioning of their council.

f. Attend other organizations' meetings A number of FPCs engage with other organizations by attending their meetings, rather than by asking the other organizations' staff, clients, or members to attend the FPC meetings. They use these opportunities to gather stakeholder opinions without requiring long-term FPC participation, and also as a method of recruiting more FPC members. FPC members are sometimes invited to attend meetings to present council research or inform various government officials or community organizations. Two interviewees feel strongly that taking this more delicate approach is required when seeking the input of specific communities and in working with people of color, who may be distrustful of white leaders working in communities of color.

2. Project-based techniques Project-based techniques include activities that take place outside regular FPC meetings during the course of policy-making or projects that the council is engaged in.

a. Plan events and projects to intentionally and strategically involve community residents In a few cases, FPCs have planned projects and events that are aimed at understanding the condition of the local food system and have intentionally involved diverse community residents in those events. One FPC sponsored a research report on food insecurity that specifically recruited food-insecure people to design and oversee the project. Those participants helped design the research and participated in collecting the data 'which hopefully leads to better ways of meeting the needs that [the food insecure] have.' This FPC also engaged Hmong farmers in the community by planning a tour of farms that brought food system stakeholders, including elected officials, to farms on the outskirts of their community to help them understand the impact of residential sprawl on farms. This event led to additional projects that involved the FPC and Hmong growers acting together to improve the farmers' market access. Two other examples are community food assessments (CFAs) and participatory budgeting activities:

- *Perform CFAs.* CFAs are among the first activities that FPCs undertake. A CFA is a 'process that systematically examines a broad range of community food issues and assets, so as to inform change actions to make the community more food secure' (Pothukuchi et al. 2002, 11). Researchers combine information on food outlets with poverty, health, and transportation data. Interviewees say their assessments included conducting focus groups in food deserts and with specific community groups, such as Hmong farmers. These communities can be empowered through their involvement in actively mapping their community resources, analyzing the health indicators, and working with the FPC to develop solutions. FPCs have even hired community members to conduct surveys that contribute to a CFA.

- *Hold participatory budgeting activities.* One FPC suggested that a way to meaningfully engage community residents might be through a participatory budgeting activity where the participants from the community make decisions on public spending. One interviewee describes the potential for a participatory budgeting process for school lunches.

  Everybody is always screaming about school lunches saying: 'They're so terrible, can't you do any better?' Most people don't understand how affected by federal policy it is ... If I could find $25,000 of discretionary money in the school lunch program in the high school, and then we create a participatory budgeting process. So you set up a six-month process where, at the end of the day, that $25,000 will be spent on what the group of people who spend the time and come to the meetings ... the high school would have to agree that the money would get spent the way the public wants. It's a learning process. People get very educated about the policies very fast by doing that.

b. Establish synergistic relationships with existing community processes

FPCs often work through the organizations their members represent to reach community members. FPCs also make strategic partnerships with current processes that are active within a certain community. One council was focusing its efforts on a farmers' market in a community that was in the process of an official revitalization effort and was able to take advantage of the community gatherings and festivals that were part of the separate effort. This helped the council to better understand the community and realize that the farmers' market 'didn't feel like "theirs" even though they were close enough to be able to access it.' This FPC also developed specific relationships with community organizations that helped to shape its farmers' market coupon program for low-income shoppers. One FPC recognizes that, because its council members are professionals in the food system, it needs to maximize partnerships with organizations that are in touch with their local communities. To do so, the council provides grants to organizations that promote social inclusion and empowerment of neighborhood residents around food system issues.

A compelling example of an FPC being responsive to community need was when the council learned from a neighborhood community organizer that:

> a national fried chicken chain wanted to come in and the neighborhood didn't want it, and that was expressed at the meeting. They already had two other fried chicken places in the area and ten fast food places in the area, so they had plenty of that. There are no full-fledged supermarkets.

The FPC wondered what they could do to support the community:

> What could we do to help stand with them, shoulder to shoulder, to express this, in a very peaceful way. What we decided to do is [we] picked a day and a time where we would all gather on that corner and we put it out so that the media knew that we were going to be there. And they were. TV, print, radio all picked up on the story and were there and broadcast this. The decision was coming up before the board of zoning appeals in the next week or two after that, so it was well timed. The board of zoning appeals did give approval to the fried chicken place, which was really disappointing after we had galvanized this great effort. But the rest of the story is the fried chicken place decided to pull out. So they took themselves off the table when they realized that the community with broad support, when people from outside of that particular neighborhood, really thought that there was some injustice, that this was not what they wanted. Maybe it would have added five or ten jobs to the neighborhood. It was worth it for them to stand for better quality food.

c. Use focus groups In addition to participating in ongoing, community-driven processes, many of the councils interviewed solicit community input through focus groups on specific topics that are selected by the FPCs. These focus groups allow FPCs to be representative of the 'grassroots community' in spite of not having 'great representation from a grassroots level on the council.' FPCs use focus groups and community meetings as a way to 'check themselves,' get public input on their proposed policies and priorities, and 'let it be known that we're working on these issues and people have concerns and they can come to us.'

d. Offer public education FPCs often sponsor community education events such as film nights and workshops. Some interviewees mention strategies they use to achieve high levels of community participation, which sometimes carry over into more long-term engagement with the council. Some councils successfully reach new audiences for their film screenings and workshops by specifically partnering with another organization or community or by intentionally recruiting workshop leaders from the community. Besides acting as a consciousness-raising activity, film nights have also catalyzed engagement with local food policy among participants. One FPC screened *Mad City Chickens*, a film about raising backyard poultry, which they used to launch their campaign to alter the city's zoning to allow for backyard chickens. 'You could draw the dots,' the interviewee said.

e. Offer incentives Several FPCs describe the incentives that they use to compensate community members for their participation in council activities – both project-based and council-based. Focus group participants often receive gift certificates, and many meeting co-ordinators make sure that food (either snacks or a full meal) is part of the meeting or community focus group. The most innovative US example of incentives involved accessing funding from the Temporary Assistance for Needy Families (TANF)[6] program in their state to pay low-income participants (who are eligible for TANF funding) to attend council meetings and for their time spent creating a report on food insecurity in their community.

> We appealed by writing a letter to the state [TANF] office to request that all the hours put into the research project by the participants would be counted towards their work, much like going in to interview for a job … This was our rationale: if it was a professional representing an organization, the organization pays for their time to go to meetings. So our thought was that was also true of anyone who goes to meetings and carries out the parts of the project.

The FPC also obtained additional grant funding to supplement the

TANF funding and collaborated with their food co-op to also offer gift certificates with the food co-op in exchange for participation on the council. This subsidy succeeded in incentivizing residents who might not have otherwise participated, although only for the duration of the funding.

Another FPC held a regional food summit and secured a $1,000 grant to subsidize food-insecure residents to be compensated $25 for attending. They estimated that 30 percent of the participants who attended identified having experienced food insecurity in their lives. The participation of people who had the lived experience of food insecurity (but may not have been as well versed in food policy) impacted the tone of the summit. At the end of the summit, participants all signed a joint declaration with the goals developed during the summit, which has directed the work of the FPC since.

Challenges Many of the challenges that FPCs face have been addressed already by other authors (Harper et al. 2009; Schiff 2007; Hamilton 2002; Gottlieb and Fisher 1995), including:

- overall challenge of working with diverse membership and constituencies;
- designing an effective organizational structure;
- balancing focus between policy and program work and between a structural and a narrow focus;
- measuring and evaluating a council's impact;
- financial and political challenges;
- lack of institutional support;
- complex local political environments;
- lack of dedicated staff, or a reliance on volunteers or on sharing staff with governmental departments; and
- lack of data on a variety of issues relevant to a local food system.

Many interviewees reiterate these challenges, but also discuss others that specifically relate to the inclusion of diverse community residents.

1. The structure is not yet conducive to community inclusion Some FPCs have conducted community outreach or held public events that attracted participants to the next council meeting. However, these councils realized that they were in need of more formal structures or frameworks that would enable them to better support new council members.

> After the film series, we started having 15 new people, 20 new people ... I think our February meeting had 25 people and we didn't have anything to say to these people! We had no real plan for how to make them feel included in our group and make them feel like we're accomplishing things and so on.

2. Reliance on volunteer council members A few FPCs mention that their ability to engage community residents is hindered by their reliance on an all-volunteer council or minimal staff time donated from member organizations. Community engagement is time-consuming work and one FPC says that the problem is not a lack of recognition of the value of the community voice, but rather that 'people don't do it because they don't have time.'

3. Lack of financial resources In addition to limited time available for members to contribute to FPC-related work, a lack of financial resources hinders the councils' ability to initiate and maintain community engagement. This lack of resources, both of time and financial, limits a council's capacity to go beyond email communication and to reach communities that do not have regular internet access with printed flyers or door-to-door recruitment, for example.

4. Culture and language barriers One FPC states that it was interested in increasing the diversity of its council members, but that the Hmong community in particular is a very insular society and both differences in culture and language were barriers to their involvement on the council. In addition to language, communication style is mentioned as a potential challenge to including more diverse voices on the council.

5. Suitable meeting times and locations Many FPCs hold their meetings during the day, which is beneficial for members whose involvement on the council is part of their work responsibilities, but would exclude potential members who work daytime jobs that do not allow for their participation. Even though councils are technically 'open to everybody,' 'structurally some of the ways that we do our work makes it tough for people to become involved ... if you're working during the day.'

6. A limited number of seats available, and a focus on food system sector diversity Many FPCs say having racially and economically diverse council members is important, but councils primarily prioritize diversity of food sectors. FPCs struggle with balancing the desire to be inclusive of racial and age demographics with the need to be efficient by incorporating representatives from selected food system sectors or by keeping the number of council members at a manageable level. One interviewee cautions that, while it is important that the FPC address low-income residents' concerns, 'it's important that we don't pack the board with low-income people because that's not all we do.'

7. Effectively engaging people in 'food policy' Some FPCs mention that a challenge of their work is the focus on 'food policy' and 'food systems thinking.' Policy is 'less tangible and in some ways less accessible' than projects. Naturally:

> people who know the most about this nascent food economy are the ones who are actually in it … probably the average consumer going to a big box for their groceries is not likely to resonate with the values behind the policies or not likely to be like 'Oh, I see this major problem and I want to address it with this policy …' The policies are … not likely to come from the folks who don't see a problem.

FPC members describe instances where community members without a policy background who participate on FPCs haven't been able to 'get' policy, despite honest attempts by other members to frame food policy in an understandable way, and they drop out within a year. Understanding the complexity of many local policy processes has challenged even the food systems professionals on the FPCs, many of whom have not worked with local governments before. Additionally, because policy change happens gradually, it requires a 'long-term commitment to the process. One policy change can take 12 to 18 months.' This drawn-out process can make it difficult to keep even the most passionate people 'motivated to push, work, research, inform, advocate for that entire time for one thing.'

8. Working in an environment of anti-government sentiments Some FPCs feel that their association with the government and with policymakers makes them appear less welcoming to community members, especially community members who may have previously felt ignored due to structural discrimination.

At the table, or setting the table? Allen (2010, 303) writes that social justice cannot be achieved without addressing the empowerment of the food insecure and those who are 'most vulnerable and have benefited the least from current arrangements.' Therefore, FPCs, especially those espousing the support of social justice goals, have a real necessity to think about how their policies, programs, and structures are supporting a more just food system. The following are six recommended areas for increasing inclusion.

1. Knowing the community FPCs often start with a CFA that combines demographic information with market and survey data to paint a picture of the local food system. Combining this information with ethnographic interviews would help to achieve a deeper understanding of attitudes to food and foodways, which are fundamental to people's individual and collective identities, especially in 'new' populations and other marginalized groups. Hearing from community members as well as from local and national activists can help uncover some of the 'historical configurations' that have contributed to the current 'differences in wealth, power and privilege [that] exist both among and within localities' and deeply impact the food system (ibid., 296).

2. Culture of the council It is important that council members are aware of both the culture of their council and the community's perception of the council. Many respondents suggest that their councils have welcoming and open atmospheres that encourage education, critical thinking, and debate among members. These are all arguably positive attributes of FPCs. However, when considering policies and projects that affect diverse community residents, interviewees say that the orientation of the council depends heavily on the personal and professional background of the council chair.

> You can have bylaws that spell out exactly what the purpose and direction of a community group is, whether it is an FPC or any other type of community group, but what actually happens is often dependent on the leadership skills of the people who are sitting around the table. So, for instance, if you have a chairperson or FPC membership that really has no comfort level with engaging community members then even if that is part of your mission, if there aren't the capacities to deal with that in that leadership, then it's probably not going to happen in the way that it should.

The culture and make-up of a council from its initiation can have an impact on the diversity that it is able to attract in the future. One FPC mentions that the lack of diversity on its council is already impacting its ability to attract people of color because of historical experiences of communities of color being 'helped' or 'served' by all-white organizations. Additionally, on the widespread association of 'local food' with more affluent communities, one council director commented that 'the more an FPC reflects white upper middle class, the more we unintentionally reinforce that perception.' Councils need to take careful steps to address both their actual culture and the community's perception of their activities from their inception.

3. Meaningful inclusion The interviews demonstrate that FPCs are engaging residents for honest reasons. However, despite good intentions there is still a danger of tokenism and of assuming that diverse representation automatically leads to equitable outcomes. It is vital that FPCs analyze how their structures, policies, and cultures might present barriers to the full and meaningful participation of certain groups.

Allen (1999, 121) cautions that 'bringing groups with different interests together in community food security coalitions can be extremely difficult' and that inclusion of diverse community residents 'does not guarantee that their needs will be met or that they will have control over decision making and institutional accountability' (Allen 2010, 304). Participation is moderated by relationships of power and privilege that have to do with culture, race, gender, and more, which shape 'not only who is allowed to be part of the conversation but also shape who has the authority to speak and whose discursive contributions are considered worthwhile' (ibid., 303). In certain situations unequal treatment can arise due to differing speech and communication styles.

In most cases, FPCs shaped their broad goals and strategies internally, debating among the council members and working group members who had, in Guthman's terms (2008b, 388), already 'set the table.' Reaching out to their broader community was reserved for work on specific projects or policies. Harris (2007, 19) suggests that:

> including people of color and other disenfranchised groups defined in the membership in the strategic planning process helps to diminish some of the difficulty of managing a diversity of people, perspectives and positions when broad inclusion is sought.

Meaningful inclusion of vulnerable groups would require their participation in every stage of the council's work, from setting ('the table' of) priorities and goals to initiating and then later evaluating the projects. This practice is more common with environmental justice and food sovereignty groups, who have argued for the inclusion of historically marginalized people in developing long-term solutions to inequity (Loh and Eng 2010; Holt-Giménez 2009).

4. Council members' training and education Continuous education and training for council members is essential to maintain members' interest in participating and helps the council make more informed decisions. Members can learn a lot from other members, and many FPCs regularly invite community members and professionals to their meetings to share their knowledge and experience. FPCs also organize tours of their communities' farms, farmers' markets, community gardens, or food deserts. Such opportunities can increase the council members' understanding of their communities' demographics and specific food insecurity concerns. Further, these experiences can improve members' cultural competency and address structural discrimination within their local food systems.

In some instances, FPCs have asked members to participate in specific activities that raise the awareness of food security in their community. The Durham North Carolina FPC members participated in a 'Do the Math' challenge, in which their five-day food intake was limited to distribution from the local food bank in 'an effort to bring attention to the struggles faced by local residents who live on a limited income or social assistance' and raise awareness of food security issues (Follert 2010). Members described feelings of powerlessness and distress when someone else 'decided what I'm going to eat for a week and it doesn't matter if I don't like this food or I can't eat this food' (ibid.).

According to Malik Yakini of the Detroit Black Community Food Security Network, addressing structural racism in the food system is especially important given the racial inequities among the leadership in the community food security movement (in Detroit, as well as elsewhere).

> Many of the people doing the work are white people, particularly young white women, with golden intentions, but we have a problem because those young white women often come into

> African American and Latino communities and have not divested themselves of the vestiges of white supremacist thinking … In Detroit, which is a city at least 85% African American, we found that many of the key players in the Good Food Movement in the city are white people … it's not an attack on people, it's an analysis. White people who stand with us against white supremacy, we're with you. But if we can't have an open, honest discussion about white supremacy and white privilege, we don't really have much basis for a relationship. (Yakini 2010)

Because of this ongoing concern, the Detroit FPC has pledged to do annual anti-racism training with its members (Crouch, pers. comm.). A couple of other councils interviewed mentioned they were also considering holding similar training.

5. Relationship-building A number of interviewees describe the importance of relationship-building. One describes relationships as the 'key to moving the work forward,' and mentions relationships between the council and local policy-makers, between council members and community organization leaders, and among council members. Existing relationships or professional networks are important when known community leaders unite to establish the first council. On a deeper level, relationship-building among members (and between council members and community members in relevant cases) should generate an understanding of the other person's lived reality, the definitions and meanings of their life (Leigh 1998, 11). Establishing trust is crucial when mediating relationships, especially between groups where oppression has been the historical precedent (Harris 2007). Allocating time at each meeting for members to share stories helps build relationships between members and bridge people who might have seemingly dissimilar backgrounds. One council rotates meeting sites among the different represented sectors to garner a more complete understanding of each member's perspective:

> over the past 12 months we've met in 12 different places. They've always been in the conference room at the grocery store, in the conference room at the Chamber of Commerce, we went out to the brewery bottling facility, we went out to the feedlot and ate steak from their farm. We decided to visit all of the stakeholders' homes and we always had a meal over it.

Relationships are 'the vehicle through which reflective dialogue can occur' and facilitate 'the transformation of consciousness necessary for individuals to embrace active involvement' in a group environment (Anderson n.d.). These particular attributes are what make relationships a critical part of a council's ability to effectively include diverse community members.

6. Community organizing FPCs can learn a lot from community organizing methods and techniques. None of the councils in this research is consistently using a community organizing approach. At times, FPCs do partner with community-based organizations to support a specific event or policy agenda in which the constituents may be interested. Some councils have community organizers as members, who then organize their community around food system issues, which might be an appropriate technique given how labor-intensive building membership-based community organizations can be, especially among the poor (Dreier 2009, 11).

Hassanein (2003, 81) argues that 'organizing is about understanding a community's resources, and working on issues that people care about and that are easily understood and communicated,' as well as valuing the lived experience of the community residents as a type of expertise. Developing mutual trust and performing critical dialogue around shared problems are essential in developing a successful campaign (Carroll and Minkler 2000). For FPCs, taking a community organizing perspective would involve working directly with people who have the most at stake and whose self-interest is the focus of the council's work. However, the interviews revealed that when choosing what to 'take on,' councils often strategically prioritize issues that relate to the work of their current members, not necessarily issues that relate directly to a community-prioritized need. In a few cases, FPCs look at the demographics of their communities and pick projects that directly affect certain populations. For example, one council started working with Hmong growers after it recognized that they were being discriminated against at the farmers' market. It is rare, however, for councils to hold open meetings with the community and ask: 'What do you want us to work on?' How impactful might it be for council members to use their professional expertise and political connections to work on a problem defined by the community, alongside community residents?

FPCs are uniquely poised to engage in a community organizing approach because the spaces that they often help to create, such as farmers' markets, can serve as community organizing 'hubs' that attract potential participants (Alkon 2008). They are structured in a way that mimics good community organizing techniques, namely that they often use working groups, which, because of their smaller size and narrow focus on a particular topic, provide 'the ideal environment for exploring the social and political aspects of personal problems and developing strategies for work toward social change' (Gutierrez and Lewis 1997, 246).

Conclusions

In the first part of this chapter, I made the point that the local food movement, as it is framed in popular discourse, has often confused the *ends* – a more sustainable and socially just food system – with the *means* – a system of localized food production and consumption. The goal seems to be the creation of a local food system, rather than creating a more sustainable and just food system using localization as the means. This friction between ends and means is essentially the difference between the largely white middle-class local food movement, and the emerging food justice movement. 'The local' is defined and defended by privileged positionalities and portrayed as discrete, homogeneous, and static (Hinrichs 2003). In this way, it does not readily include culturally appropriate food for minority and low-income populations, nor the 'intentional connection and collaboration' with 'parallel' networks (Gibb and Whitman 2012, 15); nor does it necessarily embrace translocalism, nor the ability of immigrants to create local meaning through autotopographies. If there were a space between ends and means, a space for discussing and developing Alkon and Agyeman's (2011) concept of 'the food movement as polyculture,' perhaps that space is currently occupied by FPCs.

In our research, many of the FPCs gave a variety of reasons why they felt that the inclusion of community members was important to their work, such as 'everyone on the council wants the council to be representative of the city so that it can be effective,' or because involving people with the 'lived experience' added 'a breadth of knowledge to the research' and helped the FPC verify that it was on the 'right track.' Some FPCs were concerned about advancing a '"build it and they will come" perspective' and felt that community engagement from the start of their projects was crucial for them to be effective. In one case, an FPC chair indicated that the failure of a new grocery store that city agencies helped develop in a specific food desert might have been because 'community members were not at all engaged in the decision-making process.'

Some FPCs feel that participation would help empower local residents to 'feel like "I do have a place in this community and I can make change, positive change in the community."' In some cases, community members had never had a formal venue in which to share their opinions:

> the majority of folks are low/limited income and the kids were like, oh my gosh, I can't believe you're asking us what we think. Nobody ever asks us anything. They were excited about the opportunity to share about their community ...

Involving residents in issues that specifically relate to their lived experiences and their needs has been important in drawing support for various policies that FPCs undertake. In the case of revising a backyard chicken ordinance, for example, the FPC took on the role of conducting background research and developing the language of the actual proposal while community members were the public advocates at community and government meetings.

Ultimately, the achievement of community food security goals would represent a major step toward just sustainabilities, but this can only be realized through transformative rather than reform strategies: in this case a transformation of the current food system. Similarly, as long as race, class, cultural, and justice concerns are marginalized because of a sole focus on environmental sustainability, then certain racial, socio-economic, and cultural groups will be excluded. In the instances where FPCs are concerned with issues that impact the community directly, empowering community residents as participants in (re)prioritizing ends over means is a vital role for them. There will be resistance. This may lead FPCs into work such as anti-racist, living wage or fair farm worker labor laws, which may seem tangential to the local food system or their current work focus but is of primary importance in creating both a polycultural movement and a just and sustainable food system for all.

3 | SPACE AND PLACE

'We are in a spatial moment' (ds4si 2011). Around the world, there has never been a time when the role and possibilities of public space have been so prominent in the news and on social media. From Tahrir Square to SlutWalks, new possibilities are opening up. New spaces are being created and used as fabulous sites of re-creation, such as New York City's High Line, once a disused elevated rail bed and now a highly used urban park running along the lower west side of Manhattan. Road spaces around the world are being reimagined. In Copenhagen, as in the Dutch *woonerven* and in streets such as London's Exhibition Road, the concept of 'shared space' removes the usual separation of cars, pedestrians, and other road users and devices so that curbs, road lines, signs, and signals are integrated into a 'cities for people' understanding of public space. In this way, walking, cycling, shopping, and driving cars are integral to the 'livable street.' Spaces are also being used, as they have for millennia, as sites of protest and resistance, such as the Occupy Wall Street movement's residency in Zuccotti Park,[1] New York City, and the subsequent and rapid spread of the Occupy movement to hundreds of other cities in the US, Europe, Australia, and Latin America, with smaller numbers in Asia and Africa. Between re-creation and resistance, relaxation and reflection, public spaces offer unlimited democratic possibilities in relation to achieving just sustainabilities.

In the first half of this chapter, I examine the history, contemporary trends, and use of public spaces, places, and place-making around the world. I do not attempt to classify spaces but rather to extract themes observed in their creation and inhabitation in a rapidly urbanizing and capitalist world: spaces as *security*, space as *resistance*, and space as *possibility*. These themes, especially the more hopeful, democratic, and democratizing ones, are seen in visionary projects, for example in Dudley Street, Boston, MA, and in Bogotá, Colombia. They can serve as models, to inform the creation of new places and spaces along more just and sustainable lines. In the second half of the chapter, I look at the street, the most widely used yet overlooked public space of all. My interest here, from a just sustainabilities perspective, is in 'spatial justice' and in the 'democratization' of streets – that is, the growing success in reclaiming and reallocating space that has become allocated almost exclusively to private cars. The US narratives of 'complete streets,' 'transit-oriented development,' and 'livable streets' frame the message that streets are ultimately public spaces, and that everyone in the community should have equal rights to space within them, irrespective of whether they are in a car. Implicit in this is the recognition that those who have fewer rights are often those with lower incomes who do not own cars. However, as I will show, additional caution is needed because some low-income communities and neighborhoods of color worry that changes such as the introduction of bicycle lanes, street accessibility improvements, mass transit expansions and upgrades, and pedestrian zone placements will foster gentrification, further diminishing their rights and roles in the community.

Public spaces, places, and place-making

Introduction Historically, public spaces have been restricted by governments and reclaimed by citizens. Since the polis of ancient Greece, public spaces have been used as forums for democracy as well as organizing grounds for state repression. They were places of politics, commerce, and spectacle, where there was unmediated intermingling of strangers (Mitchell 1995). Today, in these spaces and urban areas generally, diversity has exploded, creating what Fincher and Jacobs (1998) productively call 'cities of difference.' Cities of difference are places where we are 'in the presence of otherness' (Sennett 1990, 123) – namely, our increasingly different, diverse, and culturally heterogeneous urban areas. Public spaces across the world embody this difference. They are simultaneously symbols of government, religion, culture, and economy. People around the world continue to fight for, create, and re-create public spaces. From pocket parks to PARK(ing) Day, they are carved from the commerce of urban centers, the abandoned industrial structures of yesteryear, and even the automobile-lined streets. These spaces are used for everything from people-watching to protest and political revolutions.

With Western colonization, local forms of public space in many areas of the world were lost to traditional European squares. For example, the parks and plazas valued by Europeans are not an important part of West African culture. Instead, less formal spaces such as streets are the 'living tissue' offering the gathering spaces, shade, and forums for communication, affording a rich public sphere through 'oral history, verbal navigation and the now dominating mobile technologies' that are central to West African society (Passmore 2011). On the other hand, Latin Americans adopted colonial Spanish plazas. The urban grids developed around these plazas have been key in many Central and South American countries' retention of their public spaces (Rosenthal 2000). In Europe and America, public spaces have been cyclical in their accessibility. In the late 1800s, American public spaces catered exclusively to the wealthy, with open spaces reserved for elite neighborhoods (Cranz 1989). And in eighteenth- and nineteenth-century England, Victorian-era public spaces were managed and controlled by the bourgeois, a dynamic that threatens once again to dominate (Minton 2006). In the early twentieth century, however, many parks and open spaces in cities were created for the poor in response to congested living conditions and resulting health concerns. The city of Derby has the first and oldest surviving public park in England, the Arboretum, which was donated to the city in 1840 by local mill owner and former mayor Joseph Strutt.

In the last century, the colonizing force has been Western capitalism, and cities have experienced the increasing privatization of public spaces, especially after the 1980s 'neoliberal onslaught,' which brought a 'trenchant reregulation and redaction of public space' (Low and Smith 2006, 1). Many theorists, designers, and activists lament the loss of public space. Parks, streets, squares, and markets, they fear, have been swallowed into the bloated belly of 'consumerism, the media and the intrusion of space into private life' (Crawford 1995, 4; see also Sorkin 1992). Zukin (2010, 31), however, is more reflective on the changes in her home city, New York:

> Though [Jane] Jacobs fought strenuously to preserve an ideal vision of the urban village, and [Robert] Moses just as strenuously fought to replace it with the ideal of the corporate city, their ideas have been joined to create the hybrid city that we consider authentic today: both hipster districts and luxury housing, immigrant food vendors and big box stores, community gardens and gentrification.

Indeed, the urban landscape, especially in the US, has been drastically transformed over the last 50 to 80 years by the rise of the automobile and by the land-hungry development patterns it has sparked across urban space. As Flusty (1994), Banerjee (2001), Mitchell (1995; 2003), and many others have declared, public space in particular has suffered from these planning practices as more and more parks have been bisected by expressways, as markets and promenades have been lost to parking lots, and as people not inside an automobile have been squeezed to the edge of the street or out entirely. Nonetheless, it is these (public) spaces in a city that stand to offer the most value for community empowerment, and for social (Flusty 1994) and cultural inclusion (Agyeman 2010), all of which are essential to achieving the higher quality of life and wellbeing I described in detail in Chapter 1, and, through this, just sustainabilities.

The decline of public space is a symptom of a larger neoliberal pattern of expanding marketplaces and shrinking governments that has resulted in an unequal distribution of resources (Banerjee 2001). In some places, especially but not exclusively in developed regions, public space has been co-opted by private entities. Low (2006, 84) describes countless cases of gated communities that 'manipulate municipal and town planning laws and regulations to control public space and tax dollars.' This is part of a wider shift that has resulted in a perceived decline in demand for public space that then becomes 'empty space' (Sennett 1994 cited by Madanipour 2010, 174). In other places, development patterns are to blame. The creation of new public space in quickly growing cities, suburbs, and settlements is not keeping pace with population growth, and, in some instances, public spaces are replaced by development. In the case of Nairobi, Kenya, the city authorized high-density settlements over low-density areas that would have included parklands (Makworo and Mireri 2011).

Banerjee (2001) argues that changes in public space are a lens through which to look at broader transformations of the public realm. Low and Smith (2006, 6) concur, differentiating the public sphere (also called the public realm) from public space, while recognizing that 'an understanding of public space is an imperative for understanding the public sphere' and that:

> investigating the means of making and remaking public space provides a unique window on the politics of the public sphere, suggesting an even more powerful imperative to the focus on public space. (ibid., 7)

Space as security Shaftoe (2008, 16) talks of 'inclusive' and 'exclusive' urban spaces. Inclusive spaces, he argues, are the aim of 'the New Urbanists, Urban Villagers and 24 Hour City people who want to "crowd out crime" through mixed use and maximizing activity in public areas.' Exclusive spaces, in contrast, are the domain of 'the "designing out crime" proselytisers who seek closure and limitation of use of spaces.' Shaftoe's main concern is crime: both inclusive and exclusive approaches have at their heart either 'crowding out crime' or 'designing out crime.' This is sad, although understandable given the 'anti-social behavior' debates in the UK, which have led to a raft of government reports such as the 2005 report by Sir Richard Rogers, *Towards a Strong Urban Renaissance*, which favors inclusive space approaches; on the other hand, the 2004 publication by the Office of the Deputy Prime Minister and the Home Office, *Safer Places: The planning system and crime prevention*, tries to bring inclusive and exclusive space approaches together. Shaftoe (ibid.) frequently mentions terms such as 'urban security,' 'surveillance,' 'CCTV,' and 'public safety,' and he reluctantly concedes that 'on the ground, the default drift seems to be towards closure, fortification and exclusion' (ibid., 18).

Space as resistance Public spaces have been sites of the 'geographies of protest'[2] for centuries. Tiananmen Square, Beijing's largest public space, catalyzed one of the most infamous protests in modern history as Chinese students demonstrated and died for economic and political reform in 1989. The state-sponsored violence in Argentina in the late 1970s and early 1980s spurred another globally recognized act of public space protest. The mothers of disappeared family members gathered in the main plaza of Buenos Aires in an action of desperation and fear, demanding to know where their missing loved ones had gone. These women became internationally renowned as Las Madres de Plaza de Mayo (Rosenthal 2000). These stories are among many that not only have become ingrained in the public space narratives of their native countries but have also been imprinted on the collective memory of citizens internationally.

In December 2010, with Tiananmen Square and Las Madres de Plaza de Mayo two decades past, Tunisia's uprising began against long-time president Zine El Abidine Ben Ali, followed in January 2011 by events in Tahrir Square in Cairo. The seeds of the Arab

Spring were planted. Libya, Bahrain, Syria, and Yemen, among other Middle Eastern countries, followed in Tunisia's and Egypt's footsteps. Citizens took to the streets, plazas, and squares to protest against long-standing repressive regimes. Although most of these countries are still in the throes of civil disputes, and the end result of the Arab Spring has yet to manifest itself, the role of public spaces in this movement is evident. The Arab Spring employed an entirely new public realm – social media – but the attention given to Twitter and Facebook largely overshadowed the role of the physical places in which these protests were grounded (Beaumont 2011). In fact, the Arab Spring was a reminder of the crucial role of public space in an age of social media and digital communication. Although there is some dispute over the necessity of social media in facilitating the Arab Spring (Gladwell 2011; Kravets 2011), no one has questioned the need for Tahrir Square in Egypt or the streets of Sana'a in Yemen. Residents needed these spaces to stand their ground and to press forward despite the violence of the regimes they were facing.

In Cairo, the uprising revitalized public spaces. Although Tahrir Square was at the front and center of the protests, the lasting effect of the demonstrations on Cairo's public spaces may be the transformation of neighborhood streets. During the uprising, Egyptians came down to their streets to protect their neighborhoods and homes. The streets became places of organization and participation (Goodyear 2011). With the initial protests behind them, Egyptians expressed a desire to preserve the sense of community they developed during the uprising. After the protests, Egyptian citizens are looking for ways to counter decades of privatization, traffic, and lack of funding to create better public spaces in Cairo (Viney 2011).

In Fall 2011, the Occupy Wall Street movement burgeoned in protest at the increasing inequality and wealth disparity in the US. Protestors occupied highly visible urban spaces, from Zuccotti Park in New York City to Civic Center Park in Berkeley, California. The movement didn't take long to spread to other cities in the US, Europe, Australia, and Latin America, with smaller numbers of protestors in Asia and Africa. The squares and parks selected by occupiers gave rise to organized communities. The spaces became poleis, small cities organized by general assemblies, working groups, and the vernacular of protest – 'mic checks' and hand signals (Kimmelman 2011). The Occupy movement as an act of public space reclamation was especially pertinent in New York, where the protestors occupied Zuccotti Park, a privately owned public space (POPS). The tension around Zuccotti Park helped to foreground the issue of declining public spaces (and public spheres) in America, an issue poignantly connected to the movement's central issues. Major cities such as New York, San Francisco, Portland, and Boston have used zoning laws to allow developers to break zoning codes in order to create more square footage, in exchange for the creation of public–private space. In addition to many of these spaces being inadequate and inaccessible, POPS owners have the legal prerogative to enforce their own rules in these semi-public spaces (Kayden 2011; Banerjee 2011, 12). The Arab Spring and Occupy Wall Street are reminders of the enduring 'political power of physical space' (Kimmelman 2011).

Since the 1990s, feminist geographers (McDowell 1993; Bondi 1991) and transgendered urban planners (Doan 2010) have problematized the fact that 'the majority of women have more spatially restricted lives than men' (McDowell 1993, 166), and that transgendered and gender-variant people:

> experience the gendered division of space as a special kind of tyranny – the tyranny of gender – that arises when people dare to challenge the hegemonic expectations for appropriately gendered behavior in Western society. (Doan 2010, 632)

In 2011, gendered usage of public space came to the fore. Arising from a speech by Constable Michael Sanguinetti on crime prevention to York University students in Toronto, the SlutWalk movement quickly spread around the world, aided by Facebook and Twitter. Sanguinetti argued that women dressing as 'sluts' was a key ingredient in the victimization and rape of women. A few months later, on 3 April 2011 in Queen's Park, organizers expected 100 but over 3,000 people gathered to hear speeches, before moving to the Toronto Police Headquarters. Women were requested to dress in ordinary, everyday wear, but many women dressed as 'sluts' in provocative clothing. While being problematized on a variety of fronts, from within the movement to black feminists who accused it of being exclusionary, the SlutWalk has raised the issues of rights, access to public space, safety, and personal choices to a new generation.

Space as possibility: loose and insurgent space Some public spaces are carefully planned and delineated while others emerge from the everyday space, wherein users become the architects of the space through both scripted activities (Hou 2010) and everyday uses.

Planned and unplanned public spaces alike are recognized as indicators of a healthy built environment. They are considered marks of good neighborhoods, lively cities, and healthy democracies, and are essential in fostering a high quality of life and wellbeing, and a healthy local economy. Franck and Stevens (2007) use the term 'loose space' for spaces that are most conducive to being activated by the public. These spaces are varied in their structures, diverse in their uses, and programmed by citizens rather than by authorities. Loose space can be adapted, manipulated, reimagined, and reshaped. Often they are spaces that have been abandoned by their original users and where expressive activities are common. For decades, loose spaces have been identified, in different terms, as successful public spaces. They are the spaces that Whyte (1980) famously describes in *The Social Life of Small Urban Spaces*. With a focus on New York City plazas, Whyte describes good public spaces by identifying many of the characteristics of loose spaces. Where sitting space is concerned, for example, he notes that the most popular public spaces are those that feature various levels of seating where people can lean, sit, and sprawl. Connectivity between the street and the plaza is essential to inspire pedestrians to enter. Franck and Stevens (2007) note that niches, stairs, and recesses located at the edges of public spaces encourage people to linger. These design elements allow spaces to be easily traversable; one can straddle the border of a plaza and interact in both realms. The space 'in between' is the loose space.

In the past decade, new evolutions in the appropriation and reclamation of public space have capitalized on these loose spaces and the creativity of the citizens who expose their potential. Hou (2010, 1) defines the 'small yet persistent challenges against the increasingly regulated, privatized and diminishing forms of public space' as 'insurgent acts' and the spaces these acts create as 'insurgent public spaces.' There is a growing variety of actions and practices that address the use and production of public space as a highly contested process. Hou (ibid.) continues to posit that 'the presence and making of insurgent public space serves as a barometer of the democratic well-being and inclusiveness of our present society.' Sennett (1970) captured the sentiments of contemporary public space movements in his book *The Uses of Disorder*, in which he advocates for more communal urban lives through increased disorder in cities.

It is both the disorder and the community that create vibrant, distinct, and livable cities. A sense of place results from people's interactions, and place may be measured by physical activity (Illich 2000). Through various methods of urbanism – guerilla, DIY, tactical, pop-up, and open-source to name a few – city dwellers are redefining their environments. Rather than accepting places as they 'are,' they are redefining what they can 'become' (Massey 1995b). Some of these 'insurgent tactics' are centuries old, and some brand new. Physical activities that create public space include digging, dancing, selling, building, and sitting, among many others. These movements are embodied in Jacobs's (1961, 50) description of the 'sidewalk ballet,' wherein people shape the street through a choreographed chaos. Tactical urbanism is working to revitalize the art of the public sidewalk ballet, which has been lost in many places throughout the world to private automobiles, suburbs, indoor malls, and restrictive laws. Jacobs (1958) wrote: 'Designing a dream city is easy, rebuilding a living one takes imagination.'

And it is with this imagination, this sense of possibility, that self-proclaimed urbanists and neighborhood elders are erecting parks from parking spaces, benches from shipping pallets, and gardens from rubble. Acts of 'insurgent public space' can be fleeting. Some, like the now closed Union Street Urban Orchard in London, are intended to challenge people's conceptions of their built environments. Other actions are everyday occurrences that loosen the constraints of public space. These actions include skateboarders who take advantage of the curvatures of a freeway underpass, or who have (re)claimed parts of London's South Bank, and Yangee dancers who use the streets of Beijing on a daily basis to practice their dance ritual (Chen 2010). Although not their intention, these everyday performances and actions may also shift the meaning of public spaces.

In 2005, San Francisco-based design collective Rebar transformed a downtown parking space into a park, an act of experimental public space creation that laid the foundation for many of the insurgent public space projects that have followed. Working within the existing landscape, the collective reprogrammed the space by adding street furniture, trees, and grass – fixtures denoting a traditional Western park. A small park island in a sea of concrete, the installation attracted curious passersby and promoted social interactions that a parking space fulfilling its intended purpose would not have done. Photographs of the parking space were released online and Rebar subsequently received hundreds of emails from interested people. The concept tapped into a far-reaching discontent, or curiosity, or excitement, among fellow urbanites seeking to challenge their auto-dominated concrete cities. Rebar launched an annual event, called PARK(ing) Day, which is now celebrated internationally, and made a *PARK(ing) Day Manual* available on their website (Merker 2010).

New forms of public space intervention, such as Rebar's PARK(ing) Space, have been enabled, in part, by communication technology. While technology has threatened the importance of place-based public space, it has also allowed mass mobilization and the open-source dispersion of new urbanist tactics. As part of this dispersion, the originators or users often codify their approaches in the form of how-to guides. The Streets Plans Collaborative, a planning, design, and advocacy firm based in the US, released a guide entitled *Tactical Urbanism*, which includes urban gardens, informal street furniture, and food vendors, among other methods (streetplans.org). Most of the tactics in this guide advise or necessitate the involvement of local government, which points to a trend of cities sanctioning actions that were formally left to grassroots activists. The guide calls tactical urbanism interventions a 'laboratory for experimentation,' and proposes that 'there is real merit in a municipality spending $30,000 on temporary material changes before investing $3,000,000 in those that are permanent.' Indeed, with decline of government-funded projects in a faltering economy, the responsibility for public space creation may fall increasingly on the public.

Place-making When does space become place? There are many different ways of looking at this. At the conceptual level, Tuan (1974) sees space as freedom and place as security. Massey (1995a, 188) sees places as having no fixed meaning; rather, they are 'constantly shifting articulations of social relations through time.' On the practical level, place-making seeks to shift the focus of development away from auto-centric planning (wide, high-speed streets, expansive surface parking lots between buildings, signs, and lighting that are scaled for moving cars, etc.) toward community-based places that inspire civic engagement. Kent (2008, 60) describes place-making as 'a set of ideas about creating cities in ways that result in high-quality spaces where people naturally want to live, work, and play.'

He illustrates this definition with examples from Europe, Asia, and the United Arab Emirates where cities have engaged in urban development that emphasizes the appealing qualities of a place and then builds on those qualities to create both an economically successful project and a socially successful community. Such projects have taken the form of sweeping traffic-calming measures, regenerated public spaces (parks, plazas, and markets), increased or improved transit connections, and community visioning processes (ibid.). In Masdar, south-east of Abu Dhabi in the United Arab Emirates, a planned sustainable city that will rely on solar and renewable energy and house a clean technology cluster is emerging. In Seoul, South Korea, as in Boston, space once occupied by an elevated highway was transformed into a public greenway. Boston's Rose Kennedy Greenway effectively (re)links Chinatown to North Station, Faneuil Hall to the Italian North End. Even cities that have become dominated by auto-centric planning over the last century (such as Paris, Dubai, and Hong Kong) have successfully engaged in place-making.

In most cases, the leaders of these projects – usually politicians or non-profit organizations – are driven by a common desire to increase the livability of their city and create wellbeing and an improved quality of life. Mayor Bertrand Delanoë of Paris recognized that clogged streets, muddled parking, and perilous cycling and walking conditions were detrimental to Paris's position as an international business and cultural capital and aggressively implemented a range of traffic-calming measures and public space and transit expansions that welcomed both tourists and residents back into the city. Perhaps most bravely, he changed an expressway along the River Seine into a pedestrian walkway and beach (Paris Plage). The Czech Environmental Partnership, a non-governmental organization (NGO) and partner of the US-based Project for Public Spaces, has formed a consortium of groups in Central and Eastern Europe to restore public life and public spaces that help build democracy and heal war wounds.

In Chapter 2, I developed a just sustainabilities critique of the food movement's valorization of 'the local' in which 'ecological' arguments are adduced to tell us that we should be growing only native food plants, especially plants local to a given (bio)region. I argued that this can drown out an emergent, culturally focused narrative surrounding the growth and celebration of culturally appropriate foods. Similarly, a common and not unwarranted criticism of place-making, especially in the developed world, is that it is based on middle-class visions, values, and narratives of place, and leads to gentrification. Blokland (2009), through her study of New Haven, Connecticut, builds on Massey's (1995a) 'shifting articulations' point noted above by showing how place-making can be seen as a struggle between residents' different historical narratives (which thereby define 'the community'); if any of the historical narratives are absent from the dominant picture of who the community is, that picture will therefore be distorted. I want to show two city case studies – one from the developed world (Boston) and one from the developing world (Bogotá) – where place-making was explicitly focused on shared and hopeful narratives of equity, justice, and, ultimately, just sustainabilities.

Dudley Street, Boston, Massachusetts One of the classic cases of urban place-making from a low-income, minority perspective is the redevelopment of Dudley Street by the Dudley Street Neighborhood Initiative (DSNI). Dudley Street straddles the Roxbury–Dorchester line in Boston. DSNI is an excellent example of what can happen when non-profit organizations understand that the framing of their activism should be proactive and based on a vision of place as potential – social, economic, and environmental. This is a vision that sees not 'community deficits' but rather 'community assets.' Medoff and Sklar (1994), who chronicled the DSNI effort in their book *Streets of Hope*, call this 'holistic development': a combination of human, economic, and environmental development. I would call it just sustainabilities.

DSNI's 34-member board of directors is diverse, with equal representation of the community's four major cultures (and therefore historical narratives of place): African American, Cape Verdean, Latino, and white. It works to implement resident-driven plans with partners including community development corporations (CDCs), other non-profit organizations and religious institutions serving the neighborhood, banks, government agencies, businesses and foundations. DSNI's approach to place-making is comprehensive (physical, environmental, economic, and human). It was formed in 1984 when residents of the Dudley Street area came together out of fear and anger to revive their neighborhood, which was nearly devastated by arson, disinvestment, neglect, and redlining practices,[3] and to protect it from outside speculators. DSNI is the only community-based non-profit organization in the US that has been granted eminent domain authority over abandoned land within its boundaries.

DSNI's strategic focus is in three key and related areas: sustainable and economic development, community empowerment, and youth opportunities and development. Its vision was to create an 'urban village' with mixed-rate[4] housing. However, it soon realized that retaining community-driven development would not be sufficient to halt the kind of gentrification that now displaces residents in other parts of Boston. DSNI's solution was the creation of a community land trust, Dudley Neighbors, Inc. (DNI), which uses a 99-year ground lease that restricts resale prices in order to keep the land available for affordable housing. To date, a total of 155 new homes and two community spaces or micro-centers have been built on DNI land. Within the next decade, approximately 200 new homes will have been built on DNI land.

Bogotá, Colombia

In public spaces, people meet as equals. (Enrique Peñalosa)

Among the most celebrated of urban cultural and space/place transformations, Bogotá, Colombia, underwent something of a revolution in the late 1990s when first Antanas Mockus and then Enrique Peñalosa, and then Mockus again, became mayor. Where Mockus looked to change the civic culture and citizenship by using bold social experiments (hiring 420 mime artists to control traffic, launching a 'Night for Women' and asking the city's men to stay at home and care for the children, and appearing on TV during a water shortage taking a shower and turning off the water as he soaped), both invested in public space and urban access and mobility, and revolutionized the quality of life of people living in the city. By reclaiming public space, improving public transport, promoting non-motorized transport, and implementing measures for auto-restriction (Wright and Montezuma 2004), Bogotá became a model of just sustainabilities in action. In a matter of just a few years, the city largely transformed itself from a typically gridlocked and crime-ridden third-world city in a developing country to a magnet for planners from across the world seeking examples of successful urban renewal. Mockus's concentration on the social and political features of city culture created a platform culturally and financially for Peñalosa, who focused on public space and physically altering the streetscape as a tangible means of displacing the car and further shifting behavior (Berney 2010). The main reason for these emphases was the opportunity for greater equality that public space offers (Parks and Recreation 2008).

Peñalosa strove to transform the street from a conduit for cars into shared public space because of his deep-seated belief that public spaces are a great equalizer. While those with higher incomes can afford leisure activities and retreats, all people can enjoy the space of the street or park, which is accessible, safe, and enjoyable for them (Berney 2010; Parks and Recreation 2008). Thus, Bogotá underwent an influx of public works during his tenure from 1998 to 2000 that installed a robust bus rapid transit (BRT) system called the TransMilenio (based on the lessons of Curitiba, Brazil), the addition of more park space, and the expansion of cycle lanes and pedestrianized spaces. Though controversial at times – including criticism for heavy-handed policy implementation, clearing of street vendors, and demolitions of city markets (Hunt 2009; Skinner 2004) – the benefits have generally been lauded (Berney 2010; Parks and Recreation 2008; Skinner 2004).

The Mockus administration following Peñalosa's and other elected officials in subsequent years have primarily continued efforts to promote streetscape sharing that is consistent with Colombia's history of inclusive use of public spaces (Berney 2010; Hunt 2009). Berney (2010, 540) refers to public space as the 'normative element of city form' in Latin America, and states that it is:

> related to … the right of each resident to have equal access to the city and its resources, to exercise full citizenship, and to be provided the capacity to construct his or her life and to participate in the equitable development of the city.

Not surprisingly, residents have demanded more input into public works projects via municipal plans, non-profit organizations, and universities (ibid.). Responding to one need, during the 1990s Guillermo Peñalosa, the brother of Enrique who served as Bogotá's Commissioner of Parks, Sport, and Recreation, greatly expanded Ciclovía, a weekly event since the 1970s that opens car-free streets to cyclists and pedestrians on Sundays and holidays (Watson 2009). The event has since grown to 70 miles of roadway and involves over

1.5 million participants on a weekly basis largely walking and cycling, thereby improving levels of physical activity (Rydin et al. 2012). Civic participation was integral in the success of these endeavors and the continuation of public satisfaction with the use of space.

Some of Bogotá's most notable improvements have included:

- formalizing water, electricity, and paved road service to 316 mostly low-income neighborhoods (slums);
- creating 1,200 new parks and planting 70,000 new trees;
- building a 17-kilometer bicycle and pedestrian corridor (Ciclovía) connecting lower-income communities to shops, jobs, and public services; and
- dedicating road lanes to the now famous BRT system TransMilenio (Montezuma 2005).

While all of these improvements were characterized by changes in physical space, they were simultaneously reflected in Bogotá's social conditions. Referring to the TransMilenio and adjacent Ciclovía, Peñalosa explained: 'This is not a transit system, this is an urban improvement' (Peñalosa 2009). He also said of the new network of pedestrian greenways connecting rich and poor neighborhoods: 'This is not an experiment in urban infrastructure, this is an experiment in urban social relations' (ibid.). Some of these societal 'experiments' have already been quantified and attributed to the transformations implemented by the Peñalosa and Mockus administrations (Wright and Montezuma 2004; Montezuma 2005):

- Education: school enrollment rose by 30 percent (140,000 more students).
- Safety: the murder rate fell by 42 percent and traffic deaths fell by nearly 50 percent.
- Economy: tax revenue doubled and property values rose up to 22 percent.
- Environment: ambient air emissions decreased by over 10 percent in TransMilenio's first year of service.

By linking what he calls 'urban happiness' to urban design and placing this at the forefront of his political agenda as mayor, Peñalosa successfully ushered in what appears to be a much happier Bogotá (Montgomery 2007). Ricardo Montezuma, an urbanist at the National University of Colombia, confirms with Gallup poll results that the perception of the city has indeed changed since Peñalosa's time in office (1998–2000): 'Twelve years ago, 80% of us were completely pessimistic about our future. Now, it's the opposite. Most of us are optimistic' (ibid.). However, at the time of writing, the *New York Times* was more sanguine, carrying an article: 'Past its golden moment, Bogotá clings to hope' (5 July 2012).

In seeking to return private spaces to the public, to provide both men and women with access to public space and mobility within the city, and to support the fulfillment of human potential, Peñalosa's and Mockus's political legacies distinguish themselves by a principle of equity and justice that is realized in civic cultural transformation, through urban space- and place-making. In this sense, the spirit of just sustainabilities – though absent in name from the city narrative – is the theme of the Bogotá story.

Streets and streetscapes

Introduction The street is one of the most basic elements of society. Since the early organization of modern humanity, roadways have been conduits, connecting people to their government, places of business, commerce, agriculture, leisure activities, and each other. The particular type of user best suited to traverse these roadways has evolved over time, but has generally included a mix (Loukaitou-Sideris and Ehrenfeucht 2009). Streets accommodated pedestrians on sidewalks as early as 2000 BC, though some subsequent civilizations, such as Medieval Europe, lacked sidewalks so all users were mixed together (ibid.). Soon after the mass production of the automobile in the twentieth century, car domination claimed a stranglehold over the street, and government and industry embraced this revolution.

Once the era of highways and suburbia took shape in the US in the 1950s, the default street user unquestionably became the automobile (see, for example, ibid.; Flink 1972; Flint 2006; Hess 2009; Macdonald 2008; Mohl 2004; Rae 2001). This newly dominant norm was promoted by the industries that profited from it, organized and standardized by all levels of government, and accepted by most individuals, often without any awareness of other possibilities (Rabinovitch and Leitman 1996; Flint 2006; Rae 2001). The road became synonymous with the car, and other users were squeezed out. The factors of speed, convenience, design, comfort, and safety as they relate to use of the street have been molded for the car driver

(Featherstone 2004). Bluntly, as the American Association of State Highway and Transportation Officials (AASHTO) notes, the purpose of street design is to ensure 'operational efficiency, comfort, safety, and convenience for the motorist.'

The paradigm of autonormativity, where the default is the car, was the norm in planning, and in some places it still is. Rather than being simply a tool to get from A to B in 'comfort, safety, and convenience' as AASHTO would have us believe, Henderson (2006, 304) explains the darker side in his study of Atlanta:

> Automobility embodies deeper social conflicts. One of these embodiments is secessionist automobility, or automobility as a medium for physical separation and physical expression of racialized, anti-urban ideologies. While some secessionists are both racist and anti-urban, not all secessionists are racist. Nevertheless the shared vision is one of secession from urban space, resistance to the compact patterns that support transit, and abhorrence to resolving difficult urban problems through cooperation and consensus – secession by car is easier.

Pucher and Renne (2003, 67) point out that:

> Walking is lower for whites (8.6%) than for the other three groups [Asian, Black, Hispanic], who make 12%–13% of their trips by walking. The largest differences among racial and ethnic groups are in their use of transit. Blacks are almost six times as likely as whites to take their trips by transit in general (5.3% vs. 0.9%), and they are eight times as likely to take the bus (4.2% vs. 0.5%).

It could be argued that the points made by Henderson, and Pucher and Renne, suggest that the move away from autonormativity and automobility toward walkable, 'complete streets,' 'transit-oriented/transit just,' and 'livable streets' has an implicit anti-racist and social justice/inclusion element. I do not think this was ever part of the activists' overall strategy but it is interesting to ponder nevertheless.

Even Copenhagen residents, when they had the choice in the early 1960s, wanted the car and American-style streets. Visionary planners, such as Jan Gehl, and a succession of progressive mayors and management/leadership teams in the city's services showed that a different way was possible. The Dutch love affair with the bicycle and designing streets for people is a relatively recent development spurred by the 1973 oil crisis and a series of child road deaths. In the US, the regulation, maintenance, and oversight of the roadways have fallen to a patchwork of agencies, municipalities, and commercial interests that seek to consolidate their piece of the status quo (Hess 2009; Flint 2006). An individual's right to the street as public space is sacrificed within a default system that prioritizes automobiles and automobile traffic over any other form of mobility.

But change is afoot (please excuse the pun). Realtors (real estate agents) in the US frequently use the Walk Score as an index of the walkability of any given address and, according to Christopher Leinberger in the *New York Times* (25 May 2012): 'Walking isn't just good for you. It has become an indicator of your socioeconomic status.' The US narratives of 'complete streets,' 'transit justice,' and 'livable streets' frame the message that streets are, ultimately, democratic public spaces, and that everyone in the community should have equal rights to space within them. Implicit in this is the recognition that those who currently have fewer rights are those people, often with lower incomes, who do not own cars.

Democratizing the streets Research into the social fabric of urban neighborhoods has uncovered how livability relates to the street and the importance of taking streets back from cars, for people. Much of the literature on these topics stems from visionary voices that struck chords at a time when the autonormative paradigm was peaking, at least in terms of its widespread acceptance. Jane Jacobs's seminal work, *The Death and Life of American Cities*, published in 1961, criticized the modernist, Le Corbusier-inspired, form-over-function understanding of cities. Donald Appleyard's *Livable Streets*, though not published until 1981, was based on seminal research he conducted in the early 1970s in San Francisco, in which he found that traffic volume on streets correlated with livability and social inclusion. He looked at three streets that had different traffic volumes. One had 2,000 vehicles per day, the other two had 8,000 and 16,000 vehicles per day respectively. He showed that residents on the street with lower traffic volume had three times the number of friends and twice the number of acquaintances than those living on the street with high traffic volume. In other words, higher traffic volumes lead to less livable and socially inclusive neighborhoods, and vice versa. Subsequent research has updated Appleyard's findings and has explored other places, such as Basel, Switzerland (Sauter and Huettenmoser 2008) and Bristol, UK (Hart 2008), with very similar conclusions.

The existence, significance, and enhancement of the social fabric of streets and neighborhoods are now commonly perceived as accepted and appropriate goals in urban planning. This acceptance is reflected in current literature on streetscapes. For instance, Rogers et al. (2011) found that more walkable neighborhoods and streets correlated with happier people who were more socially involved and connected. Research conducted by Putnam (2000) and others showed diminishing social capital as a result of 'isolating' technologies and habits, such as person-to-person communication and social interaction via the internet. A generational shift may alleviate this problem, however. A tech-savvy cohort of individuals under 35 (the so-called 'Millennial Generation') is experiencing the public realm differently through personal and digital technologies, increasingly preferring public transit as a means through which to remain plugged in both technologically and socially (Schwieterman 2011). Fewer own cars: more car-share, take public transit, walk, or cycle. More perceive the experience of the street as one in which they have rights as individual users to interact in myriad ways. This generational shift will further aid in the transition from car domination of the streets to streetscapes that are more democratized and just.

A tale of two streets: Södra Vägen in Göteborg, Sweden and Massachusetts Avenue in Cambridge, US Södra Vägen and Massachusetts Avenue are roughly the same width, but the streetscapes are very different. On Södra Vägen, I watched pedestrians on the broad sidewalk, non-helmeted (and elderly) cyclists on the dedicated cycle way (not a painted lane in the road), and transit users in the two-way streetcars flowing freely and regularly. The few trucks and private vehicles were relegated to a minor role in this streetscape. The streetcars came in both directions every minute or so and appeared to be full. Basically, Göteborg has completed a modal shift in which people on Södra Vägen and other streets are using modes other than the private car to get around, unlike Massachusetts Avenue. Cambridge does have a generous arrangement of bike lanes, but the bike lanes are only painted white lines on the road: they are not, for the most part, separated from the potential and actual harms of vehicular traffic. Cambridge has electric buses, and its share of the Massachusetts

Bay Transportation Authority (MBTA) subway (the Red and Green Lines), but these are not as frequent as the Göteborg streetcars.

In Göteborg, politicians and planners have (re)allocated rights to the street. These rights are in favor of the pedestrian, the cyclist, and the public transit user. On Södra Vägen, I would say that these users get priority rights over about 80 percent of the streetscape. On Massachusetts Avenue, private vehicles easily get 80 percent. Three thoughts come to mind. First, while the Swedish politicians, planners, and public do not mention this exact phrase, what has happened is that 'spatial justice'[5] has been imposed on Södra Vägen by (re)allocating rights to space in favor of the least powerful users (i.e. pedestrians, public transit users, and cyclists). Given my earlier arguments about the gendered nature of public space, this (re)allocation will disproportionately benefit women who 'are more spatially restricted' (McDowell 1993, 166) and therefore tend to use cars less. If this were to happen in the US, it would also disproportionately benefit low-income and minority groups as they walk more, are more likely to use public transit (especially buses), and cycle most for work purposes (Latino) (Pucher and Renne 2003). Second, this inverts the typical US prioritization of 'street rights,' where the bigger your vehicle, the more 'rights' you have (don't try arguing your street rights with an MBTA bus driver). Third, and probably the least researched, this street-level spatial justice, this 'democratization of the street' through the redistribution of rights to (and in) public space, may make the street look physically different, but I think it also fundamentally rewires our brains, affecting the way we think. If the street is our most commonly used public space, the one we use each day, and it has been democratized in the way Södra Vägen has, and Massachusetts Avenue hasn't, what does this say to the public who use these streets and spaces daily and become acculturated to spatial justice on Södra Vägen or spatial injustice on Massachusetts Avenue? How does the daily use of a democratized or an undemocratized street affect our behavior? How does a child growing up in a Swedish city, who encounters the more democratic, spatially just environment of a street such as Södra Vägen, differ from his or her counterpart in a US city who has experienced the complete opposite?

The complete streets movement Arguably, the most prolific and persistent product of the unfolding vision of livable streets and of its related social capital and inclusion research and practice has been the genesis and growth of the complete streets movement. Developing as part of, and related to, the wider narrative around place-making, the movement has transformed the frames of livable, walkable streets and social inclusion into a mobilizing effort that has led to coalition-building and activism, has influenced legislation and policy, and has provided the average citizen with a tangible vision of the potential of their streets beyond that of automobile conduit.

Organizations such as Streetsblog, Transportation Alternatives, 8-80 Cities, and the National Complete Streets Coalition have aided the formation and growth of the complete streets movement in North America, while Living Streets in the UK, the Bicycling Empowerment Network in South Africa, and Walk 21 and EMBARQ are international examples. Moreover, city governments are starting to lead, pioneering the integration of complete streets or similar methodology into their street design manuals and regulatory structures.

To progress beyond the narrow diktats of the AASHTO *Green Book*, which mandates standards on a federal level in the US, cities have to employ innovative strategies. San Francisco has incorporated its Better Streets Plan into its regulatory framework, for example, and New York has established its Active Design Guidelines through an interagency effort to encourage healthier participation on a complete street (Hawkes and Sheridan 2011). Legislative strategies are increasingly valid tools for promoting more complete streets. This approach helps to actualize the pressure of organizations, citizens' groups, and planning and sustainability literature into enforceable – or at least guidance – doctrines. Some examples of legislative or policy remedy include the bipartisan Safe and Complete Streets Act of 2011 (H.R. 1780), introduced by US Representatives Doris Matsui (D-CA) and Steven LaTourette (R-OH) on 5 May 2011, and, at the time of writing, referred to the Subcommittee on Highways and Transit; the City of Vancouver Transportation Plan, which integrates bike paths, pedestrian zones, and traffic-calming measures; and the Crimes Amendment (Road Accidents) (Brendan's Law) Act 2005 No. 74 in New South Wales, Australia, which increased protection for pedestrians from motor vehicles.

Health and safety One of the most salient arguments for both livability and complete streets strategies, from a just sustainabilities perspective, is the binary of the positive impacts of walking and cycling, and the negative health impacts of being in a car for long periods of time. Literature is dense with the importance of walking and with neighborhood walkability as a means of tackling physical health problems (for instance, Pucher et al. 2010; Alfonzo et al. 2008; Gordon-Larsen et al. 2006; Johnston 2008; de Nazelle and Rodríguez 2009; Dumbaugh and Li 2011), such as obesity, especially among children, and the illnesses associated with it (Gordon-Larsen et al. 2006; Johnston 2008), all of which are greater in low-income and minority residents. Health concerns come as well from the pollution emanating from vehicles and the safety issues that correspond to rising volumes of traffic (Bell et al. 2006; de Nazelle and Rodríguez 2009; Morabia et al. 2010; Mohan and Tiwari 1999). Issues of race[6] and class, although contested and complex (Kawachi et al. 2005), permeate environmental justice studies, which generally show that poorer people and people of color tend to bear a disproportionate burden of air and noise pollution and other safety and health hazards compared with more wealthy neighborhoods.

Driving can have a negative impact on one's physical and psychological health, particularly in terms of aggression and stress. Exacerbating this condition, an auto-focused built environment can lead to accidents between vehicles and more vulnerable road users, usually due to high speeds and traffic issues (Dumbaugh and Li 2011). 'Road rage' is an informal phrase used to describe aggressive behavior that many drivers exhibit when confronted with traffic, slow driving, or other hindrances (Rowden et al. 2011; Harris and Houston 2010; Dahlen and Ragan 2004). Anecdotally, most people will comment that their 'driving personality' tends to differ from their ordinary personality; it can be more aggressive, agitated, and stressed. Rowden et al. (2011, 1333) show that a 'frustration-aggression link to stress [exists] within the traffic environment' in which 'time urgency significantly influenced driver stress in both high and low congestion conditions.' These levels of agitation certainly cannot be healthy, and are likely to play a role in bad behavior on the street and beyond. The safety of other types of road users, such as pedestrians, cyclists, and mass transit riders, are also endangered in this equation since aggressive driving is more likely to injure or at least frighten them due to their relative vulnerability (Harris and Houston 2010). A setting conducive to less, and calmer, driving – that is, a democratized streetscape, especially with shared streets – might therefore have a positive effect on behavior.

Happiness Is a democratized streetscape a happier streetscape? Are the good people of Södra Vägen in Göteborg, Sweden, happier than those on Massachusetts Avenue in Cambridge, US? Even if we could answer this question, it would be difficult if not impossible to ascribe it solely to streetscape conditions. Similarly, happier people could choose to live in more democratized and walkable neighborhoods. However, perhaps we can extrapolate. In happiness studies in which happiness is a metric used to measure wellbeing and quality of life, other issues such as economic affluence (particularly in terms of income) matter only to a point. After that threshold, education, health, and community play a more influential role (for example, Veenhoven 1996; Schor 2005; Rogers et al. 2011; Dorn et al. 2007; Engelbrecht 2009; Zidansek 2007; Stiglitz et al. 2011; Frey and Stutzer 2002; Jackson 2009).

Walkability has been connected to happiness in many studies (O'Brien 2008; Rogers et al. 2011; Leyden et al. 2011). On a city-specific level, Leyden (2003) shows that happiness is associated with daily interaction within one's built environment, and significantly correlates with the convenience of public transit as well as easy access (presumably along the streetscape) to amenities such as parks, leisure activities, shopping, and dining. The cleanliness of streets and sidewalks, safety while walking at night, and safety from car accidents also correlate positively and significantly with happiness (ibid.). Social capital enters into the equation as well, since social involvement and relationships are connected to the perception of a high quality of life (Putnam 2000; Frey and Stutzer 2002; Dolan et al. 2008; O'Connell 2004; Engelbrecht 2009; Leyden et al. 2011).

Rogers et al. (2011, 202) have explicitly attached social capital to the coupling of walkability and quality of life, finding that 'levels of social capital are higher in more walkable neighborhoods.' They specifically link quality of life not only to how walkable one's community is, but also to the social inclusion benefits that result. Leyden et al. (2011, 885) find that:

> A relationship [between traditional mixed-use, pedestrian-oriented urban designs rather than car-dependent single-use areas and happiness] exists because of the importance of social connections that appear to be found in more walkable, mixed-use places.

This perceived correlation between happiness and more complete, socially inclusive streets relates to Putnam's work (2000) in which he proposes that more time spent in the car commuting from disconnected suburbs degrades community life and involvement.

Democracy has been shown to correlate explicitly with happiness and quality of life as well (Veenhoven 1996; Dorn et al. 2007; Haller and Hadler 2006; O'Connell 2004; Frey and Stutzer 2002), as has social equality. Haller and Hadler (2006, 203) point to the importance of the 'feeling of being free.' Dorn et al. (2007) further find that greater amounts of time spent in a more democratic society may lead to a greater level of happiness. These results suggest that a democratized streetscape may have a positive effect on the behavioral outlook of a person who grows up in that environment. This impact may be felt to an even larger degree than it is by the person who moves into that environment from a non-democratized one, or for whom the streetscape becomes more equally allocated during their lifetime. Intuitively, it does not seem surprising that an individual who feels that he or she has a right to the street space, whatever type of user he or she is, may possess a greater sense of wellbeing, happiness, and empowerment (and might behave differently as a consequence) than does the individual who feels excluded from that space.

(In)complete streets? Low-income and minority communities in the US and around the world have been disproportionally utilized as the loci for industrial or unwanted development and as transportation corridors that often pass through but do not stop in their neighborhoods. There are, of course, health risks and impacts associated with these developments. Interestingly, however, other just sustainabilities issues have arisen recently that ask some fundamental questions about the complete streets movement's ideas, actions, and processes, and about their practical effects.

Massey's (1995a) and Blokland's (2009) point, that places are 'shifting articulations' that represent struggles over residents' different historical narratives, thereby defining 'the community,' is as pertinent to the complete streets vision as it is to place-making. Decisions to construct or locate what might be considered by some as 'beneficial amenities' in traditionally disadvantaged neighborhoods can be seen as part of a privileged narrative. As I mentioned in Chapter 2 in relation to food, the privileged narrative of 'the local' is being challenged, and the decision to locate urban farms in Boston's Dorchester neighborhood was not greeted with unanimous applause; similarly, some low-income communities and neighborhoods of color worry that changes such as the addition of bicycle lane, street accessibility improvements, mass transit expansions and upgrades, and pedestrian zone placements will foster gentrification and further diminish their rights and roles in the community (Henderson 2006; Preston 2011; Community Cycling Center 2010).

In Portland, OR, there are two strands to a growing (in)complete streets-related controversy. One relates to cycle lanes as gentrification highways; the other to cycling as an elite activity. In terms of cycle lanes and gentrification, proposed traffic changes to increase bicycle safety along North Williams Avenue have met with resistance from locals. There is a fight against what is seen as the imposition by the city of bike lanes as an instrument of gentrification, as Debora Leopold Hutchins, who chairs an advisory committee, argues:

> The issues of gentrification and race and bicycles have kind of met right here at this location, at this intersection, but one is not cause of the other. (Preston 2011)

More searing, however, in her critique is resident Donna Maxey, who explained the frustration of people of color with Portland's bicycle support efforts:

> What is causing the anger and resentment is that it's only an issue of safety now that whites are the ones who are riding bicycles and walking on the streets. Because we have been in this community for years and it has not been an issue and now it's an issue. So that's the resentment you're hearing … years of people being told, you don't count, you don't matter … but now that there's a group of people who's coming in that look like the people who are the power brokers – now it's important. That's the anger. That's the hurt. (Shareable 2011)

Maxey's comment needs to be seen in the wider context of the gentrification of North East Portland neighborhoods, which followed 'the historical process of segregation and neighborhood disinvestment that preceded gentrification in Portland's Black community, Albina' (Gibson 2007, 3). Indeed, in a *Portland Mercury* article called 'It's not about the bikes,' Mirk (2012) argues that 'pinning the North Williams uproar over bikes misses the point – and the history.' The real point, according to Midge Purcell, policy director of the Urban League of

Portland, is that 'The City of Portland's policies want to encourage increased cycling and environmental friendliness.' She continues:

> That's all very well and good. But when people feel that those values are imposed upon them, especially when there's been all the other historic impositions on the community, then it really does become about a lot more than just putting in a bicycle lane. In a lot of ways, this is a real test. To see whether some of the lessons have been learned from previous projects where the outcomes have been really, really poor. (ibid.)

To try to build bridges, the city's Office of Neighborhood Involvement since 2008 has been running a program called the Restorative Listening Project (RLP). Based on the principles of restorative justice,[7] the RLP (now named the Restorative Action Project) uses:

> dialogue as a strategy for community formation and 'antiracist place-making' ... by (1) positioning people of color as knowledge producers about the institutional and interpersonal effects of racism in the neighborhood; (2) confronting the tactics of white denial; and (3) promoting consciousness about systemic racism. (Drew 2012, 1)

Race Talks is Multnomah County's version of the RLP, and an event was held on 8 November 2011 on North Williams Avenue under the title 'Coming together on North Williams Avenue: reconciling neighborhood's past with proposed bike lane.'

The event featured speakers as well as facilitated dialogue moderated by trained volunteers from the non-profit group Uniting to Understand Racism and from Portland's Intergroup Dialogue program. However, a friend of mine who was there noted that the majority of attendees were from outside the local area so she was unsure of the value of the dialogue in relation to North Williams Avenue. In June 2012, after 17 months of deliberation, the ethnically diverse Stakeholder Advisory Committee (SAC) for the North Williams Traffic Operations Safety Project concluded its work and approved option 4B, which in technical terms is 'left-side buffered bike lane with one motor vehicle travel lane and turn lanes (segments 2 to 5) and shared left-turn lane/bikeway in segment 4.'

In terms of cycling as an elite activity, Portland's Community Cycling Center (2010) admits:

> We could do better to understand the needs of our program participants, which are predominantly low-income and communities of color. We could do better to increase and improve programs serving a culturally diverse community. We could do better at creating employment pathways into our organization. So we developed the 'Understanding Barriers to Bicycling Project,' a community needs assessment, to better understand what were people interested in and concerned about as it related to bicycling. Since we completed the needs assessment, we have been collaborating with our community partners in north and northeast Portland to develop programs and support community leaders to broaden access to bicycling and its benefits – and to ensure that those benefits are accessible to all.

The Community Cycling Center received an Oregon Metro grant in 2010 to reach out to Portland's diverse constituencies to better understand how it could support cycling in different communities. To do this the Center partnered with Hacienda Community Development Corporation (CDC) and New Columbia, a HOPE VI[8] revitalized community in North Portland. In its report, *Understanding Barriers to Bicycling*, the Center concluded that the organization needs to:

> Increase the cultural competency of the Community Cycling Center staff;
>
> Pilot tailored programs for specific cultural groups and neighborhoods;
>
> Continue investing in community partnerships; include leadership development in our bicycle programs and shop operations to build capacity within community partner organizations;
>
> Develop strategies to influence policies that address the environmental changes and other social determinants of health that ensure equitable access to bicycling for recreation and transportation. (ibid., 10)

Similar challenges to both bicycle lanes as gentrification tools and cycling as an elite activity are being made in other cities. Chicago resident and founder of the African American Pioneers Bicycle Club, Oboi Reed, criticized Chicago's priorities in a *New York Times* article, 'City bike plan is accused of a neighborhood bias' (15 October 2011). According to Reed, 'the lion's share of the resources' of the city's $150 million bike plan 'are going to go [to the wealthier neighborhoods] downtown and to the North Side – the South and West will only see a sprinkling.' In New York City, a report by graduate students from the Urban Affairs and Planning Program at Hunter College, *Beyond the Backlash: Equity and participation in bicycle planning*, concluded that:

> Traditionally underserved areas outside of the core of Manhattan and northwest Brooklyn have inadequate bicycle infrastructure. These areas have many cyclists and residents who are largely new immigrants and people of color. (Hunter College 2011)

Clearly, there is growing alarm that bike lanes – uber-narrative and key to the infrastructure of complete streets – may be the 'new gentrification.' But I think it goes deeper, along the lines suggested by Donna Maxey in Portland, OR (above): 'It's only an issue of safety now that whites are the ones who are riding bicycles.' Consider that in the US 'bicycling is the highest among whites and Hispanics (0.9% of all trips). For whites, cycling is mostly for *recreation*, while for Hispanics, it is to reach the *workplace*' (Pucher and Renne 2003, 67, emphasis added). This is a significant point: whites are choosing to cycle and are adopting an identity as cyclists, whereas Hispanic (and black) people have no other option; they simply cycle to get to work because it is cheap. Kidder's (2005) study of cycle messengers in New York City showed that, despite the fact that the majority were male and black or Hispanic, those who built a 'lifestyle' and identity around it were often female and largely white. Steinbach et al. (2011, 1130), albeit in a study of London, make an argument that works more generally:

> In cities where cycling uptake is low, the challenge … is perhaps to de-couple cycling from the rather narrow range of healthy associations it currently has, and provide an infrastructure in which anyone can cycle, rather than just those whose social identities are commensurate with being 'a cyclist'.

Planning and technical analyses and critiques There is a more traditional technical design, engineering, and planning literature that addresses current designs, standards, and agency protocols for street planning. Yet, a growing literature discusses the standards in order to demonstrate how streets can be made more livable. How the street is governed, organized, and managed constructs the context in which people and cars interact.

Critical literature questions the continued design of the streetscape to harness or support the travel of vehicles at the highest speeds possible (CABE 2002; Dumbaugh 2005; Southworth and Ben-Joseph 1995). Hess (2009, 2) argues that current street-building practices in North America encourage conflict between road design and engineering standards, naming 'standards for lane widths, turning radii, sight lines etc. which are employed by the engineers that design streets' as the 'most common explanation for the difficulty of making more walkable streets.' He outlines Toronto's attempt to navigate this bureaucracy of competing agencies and the status quo to accommodate more complete streets as representative of the friction presently occurring in many cities.

Aside from leadership and vision, the tension among and within different municipal and state agencies, official design, safety standards and regulations, and shifting values and goals is probably the greatest tangible obstacle to a democratized streetscape (Southworth and Ben-Joseph 1995; CABE 2002). NGOs and community groups often seek either to bypass or to guide these government entities in order to enact change (Newman et al. 2008). In addition to lobbying officials, non-profit organizations have produced a range of instructional manuals (such as CLF 1998) and participatory projects to stimulate a focus on shared streets, to inform and educate, and to guide decision-making. Topics range from how to share street space, pedestrianize public spaces, reclaim pavement from the automobile, and calm traffic to the encouragement of broader definitions of the streetscape as part of a larger strategy to mobilize and build momentum for complete streets. Examples include: the American Planning Association's Great Places in America program; Living Streets' report *Making the Case for Investment in the Walking Environment*; the National Complete Streets Coalition fact sheet 'Create livable communities'; Transport and Environment's report *Q&A: Funding for transport infrastructure in the new EU budget*; Transportation Alternatives' handbook *Streets for People: Your guide to winning safer and quieter streets*; the Conservation Law Foundation's *City Routes, City Rights*; and EMBARQ's report *From Here to There: A creative guide to making public transport the way to go*.

A democratized streetscape in form Although a democratized streetscape can take many forms, an ideal complete streets policy, according to the National Complete Streets Coalition (2010), includes the following elements: community input regarding a vision for the streetscape, a broad and diverse definition of 'all users,' connectivity between transit modes, understanding that all agencies must apply the policy to all roads for all new and retrofit projects, and the measurement and monitoring of outcomes.

On the street level, a classic design for a democratized streetscape would enable one or two travel lanes for single-user vehicles as well as one or two for mass transit, such as BRT or light rail. A bicycle lane that is physically separated from these travel lanes would be included and well marked. In many of the most successful practices, this lane is separated by more than simply a line of paint (Kodransky and Hermann 2011). In Copenhagen, the cycle track is often elevated from street level and can be separated by concrete, bollards, or parked cars. In New York City, a concrete curb and row of parked cars accompany its most successful bike lanes to date, such as those along Ninth Avenue in Manhattan. Pedestrians are typically incorporated either through a designated car-free section, as in the Sunday Streets (Ciclovía) initiative in Bogotá and on Sundays on Memorial Drive in Cambridge, Massachusetts, or through safe, separate spaces along spacious sidewalks and frequent, well-marked crosswalks (Loukaitou-Sideris and Ehrenfeucht 2009; Transportation Alternatives 2004). According to Gehl Architects of Copenhagen, it is important to 'start from the building out … [and put] pedestrians first – if you get that right there's nothing to hinder priority and good quality for people on bikes' (Grassov 2008, 32).

Democratized streetscapes in practice Regardless of the many leadership, technical, and gentrification issues regarding democratized streets, they are increasingly common in cityscapes – even in countries in North America, where many thought it would be impossible to break the stranglehold of the car. The following vignettes of Copenhagen, Curitiba, Toronto, and New York City illustrate some of the challenges and opportunities.

Streetscape as beacon: Copenhagen – the gold standard

> You have to start with people. You can't add the people after you have made the cars happy. (Jan Gehl)

In the transformation of urban landscapes, there is always a leader, a visionary, a change agent. In Copenhagen, that figure was, and still is, Jan Gehl, an urban design consultant and Professor of Urban Design at Copenhagen's School of Architecture. His work as an outspoken proponent of the social importance of public space and its use as a vehicle for how people live has strongly influenced urban planners and designers around the world. In his own city of Copenhagen, his architecture firm, his research and publications, and his professor's pulpit have facilitated a shift in the priorities of the streetscape. As the Gehl Architects' website (2011) states about his philosophy:

> Our approach to design extends beyond ... advocating walking, cycling and alternative transport ... [to] prioritize life quality, health, safety and an inclusive environment for all ... regardless of ethnic background, age, socio-economic class, disability, religion, or the like.

The transformation of Copenhagen took hold in 1962 with the pedestrianization of the Strøget, a district in the city center that still represents the longest pedestrianized street in the world. Many other roads followed, until the network of pedestrianized streets was completed in 1992, and efforts moved onto squares and other spaces. Whereas residents previously sat at home to drink coffee and rarely socialized in public before the streets were democratized, the city became a much more robust, vigorous, functional, and social scene in the decades following 1962 (Tan 2006). Due at least in part to this transformation, the city has witnessed elevated commercial income, improved air and noise pollution, enhanced quality of life and health outcomes, and heightened popularity as a destination (Tan 2006; Gemzøe 2001; Grassov 2008; Bosselmann 2002).

Between 1968 and 1995, the year when pedestrian activity grew to 80 percent of transit in the city center, the number of people who gathered in the public spaces of the city center increased more than threefold. As of 2007, bikes accounted for more than one-third of all transit in Copenhagen (City of Copenhagen 2007). According to Gehl and his colleagues' research, a one-to-one relation existed between the creation of pedestrian space in the city center's streets and the increase in the number of people spending time on them:

> From 1968 to 1995 the number of people who spent time in the public space of the city centre increased three and a half times. Over the same period, the total area of car-free streets and squares increased three and a half times. (Tan 2006, 33)

Public transit has replaced a good deal of car use as well, and traffic calming and parking elimination have further dissuaded drivers from dominating the city (Kodransky and Hermann 2011; CABE 2002). The streets in Copenhagen's center represent a peak in efforts to create a spatially just streetscape in which all users are afforded access, priority, and rights to the road.

As Gehl and his colleagues have been called in to help many other cities around the world, including Melbourne and New York City, Copenhagen has also refused to be complacent, continuing to improve its public spaces and create even more livable, shared landscapes. In 2007, the city officially publicized its goal to become an Eco-Metropolis by 2015, a target determined unanimously by the Copenhagen City Council (City of Copenhagen 2007). The city claims that Copenhagen will move beyond its status as one of Europe's most environmental cities to one of the world's by 2015. The plan promotes some just sustainabilities aspects: world-class biking facilities, including path expansion and enhancement and safety initiatives; promotion of public transit and reduction of auto emissions; continued reduction of parking spaces; greater walkable access to parks, beaches, and swimming pools; and traffic calming.

In using happiness as a metric for quality of life (Veenhoven 1996), Denmark consistently ranks highly (see the World Database of Happiness and the World Map of Happiness). As happiness tends to correlate with high levels of walkability (Rogers et al. 2011), the democratization of Copenhagen's streetscape and high levels of happiness in the country could suggest that an individual's right to the street could positively affect his or her outlook. As of 2007, 36 percent of Copenhageners traveled for work or leisure via bicycle, and the Eco-Metropolis plan aspires for that number to reach 50 percent by 2015. In a relatively dark and cold country, the popularity of cycling probably reflects not only its convenience, but also the freedom one feels to claim one's own space and share the street safely with cars and many other users.

Streetscape as laboratory: Curitiba

> A car is like your mother-in-law. You want to have a good relationship with her, but you can't let her conduct your life. When a city has good public transportation, it becomes for people and for cars. (Jaime Lerner)

Curitiba, like Bogotá, was the site of substantial transformations in public space – especially as related to the space of the street and transportation – that heightened its capacity to provide for the majority of its citizens, specifically the poor. The Curitiba narrative highlights the power of the individual leader as well as the role that democratized streets play in shifting entire cities toward just sustainabilities.

Jaime Lerner, an architect, urban planner, and three-time mayor of Curitiba, Brazil, was a visionary not only for the concept of BRT that he introduced and the pedestrianization and street-sharing that accompanied it, but also for his vision of the city as an integrated system. During his administrations, he helped to produce a city that is healthier and more inclusive of and attuned to its citizens. The city's transformation began through a focus on first two then four main corridors that included car-free streets, bicycle path expansion, progressive density zoning, affordable housing construction, recycling initiatives, programs for low-income adults and children, and extensive park creation (Rabinovitch and Leitman 1996).

Even though car ownership is high in Curitiba, more than 25 percent of car owners ride the BRT. Daily ridership increased from 25,000 in 1974 to 2.4 million in 2008; twice as many trips in the city are taken via bus than by car, and BRT ridership is still growing (Fox 2008). The Curitiba Master Plan was approved in 1966 but did not begin implementation until Lerner's first mayoral administration in 1971. The first pedestrian area opened in 1972. The plan initially succeeded and has ebbed and flowed with public participation and changing demographics in the years since (Rabinovitch 1996; Fox 2008; East 2009). As Rabinovitch and Leitman (1996, 47) describe:

> Progressive city administrations turned Curitiba into a living laboratory for a style of urban development based on a preference for public transportation over the private automobile, working with the environment instead of against it … [and including] citizen participation in place of master planning.

Within the last decade, Curitiba has continued its leadership in streetscape democratization, transforming a highway that cut through the city and averaged 45,000 vehicles a day into a new transit corridor called the Green Line. Explicit goals for the new axis include increased pedestrian safety, the inclusion of bike paths and sidewalks, and status as a mixed-use area (Institute for Research and Urban Planning of

Curitiba 2009). Long-term participatory planning, innovative investment in public interest projects, and democratized streetscapes have cultivated an urban setting in which residents of all socio-economic levels take pride.

Streetscape and governance reimagined and reorganized: Toronto

> An urban environment that encourages and facilitates walking … will increase use of public transit; decrease car dependence; reduce conflict between vehicles and pedestrians; lead to cleaner air; green public space; and support green tourism. (Toronto Pedestrian Charter)

Toronto is a typical North American city in which engineering and urban planning design and street safety standards clash with popular movements to democratize the streetscape for a greater variety of users. Like many other cities around the world, Toronto has supported a number of public transit options for many years and has been increasingly incorporating initiatives friendlier to pedestrians and cyclists (Hess 2009). Yet, it also has encountered several hindrances in following this path, from bureaucratic decentralization and protocol inertia to grassroots limitations.

Toronto boasts not only the first pedestrian charter in North America, but also the first approved by a municipality in the world. Although the charter was adopted in May 2002, it is not statutory. It possesses no legally binding mechanism. Instead, the charter aims to influence government and other municipal organizations to create a more pedestrian-friendly and livable landscape. For instance, it encourages the city to promote, among other initiatives, 'infrastructure that gives pedestrians safe and convenient passage while walking along and crossing streets' and 'policies that reduce conflict between pedestrians and other users of the public right-of-way' (City of Toronto 2002, 1). On paper, these ideals correlate with the notion of a democratized streetscape. In reality, the movement corresponded with and served to formalize Pedestrian Sundays, an endeavor originated by citizens in the Kensington Market neighborhood of Toronto.

In July 2002, four friends and co-workers in Kensington Market decided to work to create a car-free zone to counteract the pollution and safety hazards that the large amount of traffic in the neighborhood generated (Newman et al. 2008). Through grassroots efforts, this energy grew into Streets Are for People!, a celebration of bikes, pedestrians, and the idea of a car-free Kensington Market; this later morphed into PS Kensington and Pedestrian Sundays (ibid.). Even though the pedestrian charter had been adopted two months before the community group formed, the City of Toronto's involvement in Pedestrian Sundays was limited, especially at first, and rather hands-off. The city did, however, provide some funding and staff to support the first summer of Sundays. When the city sponsored a community survey following that first summer, its role shifted from supportive to obstructive (ibid.). The survey was lengthy and complicated, and was conducted by a third party, which lacked a history in and knowledge of the community. Unsurprisingly, few returned it, and, among respondents, feedback was mixed. The community organizers persisted to overcome the disconnect between the city's outreach and the neighborhood's true perception of the street-sharing.

Another obstacle the organizers encountered was the set of entrenched regulations, which did not include provisions for pedestrian zones. As a result, the car-free zone created did not allow for cyclists or any commercial deliveries (ibid.). At the time of writing, cyclists are still asked to walk their bikes through the space and deliveries are requested before or after the hours of the event, rather than during it. However, pedestrian Sundays have expanded to the neighborhoods of Mirvish and Baldwin. According to the initiative's website (www.pskensington.ca), the car-free events facilitate the community's attempt to voice its role within the larger city. It states: 'By regularly reclaiming our streets from the mess of traffic and parking, our neighbourhood enjoys the opportunity to express its character … our community's diverse ethnicity, age and interests' (2012).

While a democratized streetscape need not be a car-free one, Toronto's segregated bureaucratic mechanisms have made it difficult to integrate shared uses (Hess 2009). Standardization of engineering conduct, street design, and maintenance codes grew out of the automobilization that occurred from the 1930s to the 1950s (Southworth and Ben-Joseph 1995). The standards constitute long-standing codes for convenience, speed, safety, and efficient vehicle flow (ibid.), such as the right of way as apportioned by the curb line, for which 'many of the geometric dimensions provided are very narrowly if not precisely defined' (Hess 2009, 25). In Toronto, like in many cities, this standardization has increasingly conflicted with communities' desire for more livable, shared spaces, thus creating 'competing rationalities of "flow and place"' (Patton 2007, quoted in Hess 2009). To add to the complexity, Hess (ibid.) lists the many different municipal agencies, departments, officials, and divisions that claim a piece of the streetscape pie in terms of design, construction, operation, maintenance, and oversight. The transportation department competes with the city council, planning divisions, and parks and other departments, among other entities, all of whom possess tight budgets and specific mandates, for time, money, energy, and project control (ibid.; Newman et al. 2008). The process of changing entrenched standards and overcoming inertia has proven a substantial challenge in Toronto (especially during the turbulent years under Mayor Ford from 2010 to 2012), and around the globe.

Streetscape as intersection of the top-down and bottom-up: New York City

> Our mission is to reclaim New York City's streets from the automobile, and to advocate for bicycling, walking and public transit as the best transportation alternatives. (Transportation Alternatives)

New York City has long hosted a large array of transit alternatives. Until recently, however, automobiles had remained dominant. As Kidder (2005, 351–2) noted:

> Cyclists are denied access to sidewalks and are refused equal rights to the roadway. As such, bicycles must ride in a liminal space – the shoulder of the road – a space suitable for neither car nor pedestrian.
>
> In addition:
>
> Pedestrians crossed the street relatively freely, but the risk of avoiding traffic remained their burden. Little space was reserved for them on the streetscape, and the space they claimed was often more dangerous than streets in similar cities. (Transportation Alternatives 2004)

Beginning in 2007, however, this landscape began to change. Mayor Michael Bloomberg's administration released its PlaNYC 2030, a master plan involving numerous municipal agencies aimed at making the city more sustainable and livable. Though top-down in nature, the projects that have resulted have gained acclaim, including receipt of the US Environmental Protection Agency's 2010 National Award for Smart Growth Achievement for Overall Excellence. The city has implemented popular pedestrianizations of major streets, including Broadway at Times Square and Herald Square, has initiated a select bus service similar to BRT, and has instigated a large number of bike lanes. According to the Institute for Transportation and Development Policy (ITDP 2011, 12), the pedestrianization of Broadway, in addition to creating a more livable, complete street, has succeeded in calming traffic on adjacent streets as well, 'despite reclaiming nearly 500,000 square feet (45,000 m^2) of public space from traffic.' Community involvement has reacted in diverse ways, praising the administration's progressive understanding of the streetscape while also criticizing the lack of public participation in a city bursting with organizations and citizen groups existing for that very purpose (Shaer 2011).

The alternative transport movement in New York is led by Transportation Alternatives, Streetsblog, and New York Bicycling Coalition, among others. These groups lobby legislators, meet with citizens and public officials, research and write reports, release press items, and broaden awareness of the need for greater street-sharing in the city. At times, the groups will partner with the city to support an initiative that both favor. An example of this in 2011 was the 'Show Your Support for Bike Share in the Big Apple' campaign, in which Transportation Alternatives encouraged its members to voice support for the Department of Transportation-led bike share program slated to launch in the summer of 2012. However, residents have also voiced disfavor regarding the city's streetscape redesign. The furor over the installation of bike lanes in Brooklyn's Prospect Park attests to the intense debate. On 16 August 2011, a judge dismissed a suit brought by two groups of Brooklyn residents, Seniors for Safety and Neighbors for Better Bike Lanes, in which they claimed that the two-way protected bike lanes installed were 'arbitrary and capricious' (Dunham 2011, 8). At the core of their objection lay their contention that car drivers were being deprived of their rights to additional lanes, more convenient traffic flow, and parking spots (Shaer 2011).

Changing perspectives on moving through space: fewer cars, more sharing?

Younger generations exhibit a preference for fewer cars as well as lifestyles that allow for convenient access to public transit, cycle, and pedestrian infrastructure. According to the Earth Policy Institute, the car fleet in the US declined for the first time ever in 2009, decreasing by 4 million, or nearly 2 percent, in one year (Brown 2010). Among factors in this decline, Brown includes 'ongoing urbanization … frustration with traffic congestion, mounting concerns about climate change, and a declining interest in cars among young people.' Brown also points to a 9 percent uptick in transit ridership in the US between 2005 and 2008.

Similar trends are also occurring in other developed countries (Litman 2012). For instance, trips taken by car as a percentage of all trips decreased from approximately 64 percent in the mid-1990s to 57 percent in 2009 in Perth, Australia (Falconer and Richardson 2010, referencing the Western Australian State Department for Planning and Infrastructure). These declines appear greatest among the younger population. Based on the US Department of Transportation's Federal Highway Administration's Licensed Total Drivers by Age statistics from 1963 to 1995 and 2000 to 2007, and the United Nations Population Division's *World Population Prospects: The 2008 revision*, the Earth Policy Institute (2010) demonstrated that teenage drivers as a share of the entire US teenage population dropped from 71.2 percent in 1983 to 56 percent in 2007. Within the last decade, average annual vehicle miles traveled was about 20 percent less in 2008 than in 2001 for those younger than 40 years old (Litman 2012).

Greater preference for alternative transportation, from mass transit to walking, plays a role in this shift (ibid.). The drop in public transit ridership that the US encountered throughout the twentieth century paralleled a rise in automobility, which peaked in 1996. Transit ridership has climbed in subsequent years as urban governments reinvest in their cores (ibid.). The planning field has recognized this shift, placing more emphasis on transit-oriented development (TOD) in which residential and commercial growth – primarily in a mixed-use form – is encouraged adjacent to a transit hub in order to promote the development, functionality, connectivity, and popularity of both. According to Cervero and Sullivan (2011, 210), TOD 'has gained popularity worldwide as a sustainable form of urbanism.' Their work highlights the even newer model of 'green TOD,' in which the car-sprawl relationship is replaced by a transit-connected development that is explicitly more ecologically, socially, and economically sustainable. While TODs can function as a prescriptive policy tool, they also attest to a movement within the planning field in which the increasing demand for more walkable, transit-diverse communities has been recognized.

The immediacy and access of technological developments, primarily wireless internet and handheld devices, are cited as a significant contributing factor to the younger generation's ease with alternative transit and walkable communities (Linn 2010; Schwieterman 2011). Due to this shift's recent emergence, the topic tends to be discussed more frequently in popular media than in academic research. Linn (2010) describes a confluence of environmental awareness, economic uncertainty, and a preference for the convenience and interaction that accompanies technological gadgets and urban lifestyles. Younger people are also generally more reluctant to deal with rush-hour congestion, insurance costs, and fuel costs (Litman 2012). Referred to as 'techno-travelers' by Schwieterman (2011), many millennials (under age 35) feel less attached to a consistent place or travel mode – such as one's car – because they can be connected via the internet, carry their work computers with them, watch or listen to entertainment or read a book, make plans, chat with colleagues, and take calls or meetings flexibly, conveniently, and (most importantly) remotely on their handheld devices and smart phones.

Many techno-travelers of this generation often prefer to use car shares (ibid.), such as Zipcar or car2go, which are available throughout much of North America, Europe, and Australia, rather than owning a car (ibid.). This model has recently extended to peer-to-peer car-sharing, including RelayRides in the US, Buzzcar in France and SnappCar in the Netherlands. Bicycle-sharing has also entered the mainstream because of a preference for both cycling and sharing. Numerous cities around the world operate successful bike-sharing programs, including BIXI in Montreal, Vélib' in Paris, Bicing in Barcelona, Hubway in Boston, Capital Bikeshare in Washington D.C., and Guangzhou Public Bike in China, which attest to the shift in generational priority and public policy.

Conclusions

Space and place are at the top of political agendas on many scales. Whether we are talking about space as security (inclusive and exclusive space), space as resistance (the Arab Spring uprisings or SlutWalks), or space as possibility (loose or insurgent space, guerilla, DIY, tactical or pop-up urbanism), the spatial turn in the social sciences has hit the streets and the media. The visions of 'complete streets' and 'livable streets' are part of the wider discourse around place-making: the point at which urban planning tools and techniques are honed and focused by community knowledge and vision. Place-making can be guided by brave politicians such as Mockus and Peñalosa in Bogotá, Colombia, or it can be genuinely bottom-up in the case of Dudley Street, Boston, MA.

However, municipal structures, codes, lack of political vision, capacity for community input, and bureaucratic hindrances all play a role in the creation, or not, of democratized or more spatially just streets. Likewise, the involvement of grassroots voices and the ability of concerned citizens to mobilize within a neighborhood (such as those worried about the gentrifying effects of bike lanes in Portland, OR) influence the degree to which a community facilitates, resists, or advances the status quo of equality and democracy on its streets.

Pilot projects, such as Toronto's Kensington Market and Broadway/ Times Square in New York, or long-term successes such as Södra Vägen in Göteborg, Sweden, or Copenhagen, Denmark, have helped in advancing the case for more spatially just streets worldwide. It is no coincidence that Mayor Bloomberg of New York hired Jan Gehl Architects when conceptualizing PlaNYC. These successes, together with London's congestion charge, demonstrate to shopkeepers that reductions in car traffic will not lead sales to suffer. Along with the increase in foot and bicycle traffic, a calmer, more pleasant, and laid-back atmosphere has tended to follow, leading to greater recreational and commercial activity, as the popularity of cafes in Copenhagen's city center following its transformation demonstrates (CABE 2002; Gemzøe 2001). However, in the US, transport is heavily racialized, as evidenced by Henderson's (2006, 304) study of 'secession by car' in Atlanta, and the debates around North Williams Avenue in Portland, OR. This, coupled with Pucher and Renne's (2003, 67) point that 'blacks are … eight times as likely [as whites] to take the bus (4.2% vs. 0.5%),' shows that there is a long way to go if the US truly wants to democratize its streets.

4 | CULTURE

Introduction

In Chapter 3, I mentioned Fincher and Jacobs's (1998) concept of 'cities of difference,' places where we are 'in the presence of otherness' (Sennett 1990, 123) – namely, our increasingly different, diverse, and culturally heterogeneous urban areas. In this chapter I want to probe more deeply the implications of culture, difference, and interculturalism, and how I believe the concept of just sustainabilities can help us recognize, understand, and engage difference, diversity, and cultural heterogeneity in inclusive, creative, and productive ways.

In this chapter, what I refer to as 'culture' is more broadly based than the concept of culture in, for example, 'multiculturalism' or 'ethnocultural diversity' (see, for instance, Pestieau and Wallace 2003; Burayidi 2003). In my view, culture is predicated on difference and on otherness, and is a complex, dynamic, and embodied set of realities in which people (re)create identities, meanings, and values. Overlaying this is the reality of hybrid or multiple cultural and group affiliations. In this sense, no one person can be reduced to one single or fixed cultural or other form of identity.

There is an excellent and growing literature in urban planning around the concepts of difference[1] and diversity,[2] and there are, of course, overlaps. In general, the concept of 'difference' in planning literature is more recent than that of 'diversity,' which in turn postdates that of earlier planning-focused discussions around equality and equity (Davidoff 1965; Krumholz 1982; Clavel and Wiewel 1991; Metzger 1996). I prefer the term 'difference' to 'diversity' because diversity, like multiculturalism or ethnocultural diversity, has become virtually synonymous with issues of race, or race and gender (Sweet and Etienne 2011, for example), rather than the more expansive conception of difference outlined by Sandercock (2000, 15):

> Difference … takes many forms. It acknowledges that population groups, differentiated by criteria of age, gender, class, dis/ability, ethnicity, sexual preference, culture and religion, have different

claims on the city for a full life and, in particular, on the built environment.

Yet, as Pestieau and Wallace (2003, 255) note:

> surprisingly little attention has been paid to the implications of immigration and ethnocultural diversity for local planning. There is a wide gap between planning practice, in the broadest definition, and the important contribution that planning theory has made to our understanding of cultural diversity.

Some authors go further, noting an official blindness to difference, both cultural and otherwise (Howe and Kaufman 1981; Qadeer 1997; Harwood 2005).

In this chapter I will look again at space and place, but through a more specifically intercultural lens. There are many obstacles and challenges in designing public space in a way that engages difference, diversity, and cultural heterogeneity in creative and productive ways. Loukaitou-Sideris (2003, 131) argues that many public areas have 'reinforced divisions based upon class, race, age, or ethnicity.' Low et al. (2005, 1) are even more forthright:

> In this new century, we are facing a different kind of threat to public space – not one of disuse, but of patterns of design and management that exclude some people and reduce social and cultural diversity.

My argument is that it is possible to plan, design, and maintain 'culturally inclusive spaces.' In addition, though, I ask how we do this in a way that inculcates *culturally inclusive practice*. This has implications both for the difference, diversity, and cultural make-up of urban design, planning and policy-based professions, and for the cultural competency of those professionals who practice them.

Interculturalism

Along with authors such as Tully (1995), Sandercock (1998; 2000; 2003), Amin (2002), Bloomfield and Bianchini (2002), and Wood and Landry (2007), I believe that multiculturalist discourses have fallen short of promoting an active and explicit consideration of the impacts of broader interpretations of culture on planning and sustainability. In part, the multi- and ethnoculturalist discourses generally foreground race and ethnic diversity but tend to overlook other points of difference such as gender, age, class, sexual orientation, cultural heterogeneity, and (dis)ability.

Building on McDowell's (1993, 166) point quoted in Chapter 2 that 'the majority of women have more spatially restricted lives than men,' Sandercock and Forsyth (2005) assert that male dominance is embedded in the internal culture of planners and that it reveals itself in the theories, standards, and ideologies used to guide planners' work. This gendered perspective is typically left out of multicultural discourses. Indeed, Bridgman (2001, 102) notes of Burayidi's (2000a) *Urban Planning in a Multicultural Society* – one of the most widely read texts in this field – 'It is quite extraordinary that all contributors to the volume are male. This intense irony goes completely unacknowledged, it would seem, anywhere in the book.' Furthermore, as Hayden (2005) shows, there are many examples of how planning is culturally incompetent to the needs of women and families, as evidenced by mainstream, traditional approaches to housing, neighborhood, and community development.

Tully (1995) has also noted that multiculturalism as it has been conceived has not required any fundamental change in thinking. In order to change our thinking, he argues, we need to be more sensitive to how cultures overlap, interact, and are internally negotiated. Like Amin (2002), he argues that our societies are intercultural rather than multicultural because of the cross-cultural overlap, interaction, and negotiation – the 'politics of recognition' – that occur out of necessity in the formation of our society. This is what Amin (ibid., 960) calls the 'negotiation of difference within local micropublics of everyday interaction.' An acknowledgment of this dynamic cultural nature of society – both the 'politics of recognition' and 'negotiation of difference' – is a key distinction between intercultural and multicultural theory, between just and environmental sustainability, and demands a culturally competent approach to both planning and policy-making for sustainability.

During the last decade, a collective of urban geography and planning scholars (including Ash Amin, Peter Hall, and Leonie Sandercock) and practitioners (including Charles Landry, Phil Wood, Richard Brecknock, and G. Pascal Zachary) have been researching and promoting interculturalism. The group noted that approaches rooted in the multiculturalism frame have been effective for cultural preservation, celebration, and tolerance yet have produced culturally and spatially distinct communities (Intercultural Cities website[3] 2004). Bloomfield and Bianchini (2002, 6) make perhaps the most eloquent argument, the full implications of which should be fully understood by politicians, planners, and sustainability advocates:

> The interculturalism approach goes beyond opportunities and respect for existing cultural differences, to the pluralist transformation of public space, civic culture and institutions. So it does not recognise cultural boundaries as fixed but as in a state of flux and remaking. An interculturalist approach aims to facilitate dialogue, exchange and reciprocal understanding between people of different cultural backgrounds. Cities need to develop policies which prioritise funding for projects where different cultures intersect, 'contaminate' each other and hybridise ... In other words, city governments should promote cross-fertilisation across all cultural boundaries, between 'majority' and 'minorities', 'dominant' and 'sub' cultures, localities, classes, faiths, disciplines and genres, as the source of cultural, social, political and economic innovation.

Sandercock (2003, 207–8), however, appeals to our emotions:

> I dream of a city of bread and festivals, where those who don't have the bread aren't excluded from the carnival. I dream of a city in which action grows out of knowledge and understanding; where you haven't got it made until you can help others to get where you are or beyond; where social justice is more prized than a balanced budget; where I have a right to my surroundings, and so do all my fellow citizens; where we don't exist for the city but are seduced by it; where only after consultation with local folks could decisions be made about our neighbourhoods; where scarcity does not build a barb-wire fence around carefully guarded inequalities; where no one flaunts their authority and no one is without authority; where I don't have to translate my 'expertise' into jargon to impress officials and confuse citizens.

Imagine, for a moment, a mayor or city leadership group who had the courage to move in these directions; to contaminate and hybridize across cultures; to feel seduced by the city; a mayor or leadership group that refused to go with the status quo, with what is probable, but instead focused on vision, on what is possible. The transformation of Broadway and the High Line in New York City under Mayor Bloomberg are small but highly significant examples of possibility, as was the more ambitious development and implementation of London's congestion charge under Mayor Livingstone, or the 'Copenhagen Miracle' under a succession of mayors and the iconic urbanist Jan Gehl. However, the only citywide, culture-shifting example that even comes close to Bloomfield and Bianchini, and to Sandercock's moving paeans, is the double act of Antanas Mockus and Enrique Peñalosa who literally performed (in the case of Mockus) the most celebrated of urban transformations, in Bogotá, Colombia, which I mentioned in Chapter 3.

Interculturalism and culturally inclusive space: challenges and opportunities

Challenges: contact, conflict, separation, segregation[4] How do we get to Bloomfield and Bianchini's (2002, 6) intercultural dream where 'different cultures intersect, "contaminate" each other and hybridise'? Clearly, parks, public spaces, and streets have a role to play in this. Unfortunately, however, culturally inclusive spaces, those designed *intentionally* around the recognition of difference, diversity, and cultural heterogeneity, have not been a major focus of study in the planning literature nor are they well understood by practicing urban designers, planners, and policy-makers (Kumar and Martin 2004).

A notable exception is the now defunct Commission for Architecture and the Built Environment (CABE) in the UK, which went further than most in improving practice. In *The Principles of Inclusive Design* (CABE 2006, 9), the Commission notes promisingly: 'Inclusive design acknowledges diversity *and* difference,' but then proceeds to focus solely on issues of mobility and disability, not on other forms of difference. Indeed, many planners' and urban designers' conception of 'inclusion' focuses on Universal Design, making spaces that are accessible to people with varying physical ability, learning and emotional disabilities, sensory impairments, and communication limitations. Most parks and leisure research focuses on the more common, and, as I've argued elsewhere (see Agyeman and Erickson 2012), more restrictive term 'diversity' (for example, Byrne and Wolch 2009; Dines and Cattrell 2006; Dwyer and Hutchinson 1990; Floyd et al. 1993; Gobster 2002; Low et al. 2005, Lanfer and Taylor 2005; Loukaitou-Sideris 1995; Sanchez 2010). Few publications addressing park or open space design specifically mention difference, interculturalism or cultural inclusion. Notable here is the work of Sofoulis et al. (2008) in the City of Penrith, Metro Sydney, Australia.

Traditionally, a city's parks, plazas, market squares, and streets have been 'the core of the urban society' (Madanipour 2010, 5) and offered people the opportunity to discuss current events, philosophy, and everything else. However, historically, many people were excluded from these spaces; women, foreigners, and slaves had no place in the Greek agora, and intergroup interactions in the medieval square were dominated by social rules and hierarchies (ibid.). Additionally, many park designers and urbanists shared a deterministic concept of public space (Amin 2008) and believed that exposure to nature and elite visitors would uplift the working class and immigrant users (Byrne and Wolch 2009). The United States' first public park-makers, men such as Frederick Law Olmsted and Calvert Vaux, believed that by offering greater opportunities for interclass mingling in parks, democracy and inclusion would be advanced (Rosenzweig and Blackmar 1992). Taylor (2009, 229) notes: 'Some park advocates saw the parks as a gentler way to improve the poor while assimilating them into mainstream society.'

These beliefs underlie 'contact theory,' which posits that interactions between members of different groups reduce intergroup prejudice under the right conditions (Dixon et al. 2005; Talen 2008). However, there may be limits in the ability of open space to foster democratic inclusion. Unlike Bogotá's former mayor Enrique Peñalosa, who notes that 'In public spaces, people meet as equals,' Amin (2008, 7) argues that it is 'too heroic a leap' to assume that a city's democracy will be automatically improved by making its public spaces more vibrant. Most public spaces serve as meeting places for people who already know each other, although familiarity with strangers may be built over frequent encounters (ibid.).

Shinew, Glover, and Parry (2004, 338) have noted:

> Contact theory posits that … interracial interactions that occur in leisure settings [e.g. parks and public spaces] have the potential to be more genuine and sincere compared with the more obligatory interactions that take place in formal settings.

Contact theory, however, offers little or no guidance on *how* to achieve culturally inclusive space, let alone how to achieve such spaces in places where social inequality is deeply entrenched (Dixon et al.

2005). Additionally, contact with diverse groups may serve to make shifts in personal prejudice, but it has been shown to have little impact on structural discrimination (ibid.), which may have a much greater impact on a particular group's use of public space (Floyd et al. 1993; Arnold and Shinew 1998). Instead, many open spaces can align more with *conflict theory*: they are sites of tension and racism that reinforce intergroup separation (Dines and Cattrell 2006).

In addition to intergroup separation, studies examining race-based[5] differences in park usage offer evidence for significant differences among various ethnic, racial, and cultural groups in their usage of public spaces. Gobster's (2002) study of Lincoln Park, the largest and most heavily used park in Chicago, IL, found that white park users were more likely to be involved in active, individual sports, while minority users were more likely to engage in passive, social activities. In the same study, Gobster observed differences among user groups in water activities: whites and Latinos were more active in swimming, Asians more active in fishing, and whites more active in boating than any other group. Both Dwyer and Hutchinson (1990), who looked at recreation participation data for Illinois generally, and Gobster (2002) reported that white Americans tended to prefer more natural or wild areas, for camping or hiking, while African Americans were drawn to more urban recreational facilities, for ball-playing and picnicking.

The study of four neighborhood parks in areas of differing ethnicity in Los Angeles by Loukaitou-Sideris (1995) found that African Americans primarily visited parks in peer groups, generally male-only groups. The younger males tended to hang out at the park entrances, parking lots, or around athletic facilities. Most often the groups were talking, joking around, and girl-watching. Most African Americans used the park how they found it, and did not adjust the physical space to meet their needs. As was found in previous studies, Caucasian users tended to be engaged in reclusive, self-oriented uses; more than 30 percent of whites came to the park alone. Exceptions to this trend were elderly white users who were often engaged in small groups playing games such as cards or croquet. Asian users were the least represented in the study and were notably absent from the parks. The Asian users observed were mostly older men who were relaxing, socializing, and performing t'ai chi. Parent–child visitors were relatively common in each of the ethnic groups, but families were rare among Chinese users. Ethno-racial differences such as these have been identified in all kinds of parks and public spaces (Gobster 2002; Byrne and Wolch 2009; Sanchez 2010).

One study found that the Hispanic population brings another pattern to these studies: African Americans and whites have more recreational and leisure preferences in common than either group has with the Hispanic population (Cheek et al. 1976, as cited in Loukaitou-Sideris 1995). In her own research, Loukaitou-Sideris (ibid.) found that Hispanics utilize parks more frequently than other users, and tend to visit in large family groups and participate in social activities such as parties, birthday and wedding celebrations, and picnics. Often, Hispanic groups arrange themselves in circular configurations centered on the group's food. Unlike other racial groups, Hispanics often changed the park space to accommodate their needs. For example, if people wanted to play soccer, and there were no fields (pitches) in the park, players would bring goal posts with them (ibid.; Sanchez 2010). Almost 60 percent of Hispanics were participating in stationary activities, such as eating or watching others play a sport.

It is important to note the intra-ethnic differences and, when possible, identify different patterns between ethnic and cultural subgroups. For example, within Hispanic culture, many Puerto Ricans prefer baseball while Central and South Americans prefer soccer, so one cannot say that all Hispanics use parks for soccer (Dwyer and Gobster 1996). Indeed, one of the keys to becoming culturally competent is that planners and policy-makers cannot assume homogeneous life experiences based upon racial or ethnic similarities: doing so may deepen and entrench stereotypes (Beebeejaun 2006).

The differences discussed above in how various ethnic, racial, and cultural groups use public spaces were not found in Loukaitou-Sideris's (2003) study of children's use of parks and playgrounds. In fact, children of both genders and all cultures and ethnicities were found to prefer many of the same amenities and share similar values in their public spaces. Children most frequently valued safety and cleanliness as well as nature-like, athletic, and commercial spaces (such as laser tag, video games, recreation rooms, etc.). The fact that children appear to value the same types of spaces, however, has not been found to translate simply into intercultural cooperation and interaction.

Children's behaviors are heavily influenced by their social environments, and especially by examples set by adults. Programmatic elements, policies, and specific programs in children's play spaces can help to encourage children to play and interact with children from other backgrounds. While alleys, street corners, and plazas are important in the lives of adults, school yards are often the most impactful public spaces for children's social skills (Fielding 2009). Teachers, tutors, play leaders, and coaches can all help to bridge racial and ethnic differences by actively facilitating and creating opportunities for children to play, work, and collaborate with children from other backgrounds. Finally, children value a sense of place as much as adults (Loukaitou-Sideris 2003). Sense of place can be fostered by using non-standardized play elements and by encouraging manipulation of the play environment.

While some spaces are specifically designed and managed to be exclusive (Low et al. 2005), more are simply unintentionally unwelcoming. People may feel excluded for a variety of reasons, including lack of access to quality parks, feelings of discrimination, and lack of facilities that meet their cultural needs. Even though there are differences in how cultural and ethnic groups use parks and public spaces, in Gobster's (2002) study of Lincoln Park, all groups reported litter, vandalism, and the need for more and cleaner bathroom facilities as problems. An English study similarly found that the five most common reasons that people reported not using public spaces include: a lack of and/or the poor condition of children's play spaces; the presence of undesirable users and uses in the park; concerns about sharing the space with dogs and dog mess in the parks; the feeling of safety or other psychological issues; and litter, graffiti and/or vandalism (DTLR 2002). Additional studies have identified crime and drug-user problems as a reason why people do not use downtown parks (Stoks 1983, cited in Francis 1987).

Beyond these unintentional barriers, different groups reported distinct problems. Asians most frequently reported problems with park access and lack of parking. Latinos mentioned the lack of restrooms and other facilities. African American users cited the prejudicial behavior of other park users, park staff, and the police. Whites mentioned crowding, user conflicts, and the presence of homeless individuals as problems in the parks and public spaces they use (Gobster 2002). Muslim groups were most likely to be turned off by the presence of dogs in parks (Lanfer and Taylor 2005). Interracial tensions have been shown to have an impact on which activities and spaces minority residents prefer. Studies in the US have shown that the black community's leisure activities especially have been constrained by a lack of comfort caused by present or past patterns of discrimination (Floyd et al. 1993). Black community members have reported that the belief that they will be unwelcome or discriminated against has caused them to not participate in a particular activity (Arnold and Shinew 1998).

Another study in a variety of Chicago parks found that about 10 percent of minority park users experienced discrimination in parks. The most common incidences of racial discrimination were verbal harassment, physical gestures, assaults, and other non-verbal behaviors that caused the minorities to feel unwelcome (Gobster 1998). These interracial conflicts have been observed both between majority and minority groups as well as between minority groups. Tensions can lead to physical harm, feeling fearful or uncomfortable, and even the further segregation of park users within the park or particular groups leaving the park for good (ibid.). In focus groups, different park users mentioned a variety of examples of this type of tension. Chinese American senior citizens reported being afraid to use certain areas of parks because they were verbally harassed by African American teenagers (ibid.). In another focus group, Cambodian American adults said that white adult park users had told them they did not 'belong' in a certain area of the park (ibid.). African American adults reported that they felt that a certain park belonged to the white community and thus avoided the park (ibid.).

Leisure theorists have suggested four interconnected explanations for ethno-racially differentiated park use: 1) marginality; 2) race/ethnicity; 3) assimilation and acculturation; and 4) discrimination. The marginality hypothesis suggests that low minority participation in recreation is due to limited socio-economic resources (Washburn 1978). The ethnicity hypothesis finds that distinctive patterns of recreational participation are due to varying 'subcultural' value systems, norms, and leisure socialization patterns (ibid.). The assimilation/acculturation hypothesis also says that ethno-racial heritage is responsible for use patterns, but that these use patterns will change as the groups adopt 'the culture, behavior, and norms of more dominant social groups' (Floyd et al. 1993, as cited in Byrne and Wolch 2009, 749). Discrimination theory posits that perceived hostility and overt discrimination cause people of color to avoid parks where they feel unwelcome and that historic residential segregation patterns impact proximity to parks, effectively excluding people of color from accessing the space (Byrne and Wolch 2009).

However, others, primarily geographers, believe that these explanations are too clear-cut and site- or park-focused while overlooking wider contextual factors and structural racism. Byrne and Wolch's (ibid., 750) call to 'reconceptualise ethno-racially differentiated park use to include *space* and *place*' (my emphasis) includes mapping four other elements that affect park use and accessibility:

1 socio-demographic factors of park users and non-users as suggested by the leisure theorists;
2 the political ecology and amenities of the park itself, including design and management (see Low et al. 2005), vegetation, park facilities, and the characteristics of surrounding neighborhoods;
3 the historical and cultural landscape of park provision, for example how the park was developed and designed and whether there are discriminatory land use practices; and
4 individual perceptions of park space: is it accessible? Do I feel safe? Is it convivial and welcoming?

Byrne and Wolch continue:

> Together, these forces tend to produce spatially uneven development of park resources and access, typically to the detriment of communities of color and disadvantage, and thus disproportionately affecting their health and well-being. (ibid., 751)

This is a classic case of spatial injustice.

In addition to the unintentional barriers and the racial or ethnically specific barriers described above, certain subgroups express additional difference-based barriers. People who do not speak the area's primary language are often excluded from public space use simply because they cannot find information in a language they can understand (Sanchez 2010). People with physical or mental disabilities often face barriers that others, even with the same experience and background, do not face. Poor facilities are often more difficult to navigate for those with disabilities; physically disabled children feel especially marginalized in most public playgrounds, as many park features, such as tables, are not designed to accommodate wheelchair users (DTLR 2002; Sofoulis et al. 2008). People on low incomes often cannot afford transportation to public spaces; since economically depressed areas tend to have fewer public spaces, community members must often travel relatively long distances to get to the park or playground (Arnold and Shinew 1998).

Additionally, (trans)gender issues are not often adequately addressed in public spaces; large, open spaces often attract men but discourage women from using the space, and women are more acutely aware of safety concerns than men (Doan 2010; Westover 1986; Byrne and Wolch 2009; Arnold and Shinew 1998). Muslim women require public spaces separate from men (CABE 2010a), a feature rarely provided by public spaces in the United States and Europe. There are also barriers specific to the elderly. Vandalism and graffiti impact the elderly much more than any other age group (DTLR 2002). Physical accessibility is also very important to older park members, who are generally not as stable on their feet and may need toilet facilities more regularly than other users. Further, many grandparents are spending more time with their grandchildren, so facilities that a child would need, such as the bathroom, should also be easily accessible for elderly individuals (DTLR 2002; Sofoulis et al. 2008). All of these barriers serve to diminish the true openness or publicness of our public spaces (Lownsbrough and Beunderman 2007).

Opportunities: designing, planning, and maintaining culturally inclusive spaces Despite these conceptual challenges, public spaces can be sites of huge intercultural opportunity. They may be the only sites where various groups interact at all, and organized events such as soccer matches, festivals or youth group activities may offer important opportunities for intergroup contact (Dines and Cattrell 2006) and for generating shared experiences (Lownsbrough and Beunderman 2007). People who have emigrated from one country and culture to another tend to use public open spaces and parks to gather and congregate in ways that are reminiscent of their home country, transforming the parks of their adoptive community into familiar spaces. People grow attached to spaces, to their aromas, textures, and the overall 'feel' of a space.

Lanfer and Taylor (2005) write about Latino immigrants in Boston, MA, who transform public spaces into familiar landscapes found in the group's home countries. They have adopted Herter Park on the River Charles in Boston's Allston-Brighton neighborhood because it reminds them of the river banks and willow trees they left behind in

Guatemala. Vacant lots, especially in Boston's Brighton neighborhood, have been transformed into squares reminiscent of Latin American plazas. Dines and Cattrell (2006) found that first-generation Asians in Newham, East London, described feeling most comfortable in specific shopping corridors where there were fewer language barriers and also direct reminders of their countries of origin, such as foods and music. In the context of the challenges associated with establishing oneself in a new place, these familiar-looking, familiar-sounding, familiar-smelling places enable the transfer of comforting cultural patterns from their home landscapes to the new landscape.

Designing culturally inclusive spaces aims to remove the barriers that create undue effort (in accessing those spaces) and separation by planning and designing spaces that enable everyone to participate equally and confidently (CABE 2008a; 2008b). While a 'barrier removal' approach may seem negative, the Australian research of Sofoulis et al. (2008, 81) noted:

> The Creative Mapping workshops and Community Perceptions studies revealed that it is easier for park users (and non-users) to name what they don't like in parks than to articulate what they do like.

Creating culturally inclusive spaces contributes to interculturalism in seeking to integrate groups in ways that contribute to the construction of difference and diversity as an asset within a community, rather than a source of tension (Lownsbrough and Beunderman 2007).

When planning and (re)designing inclusive spaces, the question is not, as Guthman (2008b, 388) has asked in terms of urban agriculture, 'Who is *at* the table?' but 'Who is *setting* the table?' This is the first principle of *culturally inclusive practice*. If it is not addressed, the chances of success are dramatically lowered. It is critically important to draw from different cultures and subcultures and to include a variety of user-derived options. It is also important to focus efforts aimed at designing inclusive spaces on places that accommodate meaningful interaction among users, rather than simply on areas with the greatest number of people crossing paths (Lownsbrough and Beunderman 2007).

The UK Urban Green Spaces Taskforce report found that the needs of different user groups can be addressed through proper design, management, maintenance, and funding (DTLR 2002); indeed, each of the parties involved with park design and maintenance has some responsibility to ensure an inclusive space. CABE defines the stages of public space development as: prepare, design, construct, and use (CABE 2007a). Public agencies are also obligated to consider levels of access to public space among different residents; the preparation, design, management, and maintenance of public spaces all contribute to accessibility.

Prepare Madanipour (2010, 11) cautions: 'If public spaces are produced and managed by narrow interests, they are bound to become exclusive places.' Therefore, the planning process must be inclusive. Planners are advised to forget about the 'average' user and instead begin the open space planning process with 'deep knowledge' of the preferences of the actual communities who are likely to use those spaces (Sofoulis et al. 2008). However, echoing Beebejaun (2006), they should remember:

> Complexities exist both within and between cultures. One issue for planning in culturally diverse contexts is that different cultures, sub-cultures, and generations have different assumptions and conventions about who uses public space, with whom, how, and when. Older women can feel intimidated by young people publicly socialising in large groups. (ibid., 79)

Generating deep knowledge may involve ethnographic surveys to learn about the cultural backgrounds, perceptions, and needs of those in the local community regarding open space use (Lanfer and Taylor 2005). Equally important is an understanding of how users' past experiences in public spaces have shaped their use of or aspirations for the space now and in the future (Lownsbrough and Beunderman 2007). Kent (2008) and others believe that the best ideas for the future come from the community and that they should be actively engaged in creating public spaces at every stage of the process. However, there are ranges of community involvement; one end of the spectrum involves simple communication and information exchange while the other end involves active collaboration and decision-making (DTLR 2002).

The memory of previous failed participatory planning processes can undermine community engagement in future projects (APaNGO 2007). Facilitators must be culturally competent, and must work to build trust with community members by being clear about the decision-making process, honest about any problems that arise, and following through on commitments. They must be prepared to accept 'pluralistic viewpoints,' realizing that ordinary landscapes may be viewed entirely differently by people from various cultural backgrounds (Rishbeth 2001). Training designers and planners in public participation facilitation can help ensure that the design staff are helping to create places that are valued by the end user (CABE 2010b). CABE (2010a) suggests active consultation through events on-site, design workshops, discussion groups, and visits to quality green spaces. Such visits can help users learn 'visual literacy' and be able to recognize and express their opinions about good design (CABE 2010b). Hosting focus groups on-site has been associated with more positive perceptions of green space and more consistent survey data (CABE 2010a). Using tools such as Spaceshaper, Creative Mapping, or PhotoVoice to guide the pre-design process can be useful in engaging diverse community members and capture their existing knowledge about their environment (CABE 2007b; Sofoulis et al. 2008; PolicyLink 2011).

Design A culturally inclusive space should offer amenities, rules, and landscapes that accommodate people of all ages and backgrounds. Following good design principles is fundamental in creating high-quality open space (CABE 2007a), but not sufficient in ensuring inclusivity. Devier (n.d.) outlines additional design guidelines that can help create inclusive spaces, such as utilizing the concept of the loop,[6] protecting and caring for larger and older trees, incorporating cultural and spatial resonance, leaving room for adaptation, and accommodating particular user groups. Designers can create spaces that resemble 'home,' such as the Ryerson University student-led designs based on Bollywood for the Gerrard India Bazaar, an ethnic business enclave in East Toronto (Kumar and Martin 2004), the Chinese gardens in Portland, OR, Sydney, Australia, and Dunedin, New Zealand (van Velden and Reeves 2010), or the multicultural garden at Chumleigh Street in the London Borough of Southwark (Rishbeth 2001), where, similar to the 'autotopographies' of Mares and Peña (2011) in Chapter 2, the use of plants representative of different cultures strategically invokes beloved landscapes.

Officials can also assign culturally relevant names (toponyms) in order to promote a specific sense of identity (van Velden and Reeves

2010). Two of the best known are the renaming of Mount McKinley in Alaska as Denali (Koyukon Athabaskan for 'The High One') and Ayers Rock in Australia as Uluru (Pitjantjatjara). Parks that reflect cultural diversity can be an opportunity for other groups to learn about the diversity in their community or be a place to symbolically meld the 'old' culture with the 'new' culture (Lanfer and Taylor 2005). However, designers should be careful about overusing cultural symbols; for example, using a distinctive arch shape on street furniture, including litter bins, outraged Pakistani residents who perceived the arch to be too similar to religious symbols and felt it was disrespectful to place it on a garbage can (Rishbeth 2001). Of great importance to the accessibility to users of an open space is the 'whole journey' approach – attention needs to be paid not only to the design of the park itself but also to the pedestrian and transit links that lead users to the park. For children especially, traffic can be a major impediment to safety (Francis and Lorenzo 2006), while lack of clear signage can prevent others from finding entrances or park features.

A lack of comfortable and adequate seating is often a reason people do not use public spaces. Inclusive spaces must provide appropriate seating, not the 'standard' park bench, for individuals or the nuclear family, but also for extended families and groups of individuals simply hoping to socialize. They must provide spaces for adults and children to participate in a variety of sporting activities but also allow for individual users. Safety is a major barrier to park usage: people report feeling unsafe in spaces with overgrown vegetation, insufficient lighting, and high walls (CABE 2010a). Some of the characteristics of parks that have been found to increase feelings of discomfort are fencing, dense vegetation, and hedging that provides privacy for drug dealers and other criminals (Francis 1987). Vegetation and hedging have been particular concerns among women. This can be addressed through the judicious selection of plant species and proactive design or redesign measures. Especially in today's economic uncertainty, it is important to consider which projects and policies can create the most impact with the (relatively) smallest investment, and what will support and sustain the area's existing social diversity while encouraging new social diversity to evolve (Talen 2008).

Construct While most of the construction may require heavy machinery and trained engineers, the different publics can be engaged in a variety of volunteer activities, such as planting flower bulbs or painting murals. In one instance, collaborating on a public green space project allowed people to get to know each other and form new friendships, thereby improving the quality of life in the village (CABE 2007a). This type of involvement can support feelings of ownership over a space.

Use Many user studies have revealed that park users do not always need new facilities; sometimes simply better design (Low et al. 2005) and/or maintenance of existing facilities can resolve problems (Low et al. 2005; Sofoulis et al. 2008; Lownsbrough and Beunderman 2007). Therefore, the 'use' stage of open space development must include proper maintenance and management of facilities. Additionally, open space staff must adopt new, culturally competent approaches to interacting with diverse users. Hiring staff who reflect users or who speak the language of diverse users can go far in reducing perceptions of discrimination, which has been shown to be an important deterrent.

At the very least, park supervisors should take time to learn how sites are perceived negatively by different user groups and make their staff aware of the potential for their language and actions to be seen as offensive to certain groups (Gobster 2002). Targeted marketing strategies could be used to respond to the diverse needs of various groups in order to re-establish a park as a welcoming place for all (Arnold and Shinew 1998). Park managers might consider hosting organized activities that specifically engage diverse users, such as soccer leagues for youth, playgroups for young families, or all-female exercise groups (Sanchez 2010). Once a space is created, it is important to employ continual evaluation in order to understand changing use patterns and needs over time (Francis 1987). These evaluations should empower park users to be involved in the shaping of the park's success (Francis 1988).

Access As municipalities and other local governments have begun to realize some of the differences in park use and accessibility, many have taken the first step in developing requirements for open spaces, such as 'no person should live more than 300 m from their nearest area of natural greenspace of at least 2 ha in size' or 'there should be at least one accessible 20 ha site within 2 km from home' (Comber et al. 2008, 104). Others have developed guidelines to ensure that public spaces are used: the city should provide sitting space, programmed events, and food vendors. Yet most guidelines do not specifically account for user inclusivity (Francis 1988), which dramatically impacts accessibility. Accessibility, usability, and the quality of parks and public spaces all influence *who* uses the space and *how* they use it.

Accessibility depends not only on the location of parks, but also on the built environment that surrounds them. Good street lighting, adequate sidewalks, street interconnectivity, local land use, infrastructure, and facility maintenance all influence when and how urban residents participate in outdoor recreation (Talen 2008; Sanchez 2010). Furthermore, as Byrne and Wolch (2009) showed, the distance to parks, the quality and quantity of public spaces, and an individual's personal perception and preferences all influence park use. In addition to perception and preference, it has been found that a person's gender, socio-economic status, age, and ethnicity will influence whether a particular individual will choose to use certain public spaces (Sanchez 2010).

Numerous studies, especially in the US and UK, have shown that there are fewer accessible parks and public spaces in minority and economically disadvantaged areas. In addition, the parks and spaces in these neighborhoods also tend to be of lower quality, making quantity and quality especially important in low-income communities (CABE 2010c). Since these communities are also those with the highest incidence of obesity and other chronic diseases, providing green and other public spaces in low-income and minority neighborhoods has a much higher public health benefit than providing additional acreage of open space in more affluent areas (CABE 2010a). There is a trade-off between accessibility and inclusivity.

If the community is not helping 'set the table' during the design process, spaces attempting to cater to everyone and be fully inclusive can tend to be impersonal. Impersonal spaces do not allow people to feel a sense of ownership over the space. Unfortunately, these personal touches and characteristics that enable people to feel ownership over a space can often discourage people from outside the community from using the space. This creates a difficult dynamic for those planning inclusive spaces: familiarity decreases accessibility and vice versa (Madanipour 2010). Creating a shared identity is important in cities of difference; having a shared sense of ownership and identity can help to hold a diverse group of people together and can even serve as a 'rallying point' to provide a shared experience for diverse populations (Talen 2008, 152).

Cultural competency: towards culturally inclusive practice

What is the role of the professional in planning and urban design in the shift toward interculturalism as envisaged by Bloomfield and Bianchini (2002) and Sandercock (2003)? It is important to note that the professions most closely associated with the policy, planning, design, and development of public and open spaces are not known for their difference or diversity, nor for their cultural heterogeneity. There is a solid case to be made that the training and recruitment of professionals who more fully reflect the make-up of our 'cities of difference' would help speed the production, quality, and maintenance of culturally inclusive spaces, and, critically, the embedding and ultimately the mainstreaming of culturally inclusive practice within those professions. Planning and design professionals' cultural awareness, beliefs, knowledge, skills, behaviors, and professional practice can and do influence everything from the level and tone of outreach and representation at meetings to the interpretation of codes and the content of reports (Harwood 2005), and from the design of public spaces (Kumar and Martin 2004) to the land use regulations within a region (Lee 2002).

Until that mainstreaming happens, the current professionals must take added care to ensure that they embark on culturally inclusive practice where difference and diversity are intentional and are represented throughout the design process. The American Institute of Certified Planners' (AICP) Code of Ethics and Professional Conduct (American Planning Association 2009) notes that planners' overall responsibility to the public includes seeking 'social justice by working to expand choice and opportunity for all persons, recognizing a special responsibility to plan for the needs of the disadvantaged and to promote racial and economic integration.' Furthermore, certified planners 'shall urge the alteration of policies, institutions, and decisions that oppose such needs.' This statement can be seen as a clear mandate for professionals to become culturally competent, so that the 'aspirational principles that constitute ideals' (APA 2009) become translated into culturally inclusive practice. This responsibility does not fall only on the design and planning professionals; locally elected officials must also work to ensure that the spaces designed and developed in their municipalities include culturally inclusive design strategies.

Cultural competency has been described as both having systemic elements and being a developmental process. The five systemic elements are: 1) valuing diversity; 2) the capacity for cultural self-assessment; 3) consciousness of the 'dynamics' of cultural interaction; 4) the institutionalization of cultural knowledge; and 5) the development of adaptations to service delivery based on understanding diversity inter- and intra-culturally. Developmentally, cultural competency can be seen as occurring along a negative–positive continuum consisting of six possibilities, with the first being most negative and the last being most positive. The nodes along this continuum comprise the following: 1) cultural destructiveness; 2) cultural incapacity; 3) cultural blindness; 4) cultural pre-competence; 5) cultural competency; and 6) cultural proficiency (Cross et al. 1989).

A major challenge to some in becoming culturally competent will be Young's (1990) notion that recognition of difference should lead not to *equality* of treatment but to *different* treatment of groups or individuals based on the extent of their cultural and group marginalization, and of their lack of privilege and power, a point echoed forcefully by Wallace and Moore Milroy (1999) in terms of urban planning in multicultural cities. Harwood (2005, 367), reflecting on three controversial land use decisions in Orange County, California, acknowledges as much when she notes:

> In the name of impartiality or treating everyone the same during the process, the system is not flexible enough to handle difference. Some feel that the procedures produce either impartial or unfair outcomes on the basis of difference.

Universal Design, as I mentioned above, is about making spaces that are accessible to people with varying physical ability, learning and emotional disabilities, sensory impairments, and communication limitations. In Young's (1990) sense, one could argue that Universal Design is about *equality* of treatment, not *different* treatment based on need. Two comments, one from Australia and the other from Canada, countries that are officially multicultural, show some similar concerns. Sofoulis et al. (2008, 15) note that:

> Fostering social inclusion through Universal Design is a goal that few would dispute. Nevertheless the rhetoric of social inclusion can be questioned for presupposing some social whole into which everyone seeks to be included. This assimilationist logic – which

smacks of a populist US American view of society – is arguably not adequate for contemporary multicultural Australia.

Kumar and Martin (2004, 5) make a similar point:

> While cultural diversity is a widely acknowledged component of Canada's cities, discussion of cultural diversity is rare in urban design circles. Perhaps this neglect is because urban design practice is based on universalistic principles and is commonly oriented towards a homogeneous society. Or perhaps it is because urban design is premised on the notion that the public interest is unitary rather than composite.

Conclusions

The move toward just sustainabilities will require rethinking our policies and plans for public space and places. In Chapter 3, I took a necessarily broad look at what these policies and plans might look like through the lenses of space as security, space as resistance, and space as possibility. I argued that the sense of possibility and hope that was emerging in democratic and democratizing projects, spaces, and places around the world could serve as models, to inform the creation of new places and spaces along more just and sustainable lines. In this chapter, I am adding another layer by arguing that the provision of high-quality *culturally inclusive spaces* is essential in any society that 'embodies a dynamic and multi-faceted culture' (Rishbeth 2001, 364).

However, as Amin (2008) argues, we must not fall into a deterministic trap: we must recognize the limits of design to solve deep social injustices. There are two aspects to this. First, as Wood and Landry (2007, 260) point out:

> The intercultural city depends on more than a design challenge. It derives from a central notion that people are developing a shared future whereby each individual feels they have something to contribute in shaping, making and co-creating a joint endeavor. A thousand tiny transformations will create an atmosphere in public space that feels open and where all feel safe and valued.

Second, as Byrne and Wolch (2009, 756) note: 'The cultural landscape perspective shows us how landscapes can become racialized, shifting the scale of environmental injustice from the home, the factory or the neighborhood to entire landscapes.'

In addition, community-based planning processes surrounding open space may foster collaboration during the sessions, but may not radically alter the position of (lack of) power of disadvantaged participants after the process has concluded (Beebeejaun 2006). Similarly, there is a threat that residents engaged in planning for open space may create more exclusive, rather than more inclusive, spaces (ibid.). Clearly, there is a role for the planner to advocate on behalf of inclusivity, recognizing that this may require different treatment of individuals and groups based on need.

So, caveats aside, how do we shift toward culturally inclusive design and practice? On the city scale, Wood and Landry (2007) offer us *Five Principles of an Intercultural City*:

1 *The leader*: She or he is a person with an intercultural perspective; a person who has made the intellectual transition from 'diversity-as-deficit,' to 'diversity-as-advantage'; a person who can develop a new narrative of the city, (re)telling the city's story in a compelling intercultural way.
2 *City-making*: The wider leadership group uses an intercultural lens in city planning, consultation, school curricula, housing, and economic incentives.
3 *City management*: This is where ideas are transformed into actions, but city rules, codes, and most services were never developed for intercultural delivery; they were focused around health, safety, traffic flow, waste management, etc. The challenge is how to break down silos and introduce interdisciplinary, joined-up thinking that marries effective, efficient service delivery in an intercultural and culturally competent manner.

   Some services, such as social work in the US, already incorporate cultural competency practice objectives in their code of ethics. In relation to demonstrable racial and ethnic disparities or inequalities in US health and healthcare, Betancourt et al. (2003, 299) note: 'Given the strong evidence for socio-cultural barriers to care at multiple levels of the health care system, culturally competent care is a key cornerstone in efforts to eliminate racial/ethnic disparities in health and health care.' While the planning profession in the US is beginning to engage with intercultural and cultural competency issues (Agyeman and Erickson 2012), the UK is further down the line. Comedia's (2006) *Planning and Engaging with Intercultural*

Communities: Building the knowledge and skills base is a set of case studies of how to plan for, in, and with intercultural communities. Deriving from these cases, Agyeman and Erickson (2012) have characterized the requisite cultural competency themes as awareness, beliefs, knowledge, skills, behaviors, and professional practice.

4 *Citizenship*: Cities should be the sites of new forms of citizenship, whereas Sandercock (2003, 207–8) says 'I have a right to my surroundings, and so do all my fellow citizens'; in effect, a 'right to the city.'

5 *Bridgers and mixers*: These are the old-style activists, the social entrepreneurs, the fire souls, the younger social media nerds and crowdsourcers who make things happen. *They are us*.

Let's start from a position of humility. We don't have all the answers in how to do this, so let's begin the journey by making sure we're asking the right questions. First and foremost, do we want to live in a world where we tolerate the tedium and misery of cities of *in*difference, or do we want to live in cities where we recognize, understand, and engage with difference, diversity, and cultural heterogeneity in creative and productive ways, and in ways that could begin to transform civic institutions, the public realm, its discourses, and city management practices? As Wood and Landry (2007, 320) argue: 'If we want the intercultural city, we cannot leave it to chance.'

5 | CONCLUSIONS

In *Introducing Just Sustainabilities: Policy, planning, and practice*, I have tried to do two things. First, I wanted to acknowledge the origins of the concept of just sustainabilities while further developing and (re)conceptualizing it by reflecting on new and related thinking that now helps to permeate and strengthen the concept theoretically. I also wanted, using Chapter 1, 'Introducing just sustainabilities' as the theoretical base, to explore and develop what I consider to be three key themes within just sustainabilities: food, space and place, and culture. As I mentioned in Chapter 1, and I will reiterate here, food, space and place, and culture may seem like strange, even unrelated choices for a book about sustainability, but then, as I hope I have shown, this is no ordinary book about sustainability. I chose them for three reasons. First, each theme is fast-developing, but remains under-theorized and under-researched in terms of its contribution to achieving just sustainabilities. I hope I have shown some potential and real avenues for future reflection and research. Second, I have highlighted in each chapter, and will highlight more in this chapter, significant linkages and overlaps between food, space and place, and culture in relation to equity, justice, recognition, and inclusion. Finally, each theme has a growing literature that may not be known to, but has implications for, policy-makers, planners, practitioners, and activists alike. I have referenced a selection of what I consider to be some of the most important literature in this book.

I started by outlining four essential conditions for just and sustainable communities of any scale:

1. improving our quality of life and wellbeing;
2. meeting the needs of both present and future generations (*intra*-generational and *inter*generational equity);
3. justice and equity in terms of recognition (Schlosberg 1999), process, procedure, and outcome; and
4. living within ecosystem limits (also called *one planet living*) (Agyeman 2005, 92).

I now want to reflect on aspects of two of these as they relate to food, space and place, and culture: quality of life and recognition.

Quality of life

There is a growing consensus around the need for 'social sustainability' issues to be foregrounded in a sustainability agenda that is still dominated by green, environmental, and stewardship narratives and concerns. Frequently, this social sustainability thread is articulated through quality of life, wellbeing, and happiness discourses. Some, such as the US city of Somerville, MA, relate these issues to issues of social justice (socio-economic and racial statistics were collected as part of its Wellbeing and Community Survey).

Some, however, such as the recent UK report *Design for Social Sustainability: A framework for creating thriving communities*, a report from the Young Foundation, do not. The report was commissioned by the UK government's Homes and Communities Agency as part of its Future Communities program (a partnership between government and the Young Foundation). The report makes no mention of social justice, and uses problematic terms such as 'social success' and 'social design' with no explanation as to what they mean or how they should be achieved:

> We need a better understanding of how to create socially successful communities and how to use planning, development and stewardship functions to achieve this goal.

> And:

> Social sustainability is an issue of public value as well as the wellbeing, quality of life and satisfaction of future residents. It demands a new approach to planning, design and development that we call social design, which needs to be integrated into policy and professional practice across all the disciplines involved in the creation of new communities – much like the way standards of environmental sustainability have become widely adopted in recent years.

The work of Wilkinson and Pickett (2009) on inequality and social justice seems to have eluded the researchers at the Young Foundation, whose conflation of 'the social' with social justice is similar to practice in some US cities' sustainability indicator projects according to Pearsall and Pierce (2010, 576), who note that: 'many cities appeared to substitute social or quality of life elements for more targeted environmental or social justice-oriented indicators.' This is clearly inimical to just sustainabilities.

In terms of food, I argued that understanding the quality of life, social justice, and cultural concerns involving the ability of refugee groups, people of color, low-income groups, and 'new' populations to produce, access, and consume healthy and culturally appropriate foods has not been a priority of the dominant 'locavore' agenda and narrative. Similarly, I argued that refugee agriculture projects – such as New Roots Community Farm in San Diego, CA; businesses such as George Bowling's farm in southern Maryland, which grows African food crops for the growing African immigrant population nearby; the concept of 'foodways' and Latino/a community garden projects as 'autotopographies' – illustrate the potential to help us be more reflexive by reimagining what constitutes both 'the local' and 'local foods' through the notion of translocalism.

In terms of space and place, there are numerous links to quality of life and wellbeing, some of which have been quantified, for example by Rogers et al. (2011, 212):

> The research presented here suggests that there is another component of the equation linking walkability to quality of life and that is social capital. Analysis of a survey of neighborhoods of varying built form revealed strong correlations between the number of locations one could walk to and indicators of social capital.

More commonly, however, the results are qualitative and simple, such as greater use of particular spaces and places such as New York City's High Line and Broadway; 'loose' and 'insurgent' spaces at London's South Bank now used by skateboarders; 'Paris Plage' or Bogotá's Ciclovía. However, not all people are happy, nor do they feel that their quality of life has been enhanced by complete streets and other place-making efforts. The residents of color on the North Williams Avenue in the Albina neighborhood of Portland, OR, are not, it seems, explicitly against bike lanes per se, but they are against the fact that they are being implemented: a) now that whites are cycling more; b) because of a history of non-consultation in the community; and c) because they are perceived to portend gentrification.

Culture, like space, is a theme where quality of life and wellbeing issues permeate. One could argue that even exclusive space improves the quality of life of some people –those who are privileged to be able to use the space – but my concept of 'culturally inclusive space,' space designed not only around Universal Design principles but around the recognition of difference, diversity, and cultural heterogeneity, offers the chance for communities and urban designers to facilitate the move toward interculturalism. Dines and Cattrell (2006) talked of the challenges associated with establishing oneself in a new place, and that familiar-looking, familiar-sounding, familiar-smelling places enable the transfer of comforting cultural patterns from home landscapes to the new landscape. However, culturally inclusive spaces will only result from culturally inclusive practice, which hopefully will come from a very much more different and diverse set of city-making professionals than we have at present; but, until then, we need a more culturally competent, if non-different and non-diverse, set of professionals.

Recognition

In Chapter 1, 'Introducing just sustainabilities,' I mentioned that recognition is a critically important dimension of justice in multicultural and intercultural societies, where other dimensions of justice might be culturally distorted. I hope, from this reflection, that just how important this is has now become apparent. I want to highlight two aspects: first, recognizing the rights of the 'other'; second, the invisibility of privilege.

In terms of recognizing the rights of the 'other,' I noted above the issues of refugee agriculture, foodways and autotopographies, but they are equally issues of recognition. There is also a silence in much of the popular discourse surrounding local food systems, an absence of an explicit recognition of just sustainabilities concerns involving the ability of people of color, immigrant communities, and low-income populations to produce, access, and consume healthy and culturally appropriate foods. I also noted that some people involved in the food policy councils (FPCs) acknowledged the absence of a 'community voice' but they felt that this was not due to 'othering' or lack of recognition but that 'people don't do it because they don't have time!' If we are to move toward Alkon and Agyeman's (2011) concept of 'the food movement as polyculture' (a more inclusive food movement in which I identified a role for FPCs), recognition of human rights, or a shared responsibility to ensure good food provisioning for all, in both production and consumption, must be the ultimate goal.

Recognition in terms of both space/place and culture is perhaps the easiest to envisage and visualize, as these chapters were premised on cities of difference as places where we are 'in the presence of otherness' (Sennett 1990, 123). Issues mentioned included culturally inclusive practice and culturally inclusive design as attempts not to integrate or placate 'the other' but to get 'different cultures [to] intersect, "contaminate" each other and hybridise' in Bloomfield and Bianchini's (2002, 6) parlance. Indeed, the whole premise of interculturalism, as Amin (2002, 967) argues:

> Is … to stress cultural dialogue, to contrast with versions of multiculturalism that … stress cultural difference without resolving the problem of communication between cultures.

Interrelated with recognition of 'the other' is the issue of the invisibility of privilege, which permeates each chapter on food, space and place, and culture. Perhaps the most useful starting point is the work of Massey (1995a, 188), who argues that places are 'constantly shifting articulations of social relations through time,' and of Blokland (2009, 1594) who argues:

> … residents' historical narratives are processes of place-making that, once dominant in a public discourse, affect what defines 'the community' and what does not. Such symbolic representations thus help to define community needs. Erasures and absent agents in such representations then weaken the voices of those with other needs.

I would like to extend this argument to show that 'privileged' or dominant narratives in effect are frames that both build movements, such as the local food, place-making, or complete streets movements, and effectively drown out counter-narratives of culturally appropriate food, food justice, and place-making and complete streets as tools of gentrification. However, I illustrated two city cases – Dudley Street, Boston, and Bogotá, Colombia – where place-making was focused *explicitly* on shared narratives of equity, justice, and, ultimately, just sustainabilities.

The privileged local foods discourse is framed from a mostly white, middle- and upper-class perspective, concerned with environmental rather than just sustainabilities, the support of small-scale family farms and the local economy, and issues of health, taste, and nutrition. Due to this dominant framing, much of the community food security work that is being done by FPCs also reflects white cultures of food and white histories that may be culturally insensitive to those being served (Guthman 2008b). Similarly, Kent (2008, 60) is unaware of the privilege in his narrative when he describes place-making as 'a set of ideas about creating cities in ways that result in high-quality spaces where people naturally want to live, work, and play.' Whose ideas? High-quality spaces according to what criteria? Which people 'naturally' will want (or even be allowed) to live, work, and play there?

Just sustainabilities: policy, planning, and practice, and the implications of reformist change or system transformation

In this book I hope I have both identified a clear need for change, and highlighted, through chapters on food, space and place, and culture, some of the policy, planning, and practice means by which the ends can be reached. Yet there are strong forces ranged against such change: wealthy elites, corporate interests, and governments playing 'race to the bottom' to attract inward investment and maintain reckless economic growth. To be clear, these groups do not resist change per se – in fact, in the modern world, their positions depend on rapid economic change, such as the commoditization of new parts of life, and the opening of new resource frontiers.

But these are not changes that promote just sustainabilities – quite the contrary. Often they are changes that sweep away existing protections, decrease rights, and increase inequality, injustice, social insecurity, and anxiety. And the incremental improvements seen in many environmental areas (such as energy efficiency, waste management, and air quality) are rarely rapid enough to make a substantial change for the better. In part, this is because the neoliberal reformist strategy of 'eco-efficiency' suffers from 'rebound effects,' as higher efficiency lowers the effective cost of the environmental resource, and thus increases consumption. To counter this, policy-makers can aim to induce efficiency by the use of green taxes, but at the risk of serious distributional impacts, as seen in the issue of 'fuel poverty' in the UK (Boardman 2009) or carbon taxation in British Columbia, Canada (Lee 2011). More generally, where people do not have the capabilities to adopt efficiency measures, because of lack of income or constraints (such as old, hard-to-heat homes, or, in other circumstances, intellectual property rights), efficiency measures can have implications for justice. On the other hand, supportive government intervention can enable the just application of efficiency policies (ibid.).

However, achieving 'just sustainabilities' will require a shift from current reformist strategies toward policy, planning, and practice for transformational change. Incremental, linear change based on reform is unlikely to seriously challenge the underlying structures that (re)produce injustice. Generational change, relying on replacing decision-makers with those of a new generation with different values (for example the millennials) might do so, but neither can be expected to deliver the necessary reductions in environmental impact swiftly enough.

Contemporary theories of change, whether at societal or organizational level, stress the uncertainty of the process, emphasizing unexpected outcomes and the grave difficulties in delivering planned, directed change. Such concerns extend from the failures of soviet central planning to the failures of independent central banks to maintain economic stability.

Delivering just sustainabilities requires a transformation of society, and an understanding of emergent and transformative change mechanisms. Arguably, non-linear change is characteristic of social and economic systems. Taleb (2007) argues that the majority of change is the product of extreme, so-called 'black swan events'; Gladwell (2000) points to the contagious nature of change processes, which then trigger 'tipping points'; Ormerod (1998) proposes a 'chaos-theory' basis for a new general economic theory. All their work is based on insights into system thinking and the underlying structures of social (and physical) systems which mean that dramatic shifts between system states are possible as a result of small changes in conditions, and that such changes are not necessarily reversible without subsequent large changes in conditions.

McLaren (2011a) suggests three potential categories of mechanism for social transformation: revolution, subversion, and reinvention. Proponents of each respectively seek to 'smash,' 'flip,' or 'ignore' the current system. McLaren highlights the risks of revolution with reference to Naomi Klein's analysis of the 'shock doctrine' (2007), in which crises are created or harnessed by neoliberal elites to further centralize power. But without a crisis in the current system, a reinvented, innovative alternative would have little opportunity to flourish. McLaren

The Occupy movement

In 2011, protest groups camped out in public spaces in hundreds of cities around the world, under the banner of 'Occupy' – a term coined by the Occupy Wall Street protest in New York. The protests follow a model used earlier in 2011 by Los Indignados, whose protests were apparently self-organized, using social media to arrange the occupation of public squares in Barcelona and Madrid, inspired by the Arab Spring revolutions. Los Indignados (the indignant ones) were protesting against the lack of real democratic choice because all major parties support similar neoliberal economic policies (participants were therefore refusing to vote in the May local and regional elections in Spain). Through participatory forums, Los Indignados developed a manifesto of demands for real democracy. The protests spread to other southern European countries in May 2011. The occupation in Madrid lasted until early August 2011, when the last protesters were evicted.

The participatory models used by Los Indignados re-appeared on 17 September 2011 with the Occupy movement, first in New York and then rapidly spreading to hundreds of other cities in the US, Europe, Australia, and Latin America, with smaller numbers in Asia and Africa. The protests reflect the Arab Spring uprisings in that they are 'leaderless,' inclusive, and non-discriminatory in principle, non-violent and at least partly organized through social media. However, the Occupy movement has faced challenges from indigenous peoples activists who feel excluded from some (although not all) Occupy events.[1]

Like Los Indignados, Occupy groups have used participatory forums to agree fairly detailed demands for economic, social, and environmental justice. The unifying theme (within Occupy events and with Los Indignados) has been concern over economic injustice, and the lack of economic opportunity. The Occupy activists are predominantly young, reflecting the intergenerational injustice of high youth unemployment resulting from crises arising from decisions and actions of older people.

However, the Occupy movement has not focused solely on

the problems faced by young people, but has widely adopted the slogan 'We are the 99%' to challenge the extent to which a small global elite increasingly controls wealth and resources. Given that most of the protestors are within the global top 10 per cent, this clearly reflects Wilkinson and Pickett's (2009) analysis that even within the top decile, people would be healthier (mentally and physically) as a result of enhanced equality.

Earlier in 2011, in the May edition of *Vanity Fair*,[2] Joseph Stiglitz wrote that the societies that are vulnerable to social unrest and revolution are:

> Societies where a minuscule fraction of the population – less than 1 percent – controls the lion's share of the wealth; where wealth is a main determinant of power; where entrenched corruption of one sort or another is a way of life; and where the wealthiest often stand actively in the way of policies that would improve life for people in general.

He was indeed highlighting that the US had much in common with the Arab countries where governments had been overturned.

It seems unlikely that the outcomes will be the same in the US and in other rich nations, but the Occupy events, together with the continued sluggish global economy, suggest a real appetite for a broad-based movement for economic, social, and environmental justice, in short, for just sustainabilities, at least in a climate of global economic instability.

suggests a combination of reinvention and subversion to create spaces in which alternatives could gain traction.

The growing advocacy for just sustainabilities will need to learn to harness and guide emergent change, to achieve both the geographical and temporal scale of change needed. It will also need to resist further systemic lock-in and sclerosis, which are likely to generate conflicting approaches to reformist and incremental changes such as new environmental technologies, eco-efficiency, and corporate social responsibility; some will see them as false solutions that bolster the current system, and others as foundations for future, more rapid, change.

Existing elites deploy a culture of fear – especially about terror and economic collapse – in which xenophobic fear of 'the other' (a rejection of recognition) plays a central role. This enables more repressive controls over protest and resistance, as is happening around the world today, even in liberal democracies. What are needed are positive, inclusive narratives of change in which the entire system is 'reimagined' – narratives in which just sustainabilities are understood as a basis for security and in(ter)dependence. I hope I showed some of these possibilities in Chapter 2, 'Food,' Chapter 3, 'Space and place,' and Chapter 4, 'Culture.' Ultimately, in my view, embedding justice and the right to a clean, inclusive, and healthy environment which offers a high quality of life and wellbeing for current and future generations into existing struggles for social, economic, and political freedoms offers the best route.

It is becoming commonplace that progressive activists in different domains should work together to build large-scale, even global 'movements'; see, for example, Crompton's (2010) movement-building work around coalescing values. Harvey (2011) proposes seven spheres of activity that might constitute domains of change: labor processes, mental conceptions, our relations to nature, social relations, technology and organizational form, daily life, and administrative institutions. He makes a strong case that action in any one of these spheres will fall short of transformation, and that an effective movement must link up across the spheres to utilize the best moments of opportunity within them.

But the 'chicken and egg' problem of building both a movement and a vision is serious and severe. Without a vision, movement-building is fragmented and slow. Without a movement, visions are narrow and competing, rather than shared. Nonetheless, there are multiple initiatives wrestling with the challenge of what Cole and Foster (2001) call 'movement fusion,' with greater or lesser involvement by established non-governmental organizations (NGOs) such as the World Social Forum, the Tellus Institute's Great Transition Initiative, and the Global Citizens Movement.[3]

A promising space is being opened up by online activism: Avaaz.org and, more locally, MoveOn.org (in the US) and 38degrees.org.uk (in the UK) have created a common platform for progressive campaigning, with targets chosen by (or at least with strong involvement of) active participants. These typically mobilize much larger numbers than conventional NGOs, even those that have built online campaign networks. New vision-building opportunities might emerge in these spaces that seem to offer a greater chance of movement fusion than more conventional coalition and membership-building approaches. However, their need to choose 'achievable' targets to maintain interest from a large number of less strongly committed supporters can risk a focus on incremental change or resistance to undesirable change.

To deliver just sustainabilities, these change agents will have to engage with many challenges, including questions of value(s), difference, culture, and identity; reform or reconstruction of just and intercultural institutions; and the creation of new rules and frameworks to guide human interaction in a new economic formation. These are revolutionary changes but such a revolution need not be violent, nor will it necessarily be televised: this revolution will be co-produced.

NOTES

1 Introducing just sustainabilities

1 In November 2011, *The Atlantic* reported that it costs more to send someone to prison than to Princeton. www.theatlantic.com/national/archive/2011/11/chart-one-year-of-prison-costs-more-than-one-year-at-princeton/247629/.

2 It should be noted that in some economic schools, instability is seen as an essential element of the creative destruction central to contemporary capitalism.

3 www.sustainableseattle.org/documents/HI_Seattle_proclamation_PR.pdf.

4 www.nytimes.com/2011/05/01/us/01happiness.html?pagewanted=all.

5 Policies designed to restrict the range of choices available to consumers through regulation.

6 An independent charity with a mission to help people and organizations bring great ideas to life.

7 For example, challenging the very concept that rich countries in the global North are any more 'developed' than poor ones in the global South.

8 I am aware of the contested nature of the concept of 'race' (see, for instance, Omi and Winant 1994; Krimsky and Sloan 2011). While race may not stand scientific scrutiny as a robust categorization of humans, I use it in this chapter since it is a powerful and widely used construct among the public and in the literature.

9 See, for example, the Declaration of the Forum for Food Sovereignty, Nyéléni 2007. www.nyeleni.org/spip.php?article290.

10 Commentators such as Harvey also stress the importance of wage restraint since the 1970s in reducing the labor share of profits, and the maintenance of high levels of consumer demand through the systematic extension of credit to finance it (leading to the current financial crisis).

11 Rifkin suggests that consciousness has changed fairly dramatically in evolutionary history with the development of new needs and drivers (in ways that echo theories of human needs that we consider later).

12 Contraception is transformative in that it provides control over reproduction, which is a massive leap in women's freedom. Further, the washing machine arguably played a significant role in freeing women's time from domestic labor and enabling education as a result (see Hans Rosling at www.youtube.com/watch?v=BZoKfap4g4w).

13 It would seem self-evident that large, private, unlisted companies are not and probably cannot become 'just institutions' given their basic unaccountable governance structure.

14 Which has involved the production of a series of reports comparing the overall footprint of human society with the global productive land area, showing a trend of increasing overuse.

15 Although, of course, the loss of each individual species is in itself an irreversible event.

16 One economic alternative to redistribution rests on the claim that there is an environmental 'Kuznets curve,' as a result of which environmental quality first declines and then improves with

economic growth, the latter phase resulting from wealthier societies putting an increasing value on health and a clean environment. If this is so, then theoretically growth should be encouraged, as it would result in environmental improvement, as well as the creation of wealth to spread around. The phenomenon has been seen on national scales for local pollutants such as particulates. However, it is more questionable on a global scale, where, even for such pollutants, much of the effect seen in wealthy countries may be a result of exporting industry and emissions, and has yet to be seen for greenhouse gases, where decoupling of emissions rates from growth has been at best relative, and also subject to problems of export of production (mainly to China).

2 Food

1 McClintock (2011) questions the term 'food desert,' noting its inaccuracies (food is available but is of poor nutritional value) and that some use terms such as 'health food desert/fresh food desert' or 'junk food jungle.' He notes that others avoid the term altogether because of its racialized connotations and links to degrading or depraved environments.

2 *Portlandia* is a US TV series that spoofs the Oregon city's seriousness about sustainability.

3 For the purposes of maintaining confidentiality and to facilitate coding and analysis, we assigned each survey respondent a unique identifier: a number between 1 and 53. In some cases we interviewed multiple representatives from a council, in which case each respondent was assigned a designated letter following their council's number. To protect confidentiality, survey respondents and interviewees are intentionally not identified by their geopolitical region.

4 WIC provides US federal grants to states for supplemental foods, healthcare referrals, and nutrition education for low-income pregnant, breastfeeding, and non-breastfeeding postpartum women, and to infants and children up to age five who are found to be at nutritional risk.

5 SNAP provides financial assistance for food purchasing to low- and no-income people and families living in the US. It is a federal aid program, administered by the Food and Nutrition Service of the USDA, but benefits are distributed by the individual US states. Until 2008 it was known as the Food Stamp Program.

6 TANF is one of the US's federal assistance programs providing temporary financial assistance while aiming to get people off that assistance, primarily through employment.

3 Space and place

1 Zuccotti Park is not a publicly owned space, but is referred to as a POPS, a privately owned public space.

2 Geography of protest is a term used by Rosenthal (2000) in 'Spectacle, fear, and protest: a guide to the history of urban public space in Latin America.'

3 Redlining is where services such as banking, insurance, access to healthcare, or even supermarkets and jobs, are denied, or charged at a premium, for residents in certain, frequently racially defined areas.

4 A mix of market-rate housing with lower-cost units.

5 British MP David Lammy (2004, 1) notes: 'Just as social justice requires that like chances are not distributed along class lines, spatial justice requires that they are not distributed geographically.'

6 Although a problematic concept, 'race' is used here as it is frequently used in the health disparities literature.

7 Restorative justice, also called reparative justice, focuses on the needs of both victims and offenders and the wider community, not on legal principle or punishment.

8 HOPE VI is a plan by the US Department of Housing and Urban Development that aims to revitalize the worst public housing projects and transform them into mixed-income developments.

4 Culture

1 For example, Fincher and Jacobs 1998; Sandercock 1998, 2000, 2003; Burayidi 2000a; 2000b; Amin 2002; Goonewardena et al. 2004; Milroy 2004; Rahder and Milgrom 2004; Harwood 2005.

2 For example, Krishnarayan and Thomas 1993; Forsyth 1995; Thomas and Ritzdorf 1997; Looye and Sesay 1998; Burayidi 2000a; 2000b; Umemoto 2001; Day 2003; Umemoto and Igarashi 2009; Goonewardena et al. 2004; Milroy 2004; Uyesugi and Shipley 2005; Sen 2005; Talen 2008; Sweet and Etienne 2011.

3 www.coe.int/t/dg4/culture heritage/culture/Cities/Default_en.asp.

4 The language used to define different ethnic and racial groups is that of the author I cite or quote. In other literatures terms such as 'Hispanic' and 'Caucasian' would be challenged.

5 Although a deeply problematic concept, 'race' is used here as it is frequently used in the public space, parks, and leisure literature.

6 'The idea of coming full circle, beginning where one begins, is a common quality appreciated across cultures' (Devier n.d., 3).

5 Conclusions

1 Occupy Denver reportedly has incorporated a ten-point platform from the Denver American Indian Movement into its demands.

2 www.vanityfair.com/society/features/2011/05/top-one-percent-201105.

3 See http://wsfpalestine.net/world-social-forum, http://gtinitiative.org, and www.wideningcircle.org.

REFERENCES

Abdallah, S., Thompson, S., Michaelson, J., Marks, N., and Steuer, N. (2009) *The Unhappy Planet Index 2.0: Why good lives don't have to cost the earth*. London: New Economic Foundation.

Agyeman, J. (2005) *Sustainable Communities and the Challenge of Environmental Justice*. New York, NY: New York University Press.

— (2007) 'Environmental justice and sustainability'. In: Atkinson, G., Dietz, S., and Neumayer, E. (eds) *Handbook of Sustainable Development*. Cheltenham: Edward Elgar Publishing, pp. 171–88.

— (2010) 'Inclusive or exclusive spaces?' [online] Available at: http://julianagyeman.com/2010/10/inclusive-or-exclusive-spaces/ [Accessed 27 November 2012]

— (2011) 'Grow Canada?' [online] Available at: http://julianagyeman.com/2011/03/multiculturalism-environmental-policy-and-planning/ [Accessed 27 November 2012]

— and Erickson, J. (2012) 'Culture, recognition and the negotiation of difference: some thoughts on cultural competency in planning education'. *Journal of Planning Education and Research* 32(3): 358–66.

— and Evans, B. (1995) 'Sustainability and democracy: community participation in Local Agenda 21'. *Local Government Policy Making* 22(2): 35–40.

— (2004) '"Just sustainability": the emerging discourse of environmental justice in Britain?' *Geographical Journal* 170(2): 155–64.

— Bulkeley, H., and Nochur, A. (2007) 'Just climate: towards a reconstruction of climate activism?'. In: Isham, J., and Waage, S. (eds) *Ignition: What you can do to fight global warming and spark a movement*. Washington, DC: Island Press, pp. 135–44.

— Bullard, R., and Evans, B. (2002) 'Exploring the nexus: bringing together sustainability, environmental justice and equity.' *Space and Polity* 6(1): 70–90.

— (eds) (2003) *Just Sustainabilities: Development in an unequal world*. Cambridge, MA: MIT Press.

— Devine-Wright, P., and Prange, J. (2009) 'Close to the edge, down by the river? Joining up managed retreat and place attachment in a climate changed world'. *Environment and Planning A* 41(3): 509–13.

Alfonzo, M., Boarnet, M. G., Day, K., McMillan, T., and Anderson, C. L. (2008) 'The relationship of neighbourhood built environment features and adult parents' walking'. *Journal of Urban Design* 13(1): 29–51.

Alkon, A. (2008) 'Paradise or pavement: the social constructions of the environment in two urban farmers' markets and their implications for environmental justice and sustainability'. *Local Environment* 13(3): 271–89.

— (2012) *Black, White and Green. Farmers markets, race and the green economy*. Athens, GA: University of Georgia Press.

— and Agyeman, J. (2011) *Cultivating Food Justice: Race, class and sustainability*. Cambridge, MA: MIT Press.

Allen, P. (1999) 'Reweaving the food security safety net: mediating entitlement and entrepreneurship'. *Agriculture and Human Values* 16(2): 117–29.

— (2004) *Together at the Table: Sustainability and sustenance in the American agrifood system*. University Park, PA: Penn State University Press.

— (2008) 'Mining for justice in the food system: perceptions, practices, and possibilities'. *Agriculture and Human Values* 25(2): 157–61.

— (2010) 'Realizing justice in local food systems'. *Cambridge Journal of Regions, Economy and Society* 3(2): 295–308.

— and Guthman, J. (2006) 'From 'old school' to "farm-to-school": neoliberalization from the ground up'. *Agriculture and Human Values* 23(4): 401–15.

— FitzSimmons, M., Goodman, M., and Warner, K. (2003) 'Shifting plates in the agrifood landscape: the tectonics of alternative agrifood initiatives in California'. *Journal of Rural Studies* 19(1): 61–75.

Amin, A. (2002) 'Ethnicity and the multicultural city: living with diversity'. *Environment and Planning A* 34(6): 959–80.

— (2008) 'Collective culture and urban public space'. *City* 12(1): 5–24.

Anderson, D. (n.d.) 'M-POWER: a case study – people with psychiatric disabilities organize'. Unpublished. Boston, MA: Boston University School of Social Work.

Anderson, M. D. (2008) 'Rights-based food systems and the goals of food systems reform'. *Agriculture and Human Values* 25(4): 593–608.

APaNGO (2007) *Community Engagement in Planning – exploring the way forward: summary report*. London: Town and Country Planning Association. Available at: www.tcpa.org.uk/data/files/apango_summary.pdf [Accessed 27 November 2012]

Appleyard, D. (1981) *Livable Streets*. Berkeley, CA: University of California Press.

Arnold, M., and Shinew, K. (1998) 'The role of gender, race and income on park use constraints'. *Journal of Park and Recreation Administration* 16(4): 39–56.

Baer, P., Athanasiou, T., Kartha, S., and Kemp-Benedict, E. (2008) *The Greenhouse Development Rights Framework: The right to development in a climate constrained world*. Berlin: Heinrich Böll Foundation.

Baker, L. E. (2004) 'Tending cultural landscapes and food citizenship in Toronto's community gardens'. *Geographical Review* 94(3): 305–25.

Banerjee, T. (2001) 'The future of public space: beyond invented streets and reinvented places'. *Journal of the American Planning Association* 67(1): 9–24.

Bauman, Z. (2005) *Liquid life*. Cambridge: Polity Press.

Beaumont, P. (2011) 'The truth about Twitter, Facebook and the uprisings in the Arab world'. *Guardian*, 25 February. Available from: www.guardian.co.uk/world/2011/feb/25/twitter-facebook-uprisings-arab-libya [Accessed 28 November 2012]

Beckmann, J. (2001) 'Automobility – a social problem and theoretical concept'. *Environment and Planning D: Society and Space* 19(5): 593–607.

Bedore, M. (2010) 'Just urban food systems: a new direction for food access and urban social justice'. *Geography Compass* 4(9): 1418–32.

Beebeejaun, Y. (2006) 'The participation trap: the limitations of participation for ethnic and racial groups'. *International Planning Studies* 11(1): 3–18.

— (2009) 'Making safer places: gender

and right to the city'. *Security Journal* 22: 219–29.

Bell, S., Montarzino, A., and Travlou, P. (2006) *Green and Public Space Research: Mapping and priorities*. Edinburgh and London: OPENspace Research Centre and Department for Communities and Local Government. Available at: www.openspace.eca.ac.uk/pdf/appendixf/OPENspace website_APPENDIX_F_resource_17.pdf [Accessed 30 November 2012]

Bellows, A., and Hamm, M. (2002) 'U.S.-based community food security: influences, practice, debate'. *Journal for the Study of Food and Society* 6(1): 31–44.

Berney, R. (2010) 'Learning from Bogotá: how municipal experts transformed public space'. *Journal of Urban Design* 15(4): 539–58.

Betancourt, J., Green, A., Carrillo, E., and Ananeh-Firempong, O. (2003) 'Defining cultural competence: a practical framework for addressing racial/ethnic disparities in health and health care'. *Public Health Reports* 118(4): 293–302.

Blokland, T. (2009) 'Celebrating local histories and defining neighbourhood communities: place-making in a gentrified neighbourhood'. *Urban Studies* 46(8): 1593–610.

Bloomfield, J., and Bianchini, F. (2002) *Planning for the Cosmopolitan City: A research report for Birmingham City Council*. Leicester: Comedia, International Cultural Planning and Policy Unit.

Boardman, B. (2009) *Fixing Fuel Poverty: Challenges and solutions*. Abingdon: Earthscan.

Bondi, L. (1991) 'Gender divisions and gentrification: a critique'. *Transactions of the Institute of British Geographers* 16(2): 190–8.

Born, B., and Purcell, M. (2006) 'Avoiding the local trap: scale and food systems in planning research'. *Journal of Planning Education and Research* 26(2): 195–207.

Boschmann, E. E., and Kwan, M. P. (2008) 'Toward socially sustainable urban transportation: progress and potentials'. *International Journal of Sustainable Transportation* 2(3): 138–57.

Bosselmann, P. (2002) 'Transformations and city extensions: some observations of Copenhagen's city form at a time of global change'. *Journal of Urban Design* 7(1): 75–97.

Boston Parks and Recreation Department (2002) *Open Space Plan for Boston 2002–2006*. 'Appendix 6: Open Space Opinion Survey'. Boston, MA: City of Boston.

Bovaird, T. (2006) *The Commission for Rural Community Development: Beyond engagement and participation – user and community co-production of services*. Dunfermline: Carnegie UK Trust.

Brewer, M. B. (2003) 'Optimal distinctiveness, social identity, and the self'. In: Leary, M., and Tangney, J. (eds) *Handbook of Self and Identity*. New York: Guilford Press, pp. 480–91.

Bridgman, R. (2001) 'Review of *Urban Planning in a Multicultural Society* by Michael Burayidi, Editor'. *Canadian Journal of Urban Research* 10(1): 98–102.

Brown, L. (2010) 'U.S. car fleet shrank by four million in 2009' *Grist*, 7 January. Available from: http://grist.org/article/u-s-car-fleet-shrinks-by-four-million-in-2009/ [Accessed 28 November 2012]

Brown, P. L. (2011) 'When the uprooted put down roots'. *New York Times*, 9 October. Available at: www.nytimes.com/2011/10/10/us/refugees-in-united-states-take-up-farming.html?_r=3&emc=eta1 [Accessed 28 November 2012]

Bührs, T. (2004) 'Sharing environmental space: the role of law, economics and politics'. *Journal of Environmental Planning and Management* 47(3): 429–47.

Burayidi, M. (ed.) (2000a) *Urban Planning in a Multicultural Society*. Westport, CT: Praeger.

— (ed.) (2000b) 'Tracking the planning profession: from monistic planning to holistic planning for a multicultural society'. In: Burayidi, M. (ed.) *Urban Planning in a Multicultural Society*. Westport, CT: Praeger.

— (2003) 'The multicultural city as planners' enigma'. *Planning Theory and Practice* 4(3): 259–73.

Burnham, J. C. (1961) 'The gasoline tax and the automobile revolution'. *The Mississippi Valley Historical Review* 48(3): 435–59.

Byrne, J., and Wolch, J. (2009) 'Nature, race, and parks: past research and future directions for geographic research'. *Progress in Human Geography* 33: 743–65.

Cabbil, L. (2010). Community Food Security Conference: Food Movements Unite panel. Available at: http://vimeo.com/16464046 [Accessed 28 November 2012]

CABE (2002) *Paving the Way: How we achieve clean, safe and attractive streets*. London: Commission for Architecture and the Built Environment (CABE).

— (2004) *What Would You Do with This Space? Involving young people in the design and care of urban spaces*. London: Commission for Architecture and the Built Environment (CABE).

— (2006) *The Principles of Inclusive Design (They Include You)*. London: Commission for Architecture and the Built Environment (CABE).

— (2007a) *It's Our Space: A guide for community groups working to improve public space*. London: Commission for Architecture and the Built Environment (CABE).

— (2007b) *Spaceshaper: A user's guide*. London: Commission for Architecture and the Built Environment (CABE).

— (2008a) *Inclusion by Design: Equality, diversity and the built environment*. London: Commission for Architecture and the Built Environment (CABE).

— (2008b) *Civilised Streets*. Briefing. London: Commission for Architecture and the Built Environment (CABE).

— (2009) *Open Space Strategies: Best practice guidance*. London: Commission for Architecture and the Built Environment (CABE).

— (2010a) *Community Green: Using local spaces to tackle inequality and improve health*. London: Commission for Architecture and the Built Environment (CABE).

— (2010b) *Ordinary Places*. London: Commission for Architecture and the Built Environment (CABE).

— (2010c) *Urban Green Nation: Building the evidence base*. London: Commission for Architecture and the Built Environment (CABE).

Carroll, J., and Minkler, M. (2000) 'Freire's message for social workers: looking back, looking ahead'. *Journal of Community Practice* 8(1): 21–36.

Castells, M. (2010) *The Power of Identity: The information age: Economy, society, and culture*. Chichester: Wiley-Blackwell.

Cervero, R., and Sullivan, C. (2011) 'Green TODs: marrying transit-oriented development and green urbanism'. *International Journal of Sustainable Development & World Ecology* 18(3): 210–18.

Chambers, N., Simmons, C., and Wackernagel, M. (2000) *Sharing Nature's Interest: Ecological footprints as an indicator of sustainability*. London: Earthscan.

Cheek, N., Field, D., and Burdge, R. (1976) *Leisure and Recreation Places*. Ann Arbor, MI: Ann Arbor Science, pp. 113–30.

Chen, C. (2010) 'Dancing in the streets of Beijing: improvised uses within the urban system'. In: Hou, J. (ed.) *Insurgent Public Space: Guerilla urbanism and the remaking of contemporary cities*. New York: Routledge, pp. 47–57.

City of Copenhagen (2007) *Eco-Metropolis: Our vision for Copenhagen 2015*. Copenhagen: Technical and Environmental Administration.

City of Toronto (2002) *Toronto Pedestrian Charter*. Toronto: Toronto City Council.

Clavel, P., and Wiewel, W. (eds) (1991) *Harold Washington and the Neighborhoods*. New Brunswick, NJ: Rutgers.

CLF (1998) *City Routes, City Rights: Building livable neighborhoods and environmental justice by fixing transportation*. Boston, MA: Conservation Law Foundation (CLF).

Cobb C., Goodman, G. S., and Wackernagel, M. (1999) *Why Bigger Isn't Better: The genuine progress indicator – 1999 update*. San Francisco, CA: Redefining Progress. Available at: www.nber.org/~rosenbla/econ302/lecture/GPI-GDP/gpi1999.pdf [Accessed 28 November 2012]

Cohen, J. (2008) 'Calming traffic on Bogotá's killing streets'. *Science* 319(5864): 742–3.

Cole, L., and Foster, S. (2001) *From the Ground Up: Environmental racism and the rise of the environmental justice movement*. New York, NY: New York University Press.

Comber, A., Brunsdon, C., and Green, E. (2008) 'Using a GIS-based network analysis to determine urban greenspace accessibility for different ethnic and religious groups'. *Landscape and Urban Planning* 86(1): 103–14.

Comedia (2006) *Planning and Engaging with Intercultural Communities: Building the knowledge and skills base*. Available at: www.coe.int/t/dg4/cultureheritage/culture/cities/planningandengaging.pdf [Accessed 30 November 2012]

Community Cycling Center (2010) *Understanding Barriers to Bicycling: Interim report*. Portland, OR: Community Cycling Center. Available at: www.communitycyclingcenter.org/index.php/understanding-barriers-to-bicycling/ [Accessed 28 November 2012]

Cranz, G. (1989) *The Politics of Park Design: A history of urban parks in America*. Cambridge, MA: MIT Press.

Crawford, M. (1995) 'Contesting the public realm: struggles over public space in Los Angeles'. *Journal of Architectural Education* 49(1): 4–9.

Crompton, T. (2010) *Common Cause: The Case for working with our cultural values*. Godalming: WWF-UK. Available at: http://assets.wwf.org.uk/downloads/common_cause_report.pdf [Accessed 28 November 2012]

Cross, P., Edwards, R. T., Opondo, M., Nyeko, P., and Edwards-Jones, G. (2009) 'Does farm worker health vary between localised and globalised food supply systems?'. *Environment International* 35(7): 1004–14.

Cross, T., Bazron, B., Dennis, K., and Isaacs, M. (1989) *Towards a Culturally Competent System of Care: Volume I*. Washington, DC: Georgetown University Child Development Center, CASSP Technical Assistance Center.

Crouch, P. (2011) Personal communication with the author, 20 April.

Cunningham, C. J., and Jones, M. A. (2000) 'How a community uses its parks: a case study of Ipswich,

Queensland, Australia'. *Leisure/Loisir* 24(3–4): 233–53.

Dahlen, E. R., and Ragan, K. M. (2004) 'Validation of the propensity for angry driving scale'. *Journal of Safety Research* 35(5): 557–63.

Davidoff, P. (1965) 'Advocacy and pluralism in planning'. *Journal of the American Institute of Planners* 31(4): 331–8.

Day, K. (2003) 'New urbanism and the challenges of designing for diversity'. *Journal of Planning Education and Research* 23(1): 83–95.

— (2006) 'Active living and social justice: planning for physical activity in low-income, black, and Latino communities'. *Journal of the American Planning Association* 72(1): 88–99.

de Nazelle, A., and Rodríguez, D. A. (2009) 'Tradeoffs in incremental changes towards pedestrian-friendly environments: physical activity and pollution exposure'. *Transportation Research Part D: Transport and Environment* 14(4): 255–63.

de Zeeuw, D., and Flusche, D. (2011) 'How a bill becomes a bike lane: federal legislation, programs, and requirements of bicycling and walking projects'. *Planning & Environmental Law* 63(8): 8–11.

Desmarais, A. A. (2008) 'The power of peasants: reflections on the meanings of La Vía Campesina'. *Journal of Rural Studies* 24(2): 138–49.

Devier, G. (n.d.) 'Cultural and ethnic minority use of open space'. *CULTURE*.

Dines, N., and Cattrell, V. (2006) *Public Spaces, Social Relations and Well-Being in East London*. Bristol: The Policy Press.

Dixon, J., Durrheim, K., and Tredoux, C. (2005) 'Beyond the optimal contact strategy: a reality check for the contact hypothesis'. *American Psychologist* 60(7): 697–711.

Doan, P. (2010) 'The tyranny of gendered spaces – reflections from beyond the gender dichotomy'. *Gender, Place & Culture: A Journal of Feminist Geography* 17(5): 635–54.

Dolan, P., Peasgood, T., and White, M. (2008) 'Do we really know what makes us happy? A review of the economic literature on the factors associated with subjective well-being'. *Journal of Economic Psychology* 29(1): 94–122.

Dorn, D., Fischer, J. A. V., Kirchgässner, G., and Sousa-Poza, A. (2007) 'Is it culture or democracy? The impact of democracy and culture on happiness'. *Social Indicators Research* 82(3): 505–26.

Douglass, M. (1996) *Purity and Danger: An analysis of the concepts of purity and taboo*. New York, NY: Taylor.

Dreier, P. (2009) 'Community organizing, ACORN, and progressive politics in America'. In: Fisher, R. (ed.) *The People Shall Rule: ACORN, community organizing, and the struggle for economic justice*. Nashville, TN: Vanderbilt University Press.

Drew, E. (2012) 'Listening through white ears: cross-racial dialogues as a strategy to address the racial effects of gentrification'. *Journal of Urban Affairs* 34(1): 99–115.

ds4si (2011) Spatial Justice. See http://ds4si.org/storage/SpatialJustice_ds4si.pdf [Accessed 12 April 2012]

DTLR (2002) *Improving Urban Parks, Play Areas and Open Spaces*. Final report of the Urban Green Spaces Taskforce. London: Department for Transport, Local Government and the Regions (DTLR).

Dumbaugh, E. (2005) 'Safe streets, livable streets'. *Journal of the American Planning Association* 71(3): 283–98.

— and Li, W. (2011) 'Designing for the safety of pedestrians, cyclists, and motorists in urban environments'. *Journal of the American Planning Association* 77(1): 69–88.

Dunham, M. (2011) 'Where the shoe leather meets the road: learning from experience in crafting a complete streets ordinance'. *Planning & Environmental Law* 63(8): 3–8.

DuPuis, E. M., and Goodman, D. (2005) 'Should we go "home" to eat?: Toward a reflexive politics of localism'. *Journal of Rural Studies* 21(3): 359–71.

Dwyer, J., and Gobster, P. (1996) 'The implication of increased racial and ethnic diversity for recreation resource management, planning, and research'. Paper presented at Ethnicity and Parks and Recreation: Keynote Session, Bolton Landing, New York. Available at: www.fs.fed.us/ne/newtown_square/publications/technical_reports/pdfs/scanned/gtr232a.pdf [Accessed 28 November 2012]

Dwyer, J., and Hutchison, R. (1990). 'Outdoor recreation participation and preferences for black and white Chicago households'. In: Vining, J. (ed.) *Social Science and Natural Resource Recreation Management*. Boulder, CO: Westview Press, pp. 49–67.

Dyjur, P. (2004) *Inclusive Practices in Instructional Design*. Saskatchewan: University of Saskatchewan, Department of Education Communications and Technology.

Earth Policy Institute (2009) 'US car fleet shrank by 4 million in 2009 – after a century of growth, US fleet entering era of decline'. Available at: www.earth-policy.org/plan_b_updates/2010/update87 [Accessed 30 November 2012]

Elkin, T., McLaren, D. P., and Hillman, M. (1989) *Reviving the City*. London: Friends of the Earth and Policy Studies Institute.

EMBARQ (2011) *From Here to There: A creative guide to making public transport the way to go*. Washington, DC: EMBARQ. Available at: www.embarq.org/en/from-here-there-a-creative-guide-making-public-transport-way-go [Accessed 28 November 2012]

Engelbrecht, H.-J. (2009) 'Natural capital, subjective well-being, and the new welfare economics of sustainability: some evidence from cross-country regressions'. *Ecological Economics* 69(2): 380–8.

Ewing, R., Pendall, R., and Chen, D. (2002) *Measuring Sprawl and Its Impact*. Washington, DC: Smart Growth America. Available at: www.smartgrowthamerica.org [Accessed 28 November 2012]

Falconer, R., and Richardson, E. (2010) 'Rethinking urban land use and transport planning – opportunities for transit oriented development in Australian cities: case study Perth'. *Australian Planner* 47(1): 1–13.

Farr, D. (2008) *Sustainable Urbanism: Urban design with nature*. New York, NY: John Wiley and Sons.

Featherstone, M. (2004) 'Automobilities: an introduction'. *Theory, Culture & Society* 21(4/5): 1–24.

Ferris, J., Norman, C., and Sempik, J. (2001) 'People, land and sustainability: community gardens and the social dimension of sustainable development'. *Social Policy & Administration* 35(5): 559–68.

Fielding, M. (2009) 'Public space and educational leadership: reclaiming and renewing our radial traditions'. *Educational Management, Administration and Leadership* 37(4): 497–521.

Fincher, R., and Jacobs, J. (1998) *Cities of Difference*. New York, NY: Guilford Press.

Flink, J. J. (1972) 'Three stages of American automobile consciousness'. *American Quarterly* 24(4): 451–73.

Flint, A. (2006) *This Land: The battle over sprawl and the future of America*. Baltimore, MD: Johns Hopkins University Press.

Floyd, M. F., Gramann, J. H., and Saenz,

R. (1993) 'Ethnic factors and the use of public outdoor recreation areas: the case of Mexican Americans'. *Leisure Sciences* 15(2): 83–98.

Flusty, S. (1994) *Building Paranoia: The proliferation of interdictory space and the erosion of spatial justice*. Los Angeles, CA: Los Angeles Forum for Architecture and Urban Design.

Follert, J. (2010) 'Durham leaders learned a lot from five days on food bank diet'. 8 November. Available at: www.durhamregion.com/durham region/article/991248 [Accessed 30 November 2012]

Food, Inc. (2008) [Film] Directed by Robert Kenner. USA: Participant Media.

Food Project (n.d.). See http://thefood-project.org/ [Accessed 28 November 2012]

Ford, L. R. (2000) *The Spaces Between Buildings*. Baltimore, MD: Johns Hopkins University Press.

Forsyth, A. (1995) 'Diversity issues in a professional curriculum: four stories and suggestions for a change'. *Journal of Planning Education and Research* 15(1): 58–63.

Fotel, T. (2006) 'Space, power, and mobility: car traffic as a controversial issue in neighbourhood regeneration'. *Environment and Planning A* 38(4): 733–48.

Fox, M. (2008) 'Get on the bus: Curitiba, Brazil rolls out a transit solution'. *Earth Island Journal*, Summer: 59–62.

Francis, M. (1987) 'Urban open spaces'. In: Zube, E. and Moore, G. (eds) *Advances in Environment, Behavior, and Design: Vol. 1*. New York, NY: Plenum, pp. 71–106.

— (1988) 'Changing values for public spaces'. *Landscape Architecture* (78)1: 54–9.

— and Lorenzo, R. (2006) 'Children and city design: proactive process and the renewal of childhood'. In: Spencer, C. and Blades, M. (eds) *Children and Their Environments*. Cambridge: Cambridge University Press.

Franck, K., and Stevens, Q. (2007) *Loose Space: Possibility and diversity in urban life*. London: Routledge.

Frank, R. (1999) 'Market failures'. *Boston Review*, Summer.

Frey, B. S., and Stutzer, A. (2002) 'What can economists learn from happiness research?' *Journal of Economic Literature* 40(2): 402–35.

Friends of the Earth (2011) 'Is a just transition possible within safe global carbon limits?' Draft paper for the Joseph Rowntree Foundation.

Gemzøe, L. (2001) 'Are pedestrians invisible in the planning process? Copenhagen as a case study'. Presentation at the Australia: Walking the 21st Century conference, Perth, Australia, 20–22 February.

Gibb, N., and Wittman, H. (2012) 'Parallel alternatives: Chinese-Canadian farmers and the Metro Vancouver local food movement'. *Local Environment: The International Journal of Justice and Sustainability*, DOI:10.1080/13549839.2012.714763.

Gibson, K. (2007) 'Bleeding Albina: a history of community disinvestment 1940–2000'. *Transforming Anthropology* 15(1): 3–25.

Gladwell, M. (2000) *The Tipping Point: How little things can make a big difference*. New York, NY: Little, Brown and Company.

— (2011) 'Does Egypt need Twitter' *The New Yorker*, News Desk blog. Available at: www.newyorker.com/online/blogs/newsdesk/2011/02/does-egypt-need-twitter.html [Accessed 28 November 2012]

Global Footprint Network (2011) *Annual Report: What happens when an infinite growth economy runs into a finite planet?* Oakland, CA: Global Footprint Network.

Gobster, P. (1998) 'Urban parks as green

walls or green magnets?' *Landscape and Urban Planning* 41(1): 43–55.
— (2002) 'Managing urban parks for a racially and ethnically diverse clientele'. *Leisure Sciences* 24: 143–59.
Godfray, H. C. J., Beddington, J. R., Crute, I. R., Haddad, L., et al. (2010) 'Food security: the challenge of feeding 9 billion people'. *Science* 327(5967): 812–18.
Goodyear, S. (2011) 'The streets and squares of Cairo should belong to its people.' *Placemaking* blog. Available at: www.pps.org/blog/the-streets-and-squares-of-cairo-should-belong-to-its-people [Accessed 28 November 201]
Goonewardena, K., Rankin, K., and Weinstock, S. (2004) 'Diversity and planning education: a Canadian perspective'. *Canadian Journal of Urban Research* 13(1): 1–26.
Gordon-Larsen, P., Nelson, M. C., Page, P., and Popkin, B. M. (2006) 'Inequality in the built environment underlies key health disparities in physical activity and obesity'. *Pediatrics* 117(2): 417–24.
Gottlieb, R., and Fisher, A. (1995) *Community Food Security: Policies for a more sustainable food system in the context of the 1995 Farm Bill and beyond*. Working Paper No. 13. Los Angeles, CA: The Ralph and Goldy Lewis Center for Regional Policy Studies, UCLA School of Public Affairs.
— (1998) 'Community food security and environmental justice: converging paths toward social justice and sustainable communities'. *Community Food Security News*, Summer: 4–5.
Gould, G. (1984) 'Streisand as Schwarzkopf'. In: Page, T. (ed.) *The Glenn Gould Reader*. New York: Vintage, pp. 308–11.
Grassov, L. M. (2008) 'There's more to walking than walking: design for Copenhagen's pedestrian realm'. Presentation at Global Green Lecture Series, 'Urban Design for Walkable, Bikable Cities'. Seattle, Washington, Fall 2008.
Grazuleviciute-Vileniske, I., and Matijosaitiene, I. (2010) 'Cultural heritage of roads and road landscapes: classification and insights on valuation'. *Landscape Research* 35(4): 391–413.
Growing Power, Inc. (n.d.). See www.growingpower.org [Accessed 28 November 2012]
Gunder, M. (2006) 'Sustainability: planning's saving grace or road to perdition?' *Journal of Planning Education and Research* 26(2): 208–21.
Guthman, J. (2008a) 'Bringing good food to others: investigating the subjects of alternative food practice'. *Cultural Geographies* 15(4): 431–47.
— (2008b) '"If they only knew": color blindness and universalism in California alternative food institutions'. *The Professional Geographer* 60(3): 387–97.
— (2008c) 'Neoliberalism and the making of food politics in California'. *Geoforum* 39(3): 1171–83.
Gutierrez, L., and Lewis, E. (1997) 'Education, participation, and capacity building in community organizing with women of color'. In: Minkler, M. (ed.) *Community Organizing and Community Building for Health*. New Brunswick, NJ: Rutgers University Press.
Habermas, J. (1989) *The Structural Transformation of the Public Sphere: An inquiry into a category*. Trans. Burger, T., with Lawrence, F. Cambridge, MA: MIT Press.
Haller, M., and Hadler, M. (2006) 'How social relations and structures can produce happiness and unhappiness: an international comparative analysis'. *Social Indicators Research* 75(2): 169–216.

Hamilton, N. D. (2002) 'Putting a face on our food: how state and local food policies can promote the new agriculture'. *Drake Journal of Agricultural Law* 7(2): 408–54.

Handy, S., and McCann, B. (2010) 'The regional response to federal funding for bicycle and pedestrian projects'. *Journal of the American Planning Association* 77(1): 23–38.

Hansen, J., Sato, M., Kharecha, P., Beerling, D., et al. (2008) 'Target atmospheric CO2: Where should humanity aim?' *Open Atmospheric Science Journal* 2: 217–31.

Harper, A., Shattuck, A., Holt-Giménez, E., Alkon, A., and Lambrick, F. (2009) *Food Policy Councils: Lessons learned*. Oakland, CA: Food First/Institute for Food and Development Policy.

Harris, E. (2009) 'Neoliberal subjectivities or a politics of the possible? Reading for difference in alternative food networks'. *Area* 41(1): 55–63.

Harris, K. (2007) *Growing the Community Food Movement: From the ground up. A community food systems primer*. Fayetteville, AR: Southern Sustainable Agriculture Working Group.

Harris, P. B., and Houston, J. M. (2010) 'Recklessness in context: individual and situational correlates to aggressive driving'. *Environment and Behavior* 42(1): 44–60.

Hart, J. (2008) 'Driven to excess: impacts of motor vehicle traffic on residential quality of life in Bristol, UK'. MSc dissertation in transport planning. Bristol: University of the West of England.

Harvey, D. (2008) 'The right to the city'. *New Left Review* 53(Sep–Oct): 23–40.

— (2011) *The Enigma of Capital and the Crises of Capitalism*. Revised edition. London: Profile.

Harwood, S. A. (2005) 'Struggling to embrace difference in land-use decision making in multi-cultural communities'. *Planning, Practice and Research* 20(4): 355–71.

Hassanein, N. (2003) 'Practicing food democracy: a pragmatic politics of transformation'. *Journal of Rural Studies* 19(1): 77–86.

Hawkes, A., and Sheridan, G. (2011) 'Rethinking the streetspace: what's next?' *Planetizen*. Available at: www.planetizen.com/node/50519 [Accessed 28 November 2012]

Hayden, D. (2005) 'What would a non-sexist city be like?: speculations on housing, urban design, and human work'. In: Fainstein, S. S., and Servon, L. J. (eds) *Gender and Planning: A reader*. Piscataway, NJ: Rutgers University Press, pp. 47–66.

Health Trust (n.d.) 'Active living by design: low income populations and physical activity'. Available at: www.healthtrust.org/pdf/PhysicalActivityforLowIncomePopulations-TheHealthTrust.pdf [Accessed 28 November 2012]

Henderson, J. (2006) 'Secessionist automobility: racism, anti-urbanism, and the politics of automobility in Atlanta, Georgia'. *International Journal of Urban and Regional Research* 30(2): 293–307.

Hertz, N. (2009) 'Goodbye Gucci. It's the age of co-op capitalism'. *The Times*, 25 February. Available at: www.timesonline.co.uk/tol/comment/columnists/guest_contributors/article5798645.ece

Hess, P. (2009) 'Avenues or arterials: the struggle to change street building practices in Toronto, Canada'. *Journal of Urban Design* 14(1): 1–28.

Hester, R. T. (1984) *Planning Neighborhood Space with People*. 2nd edition. New York, NY: Van Nostrand Reinhold Company.

Hille, J. (1997) *The Concept of Environmental Space: Implications for policies, environmental reporting and assessments*. Copenhagen: European Environment Agency. Available at: www.eea.europa.eu/publications/92-9167-078-2 [Accessed 28 November 2012]

Hinrichs, C. C. (2003) 'The practice and politics of food system localization'. *Journal of Rural Studies* 19(1): 33–46.

— and Allen, P. (2008) 'Selective patronage and social justice: local food consumer campaigns in historical context'. *Journal of Agricultural and Environmental Ethics* 21(4): 329–52.

Holt, D. B. (1999) 'Postmodern markets'. *Boston Review*, Summer.

Holt-Giménez, E. (2009) 'From food crisis to food sovereignty: the challenge of social movements'. *Monthly Review* 61(3): July–August. Available at: www.foodfirst.org/en/node/2505 [Accessed 28 November 2012]

— (2011) 'Food security, food justice, or food sovereignty?: Crises, food movements and regime change'. In: Alkon, A., and Agyeman, J. (eds) *Cultivating Food Justice: Race, class and sustainability*. Cambridge, MA: MIT Press.

Hou, J. (2010) *Insurgent Public Space: Guerilla urbanism and the remaking of contemporary cities*. New York, NY: Routledge.

Howe, E., and Kaufman, J. (1981) 'The values of contemporary American planners'. *Journal of the American Planning Association* 47(3): 266–78.

Hunt, S. (2009) 'Citizenship's place: the state's creation of public space and street vendors' culture of informality in Bogotá, Colombia'. *Environment and Planning D: Society and Space* 27(2): 331–51.

Hunter College (2011) *Beyond the Backlash: Equity and participation in bicycle planning*. New York, NY: Hunter College. Available at: www.streetsblog.org/wp-content/uploads/2011/05/BeyondBacklash 2011.pdf [Accessed 30 November 2012]

Illich, I. (2000) '"The Oakland Table" conversations between Ivan Illich and friends'. Notes by Debbie Moore. 2 September.

Ingram, P., and Nyangara, F. (1997) 'Recruitment, retention, and participation of underrepresented groups on Pennsylvania Cooperative Extension Advisory Boards and Committees'. *Journal of Agricultural Education* 38(4): 21–9.

Institute for Research and Urban Planning of Curitiba (2009) *The City of Curitiba: Planning for Sustainability: An approach all cities can afford*. Curitiba, Brazil: City of Curitiba.

International Assessment of Agricultural Knowledge, Science and Technology for Development (2009). *Agriculture at a Crossroads: Global report*. Washington, DC: Island Press.

ITDP (2011) *Our Cities Ourselves*. New York, NY: Institute for Transportation and Development Policy (ITDP). Available at: www.itdp.org/documents/2010-OurCitiesOurselves_Booklet.pdf [Accessed 28 November 2012]

Iveson, K. (1998) 'Putting the public back in public space'. *Urban Policy and Research* 16(1): 21–33.

Jackson, T. (2009) *Prosperity without Growth? The transition to a sustainable economy*. London: Sustainable Development Commission.

— Marks, N., Ralls, J., and Stymne, S. (1997) *An Index of Sustainable Economic Welfare for the UK 1950–1996*. Guildford: Centre for Environmental Strategy, University of Surrey.

Jacobs, J. (1958) 'Downtown is for people'. *Fortune*, April.

— (1961) *The Death and Life of Great American Cities*. New York: Random House.

Jacobs, M. (1999) 'Sustainable

development: a contested concept'. In: Dobson, A. (ed.) *Fairness and Futurity: Essays on environmental sustainability and social justice*. Oxford: Oxford University Press.

Jaffee, D., Kloppenburg Jr., J. R., and Monroy, M. B. (2004) 'Bringing the "moral charge" home: Fair trade within the North and within the South'. *Rural Sociology* 69(2): 169–96.

Jarosz, L. (2008) 'The city in the country: growing alternative food networks in Metropolitan areas'. *Journal of Rural Studies* 24(3): 231–44.

Johnston, B. D. (2008) 'Planning for child pedestrians: issues of health, safety and social justice'. *Journal of Urban Design* 13(1): 141–5.

Jones, T., and Edwards, S. (2009) *The Climate Debt Crisis: Why paying our dues is essential for tackling climate change*. London: World Development Movement. Available at: www.wdm.org.uk/sites/default/files/climatedebtcrisis06112009_0.pdf [Accessed 28 November 2012]

Just Food (2010) Food Justice. See www.justfood.org/food-justice [Accessed 28 November 2012]

Kane, P. (2011a) 'Radical Animal: innovation, sustainability and human nature'. Available at: http://radicalanimal.ning.com/profiles/blogs/radical-animal-the-general [Accessed 28 November 2012]

— (2011b) 'English riots, Scottish stupor and the consumptive young'. Available at: www.thoughtland.info/2011/08/calmerc-englishriots.html www.thoughtland.info/2011/08/calmerc-englishriots.html

Kawachi, I., Daniels, N., and Robinson, D. E. (2005) 'Health disparities by race and class: why both matter'. *Health Affairs* 24(2): 343–52.

Kayden, J. (2011) 'Meet me at the Plaza'. *The New York Times*, opinion pages, 19 October. Available at: www.nytimes.com/2011/10/20/opinion/zuccotti-park-and-the-private-plaza-problem.html?scp=1&sq=Jerold%20S.%20Kayden&st=cse [Accessed 28 November 2012]

Kennedy, C. A. (2002). 'A comparison of the sustainability of public and private transportation systems: study of the Greater Toronto Area'. *Transportation* 29(4): 459–93.

Kent, F. (2008) 'Place making around the world'. *Urban Land*, August: 58–65.

Kidder, J. (2005) 'Style and action: a decoding of bike messenger symbols'. *Journal of Contemporary Ethnography* 34(3): 344–67.

Kimmelman, M. (2011) 'In protest, the power of place'. *The New York Times*, opinion pages, 15 October. Available at: www.nytimes.com/2011/10/16/sunday-review/wall-street-protest-shows-power-of-place.html?scp=4&sq=Occupy%20 Wall%20Street%20+%20Public%20 Spaces&st=cse [Accessed 28 November 2012]

— (2012) 'Past its golden moment, Bogotá clings to hope.' *The New York Times*, 5 July. Available at: www.nytimes.com/2012/07/08/arts/design/bogota-with-pockets-of-hope-in-recent-architecture.html?_r=1&pagewanted=alljammed [Accessed 28 November 2012]

Kingsolver, B. (2007) *Animal, Vegetable, Miracle: A year of food life*. New York, NY: Harper Perennial.

Klein, N. (2007) *The Shock Doctrine*. London: Penguin.

Kloppenburg, J. and Hassanein, N. (2006) 'From old school to reform school?' *Agriculture and Human Values* 23(4): 417–21.

Klugman, J. (2010) *Human Development Report 2010: 20th anniversary edition. The Real Wealth of Nations: Pathways to human development*. New York, NY: United Nations Development Programme (UNDP).

Kodransky, M., and Hermann, G. (2011). *Europe's Parking U-Turn: From accommodation to regulation*. New York, NY: Institute for Transportation and Development Policy (ITDP). Available at: www.itdp.org/library/publications/ european-parking-u-turn-from-accommodation-to-regulation [Accessed 28 November 2012]

Kravets, D. (2011) 'What's fueling Mideast protests? It's more than Twitter'. *Wired Politics* blog. Available at: www.wired.co.uk/news/archive/2011-01/28/middle-east-protests-twitter [Accessed 28 November 2012]

Krimsky, S., and Sloan, K. (eds) (2011) *Race and the Genetic Revolution: Science, myth and culture*. New York, NY: Columbia University Press.

Krishnarayan, V., and Thomas, H. (1993) *Ethnic Minorities and the Planning System*. London: Royal Town Planning Institute.

Krumholz, N. (1982) 'A retrospective view of equity planning: Cleveland, 1969–1979'. *Journal of the American Planning Association* 48(2): 163–83.

Kumar, S., and Martin, G. (2004) 'A case for culturally responsive urban design'. *Ontario Planning Journal* 19(5): 5–7.

Kuzio, T. (2002) 'National identity and democratic transition in post-soviet Ukraine and Belarus: a theoretical and comparative perspective'. *East European Perspectives* 4(15).

Lammy, D. (2004) 'Spatial justice and the inner city: a key component of Labour's third term narrative?' Available at: www.davidlammy.co.uk/da/21598 [Accessed 28 November 2012]

Lamont, M., and Molnár, V. (1999). Too much economics'. *Boston Review*, Summer. Available at: http://bostonreview.net/BR24.3/lamont.html [Accessed 28 November 2012]

— (2001) 'How blacks use consumption to shape their collective identity: evidence from African-American marketing specialists'. *Journal of Consumer Culture* 1(1): 31–45.

Lanfer, A. G., and Taylor, M. (2005) *Immigrant Engagement in Public Open Space: Strategies for the new Boston*. Boston, MA: Barr Foundation.

Larrain S., Leroy, J. P., and Nansen, K. (eds) (2002) *Citizen Contribution to the Construction of Sustainable Societies*. Berlin: Heinrich Böll Foundation.

Lee, J. (2002) 'Visioning diversity: planning Vancouver's multicultural communities'. MA thesis. Waterloo, ON, Canada: University of Waterloo.

Lee, M. (2011) *Fair and Effective Carbon Pricing: Lessons from BC*. Vancouver: Canadian Centre for Policy Alternatives.

— and Carlaw, K. (2010) *Climate Justice, Green Jobs and Sustainable Production in BC*. Vancouver: Canadian Centre for Policy Alternatives.

Leigh, J. (1998) *Communicating for Cultural Competency*. Long Grove, IL: Waveland Press.

Leinberger, C. (2012) 'Now coveted: a walkable, convenient place'. *The New York Times*, 25 May. Available at: www.nytimes.com/2012/05/27/opinion/sunday/now-coveted-a-walkable-convenient-place.html?_r=1 [Accessed 28 November 2012]

Lepeska, D. (2011) 'City bike plan is accused of a neighborhood bias'. *The New York Times*, 15 October. Available at: www.nytimes.com/2011/10/16/us/chicago-bike-plan-accused-of-neighborhood-bias.html?_r=1&scp=1&sq=chicago%20bicycle&st=cse [Accessed 28 November 2012]

Leyden, K. M. (2003) 'Social capital and the built environment: the importance of walkable neighborhoods'.

American Journal of Public Health 93(9): 1546–51.

— Goldberg, A., and Michelbach, P. (2011) 'Understanding the pursuit of happiness in ten major cities'. *Urban Affairs Review* 47(6): 861–88.

Linn, A. (2010) 'Carmakers' next problem: generation Y'. NBCnews.com. Available at: www.msnbc.msn.com/id/39970363/ns/business-autos/t/carmakers-next-problem-generation-y/#.T57c-ByCjap [Accessed 30 November 2012]

Litman, T. (2012) *The Future Isn't What It Used to Be: Changing trends and their implications for transport planning*. Victoria, BC, Canada: Victoria Transport Policy Institute.

Loh, P., and Eng, P. (eds) (2010). *Environmental Justice and the Green Economy: A vision statement and case studies for just and sustainable solutions*. Roxbury, MA: Alternatives for Community and Environment.

Looye, J., and Sesay, A. (1998) 'Introducing diversity into planning curriculum: a method for department-wide implementation'. *Journal of Planning Education and Research* 18(2): 161–70.

Loukaitou-Sideris, A. (1995) 'Urban form and social context: cultural differentiation in the uses of urban parks'. *Journal of Planning Education and Research* 14(2): 89–102.

— (2003) 'Children's common grounds: a study of intergroup relations among children in public settings'. *Journal of the American Planning Association* 69(2): 130–43.

— and Ehrenfeucht, R. (2009) *Sidewalks: Conflict and negotiation over public space*. Cambridge, MA: MIT Press.

Low, S. (1997) 'Urban public spaces as representations of culture: the plaza in Costa Rica'. *Environment and Behavior* 29(1): 3–33.

— (2006) 'How private interests take over public space'. In: Low, S., and Smith, N. (eds) *The Politics of the Public Sphere*. London: Routledge, pp. 81–103.

— and Smith, N. (2006) (eds) *The Politics of the Public Sphere*. London: Routledge.

— Taplin, D., and Scheld, S. (2005). *Rethinking Urban Parks: Public space and cultural diversity*. Austin, TX: University of Texas Press.

Lownsbrough, H., and Beunderman, J. (2007) *Equally Spaced? Public space and interaction between diverse communities*. London: Commission for Racial Equality.

Lynch, K. (1955) 'A new look at civic design'. *Journal of Architectural Education* 10(1): 31–3.

Macdonald, E. (2008) 'The efficacy of long-range physical planning: the case of Vancouver'. *Journal of Planning History* 7(3): 175–213.

Madanipour, A. (1996) *Design of Urban Space: An inquiry into a socio-spatial process*. New York, NY: John Wiley and Sons.

— (ed.) (2010) *International Case Studies in Urban Design and Development*. London: Routledge.

Mainwaring, S. (2011) 'The new power of consumers to influence brands'. *Forbes*. Available at: www.forbes.com/sites/simonmainwaring/2011/09/07/the-new-power-of-consumers-to-influence-brands/ [Accessed 28 November 2012]

Makworo, M., and Mireri, C. (2011) 'Public open spaces in Nairobi City, Kenya, under threat'. *Journal of Environmental Planning and Management* 54(8): 1107–23.

Malone, K. (2002) 'Street life: youth, culture and competing uses of public space'. *Environment and Urbanization* 14(2): 157–68.

Mares, T., and Peña, D. (2011) 'Environmental and food justice: toward local, slow and deep food systems'. In: Alkon, A., and Agyeman, J. (eds) *Cultivating Food Justice. Race, class and sustainability*. Cambridge, MA: MIT Press, pp. 197–219.

Maruani, T., and Amit-Cohen, I. (2007) 'Open space planning models: a review of approaches and methods'. *Landscape and Urban Planning* 81(1–2): 1–13.

Maslow, A. H. (1954) *Motivation and Personality*. New York, NY: Harper and Row.

Massachusetts Farm to School Project (n.d.) See www.massfarmtoschool.org [Accessed 30 November 2012]

Massey, D. (1995a) *Space, Place and Gender*. Minneapolis, MN: University of Minnesota Press.

— (1995b) 'Places and their pasts'. *History Workshop Journal* 39(1): 182–92.

Max-Neef, M. A. (1991) *Human Scale Development: Conception, application and further reflections*. New York, NY: Apex.

— (1992) 'Development and human needs'. In: Ekins, P., and Max-Neef, M. A. (eds) *Real-Life Economics: Understanding wealth creation*. London: Routledge, pp. 197–213.

McCann, B. (2011) 'Complete streets and sustainability'. *Environmental Practice* 13(1): 63–4.

McClintock, N. (2011) 'From industrial garden to food desert'. In: Alkon, A., and Agyeman, J. (eds) *Cultivating Food Justice: Race, class and sustainability*. Cambridge, MA: MIT Press, pp. 89–120.

McDowell, L. (1993) 'Space, place and gender relations: part I. Feminist empiricism and the geography of social relations'. *Progress in Human Geography* 17(2): 157–79.

McEntee, J. (2011) 'Realizing rural food justice: divergent locals in the Northeastern United States'. In: Alkon, A., and Agyeman, J. (eds) *Cultivating Food Justice: Race, class and sustainability*. Cambridge, MA: MIT Press.

McIntosh, A. (2008) *Hell and High Water: Climate change, hope and the human condition*. Edinburgh: Birlinn.

McLaren, D. P. (2003) 'Environmental space, equity and the ecological debt'. In: Agyeman, J., Bullard, R. D., and Evans, B. (eds) *Just Sustainabilities: Development in an unequal world*. London: Earthscan, pp. 19–37.

— (2004) 'Global stakeholders, corporate accountability and investor engagement.' *Corporate Governance: An International Review* 12(2): 191–201.

— (2011a) 'Delivering transformation: a challenge to Friends of the Earth Europe'. Unpublished, internal paper, provided by FOEE and the author.

— (2011b) *Negatonnes: An initial assessment of the potential for negative emission techniques to contribute safely and fairly to meeting carbon budgets in the 21st century*. London: Friends of the Earth. Available at: www.foe.co.uk/resource/reports/negatonnes.pdf [Accessed 28 November 2012]

— Bullock, S., and Yousuf, N. (1998) *Tomorrow's World: Britain's share in a sustainable future*. London: Earthscan.

McManus, R. (2006) 'Imagine a city with 30 percent fewer cars'. *Sierra*, January/February: 48–9.

Meadows, D. H., Meadows, D. L., Randers, J., and Behrens, W. W. (1972) *The Limits to Growth*. London: Macmillan.

Medoff, P., and Sklar, H. (1994) *Streets of Hope: The fall and rise of an urban neighborhood*. Boston, MA: South End Press.

Merker, B. (2010) 'Taking place: Rebar's absurd tactics in generous urbanism'. In: Hou, J. (ed.) *Insurgent Public Space: Guerilla urbanism and the remaking of contemporary cities*. New York, NY: Routledge, pp. 47–57.

Metzger, J. (1996) 'The theory and practice of equity planning: an annotated bibliography'. *Journal of Planning Literature* 11(1): 112–26.

Meyer, A. (2000) *Contraction and Convergence: The global solution to climate change*. Schumacher Briefing 5. London: Green Books.

Michialino, P. (2010) 'Co-production of public space in Nord-Pas-de-Calais: redefinition of social meaning'. In: Madanipour, A. (ed.) *Whose Public Space?: International case studies in urban design and development*. Abingdon: Routledge, pp. 212–36.

Milroy, B. M. (2004) 'Diversity and difference: a comment'. *Canadian Journal of Urban Research* 13(1): 46–9.

Minton, A. (2006) *The Privatisation of Public Space*. London: Royal Institution of Chartered Surveyors.

Mirk, S. (2012) 'It's not about the bikes'. *Portland* Mercury, 16 February. Available at: www.portlandmercury.com/portland/its-not-about-the-bikes/Content?oid=5619639 [Accessed 30 November 2012]

Mitchell, D. (1995). 'The end of public space? People's park, definitions of the public, and democracy'. *Annals of the Association of American Geographers* 85(1): 108–33.

— (2003) *The Right to the City: Social justice and the fight for public space*. New York, NY: Guilford Press.

Mohan, D., and Tiwari, G. (1999) 'Sustainable transport systems: linkages between environmental issues, public transport, non-motorised transport and safety'. *Economic and Political Weekly* 34(25): 1589–96.

Mohl, R. A. (2004) 'Stop the road: freeway revolts in American cities'. *Journal of Urban History* 30(5): 674–706.

Montezuma, R. (2005) 'The transformation of Bogota, Columbia, 1995–2000: investing in citizenship and urban mobility'. *Global Urban Development* 1(1).

Montgomery, C. (2007) 'Bogota's urban happiness movement'. *Globe and Mail*, 25 June. Available at: www.theglobeandmail.com/life/bogotas-urban-happiness-movement/article1087786/?page=all [Accessed 30 November 2012]

Moore Lappé, F. (2009) 'The City that ended hunger'. *YES! Magazine*. Available at: www.yesmagazine.org/issues/food-for-everyone/the-city-that-ended-hunger [Accessed 30 November 2012]

Morabia, A., Mirer, F. E., Amstislavski, T. M., Eisl, H. M., et al. (2010) 'Potential health impact of switching from car to public transportation when commuting to work'. *American Journal of Public Health* 100(12): 2388–91.

Moseley, W. (2007) 'Farmers in developing world hurt by "eat local" philosophy in US'. *San Francisco Chronicle*, 18 November. Available at: www.sfgate.com/opinion/article/Farmers-in-developing-world-hurt-by-eat-local-3301224.php [Accessed 30 November 2012]

Nair, C. (2011) *Consumptionomics: Asia's role in reshaping capitalism and saving the planet*. Singapore: John Wiley and Sons Asia.

National Complete Streets Coalition (n.d.) 'Create livable communities'. Washington, DC: National Complete Streets Coalition. Available at: www.completestreets.org/complete-streets-fundamentals/factsheets/livable-communities [Accessed 30 November 2012]

National Public Radio (2011) 'Some U.S. farms trade tobacco for a taste of Africa' by April Fulton.

NEF (2008) *Co-production: A manifesto for growing the core economy*. London: New Economics Foundation (NEF).

New Entry Sustainable Farming Project (n.d.). See http://nesfp.nutrition.tufts.edu/index.html [Accessed 30 November 2012]

Newman, L., Waldron, L., Dale, A., and Carriere, K. (2008) 'Sustainable urban community development from the grassroots: challenges and opportunities in a pedestrian street initiative'. *Local Environment* 13(2): 129–39.

Newman, P., and Kenworthy, J. R. (1999) *Sustainability and Cities: Overcoming automobile dependence*. Washington, DC: Island Press.

Nussbaum, M. C. (2000) *Women and Human Development: The capabilities approach*. Cambridge: Cambridge University Press.

O'Brien, C. (2008) 'Sustainable happiness and the trip to school'. *World Transport Policy and Practice* 14(1): 15–23.

O'Connell, M. (2004) 'Fairly satisfied: economic equality, wealth and satisfaction'. *Journal of Economic Psychology* 25(3): 297–305.

Office of the Deputy Prime Minister (2004) *Safer Places: The planning system and crime prevention*. London: Office of the Deputy Prime Minister and Home Office.

Omi, M., and Winant, H. (1994) *Racial Formation in the United States: From the 1960s to the 1990s*. London: Routledge.

Opschoor, J. B., and Weterings, R. (1994) *Environmental Utilisation Space*. Amsterdam: Boom.

Ormerod, P. (1998) *Butterfly Economics: A new general theory of social and economic behaviour*. London: Faber and Faber.

Ostrom, E. (2009) 'Beyond markets and states: polycentric governance of complex economic systems'. Nobel Prize lecture, 8 December 2009. Available at: www.nobelprize.org/nobel_prizes/economics/laureates/2009/ostrom-lecture.html [Accessed 30 November 2012]

Paciones, M. (2001) 'The future of the city – cities of the future'. *Geography* 86(4): 275–86.

Parks and Recreation (2008) 'First person: in Bogotá, the people's politician'. *Parks and Recreation*, Summer: 69–71.

Passmore, S. (2011) 'The social life of public space in West Africa'. *Planning Pool* blog. Available at: http://planningpool.com/2011/02/land-use/african-public-space/ [Accessed 30 November 2012]

Patton, J. W. (2007) 'A pedestrian world: competing rationalities and the calculation of transportation change'. *Environment and Planning A* 39(4): 928–44.

Pearce, F. (2007) *The Last Generation: How nature will take her revenge for climate change*. London: Eden Project Books.

Pearsall, H., and Pierce, J. (2010) 'Urban sustainability and environmental justice: evaluating the linkages in public planning/policy discourse'. *Local Environment* 15(6): 569–80.

Peñalosa, E. (2009) 'Towards a more socially and environmentally sustainable city'. Presentation to MIT, 6 February 2009.

People's Grocery (n.d.). See www.peoplesgrocery.org [Accessed 30 November 2012]

Pestieau, K., and Wallace, M. (2003) 'Challenges and opportunities for planning in the ethno-culturally diverse city: a collection of papers – introduction'. *Planning Theory and Practice* 4(3): 253–8.

Pharaoh, T. M., and Russell, J. R. E. (1991) 'Traffic calming policy and performance: The Netherlands, Denmark and Germany'. *The Town Planning Review* 62(1): 79–105.

PolicyLink (2011) *Why Place and Race Matter*. Oakland, CA: PolicyLink.

Pollan, M. (2006) *The Omnivore's Dilemma: A natural history of four meals*. New York, NY: Penguin.

Pothukuchi, K., Joseph, H., Burton, H., and Fisher, A. (2002) *What's Cooking in Your Food System? A guide to community food assessment*. Los Angeles, CA: Community Food Security Coalition.

Prentice, J. (2007) 'The birth of locavore'. *Oxford University Press* blog. Available at: http:// blog.oup.com/2007/11/prentice/ [Accessed 30 November 2012]

Preston, P. (2011) 'Blacks want in on discussion over city's bike proposal'. *Northeast Portland Katu*. Available at: http://northeastportland.katu.com/news/news/blacks-want-discussion-over-citys-bike-proposal/442221 [Accessed 30 November 2012]

Project for Public Spaces (n.d.) 'Houston is North America's placemaking capital'. Available at: www.pps.org/reference/houston-is-north-americas-placemaking-capital/ [Accessed 30 November 2012]

Pucher, J., and Renne, J. L. (2003) 'Socioeconomics of urban travel: evidence from the 2001 NHTS'. *Transportation Quarterly* 57(3): 49–77.

Pucher, J., Buehler, R., Bassett, D. R., and Dannenberg, A. L. (2010) 'Walking and cycling to health: a comparative analysis of city, state, and international data'. *American Journal of Public Health* 100(10): 1986–92.

Putnam, R. D. (2000) *Bowling Alone: The collapse and revival of American community*. New York, NY: Simon & Schuster.

Qadeer, M. (1997) 'Pluralistic planning for multi-cultural cities: the Canadian practice'. *Journal of the American Planning Association* 63(4): 481–94.

Rabinovitch, J. (1996) 'Innovative land use and public transport policy: the case of Curitiba, Brazil'. *Land Use Policy* 13(1): 51–67.

— and Leitman, J. (1996) 'Urban planning in Curitiba'. *Scientific American*, March: 46–53.

Rae, D. W. (2001) 'Viacratic America: Plessy on foot v. Brown on wheels'. *Annual Review of Political Science* 4: 417–38.

Rahder, B., and Milgrom, R. (2004) 'The uncertain city: making space(s) for difference'. *Canadian Journal of Urban Research* 13(1): 27–45.

Rawls, J. (1971) *A Theory of Justice*. Cambridge, MA: Harvard University Press.

Raworth, K. (2012) *A Safe and Just Operating Space for Humanity: Can we live within the doughnut?* Oxfam Discussion Papers. Oxford: Oxfam.

Reijnders, L. (1998) 'The factor X debate: setting targets for eco-efficiency'. *Journal of Industrial Ecology* 2(1): 13–22.

Ridley, M. (1996) *The Origins of Virtue*. London: Viking.

Rifkin, J. (1995) *The End of Work: The decline of the global labor force and the dawn of the post-market era*. New York, NY: Tarcher-Putnam.

— (2010) *The Empathic Civilization: The race to global consciousness in a world in crisis*. New York, NY: Tarcher.

Rishbeth, C. (2001) 'Ethnic minority groups and the design of public open space: an inclusive landscape?' *Landscape Research* 26(4): 351–66.

Roberts, P. (2003) 'Sustainable development and social justice: spatial priorities and mechanisms for delivery'. *Sociological Inquiry* 73(2): 228–44.

Roberts, W. (2010) 'Food policy encounters of a third kind: how the Toronto Food Policy Council socializes for sustain-ability'. In: Blay-Palmer, A. (ed.) *Imagining Sustainable Food Systems*. Farnham: Ashgate.

Robertson, K. A. (1993). 'Pedestrians and

the American downtown'. *The Town Planning Review* 64(3): 273–86.

Rockström, J., Steffen, W., Noone, K., Persson, Å., et al. (2009a) 'Planetary boundaries: exploring the safe operating space for humanity'. *Ecology and Society* 14(2): 1–33.

— et al. (2009b) 'A safe operating space for humanity'. *Nature* 461: 472–5.

Rogers, R. (2005) *Towards a Strong Urban Renaissance*. London: Urban Task Force.

Rogers, S. H., Halstead, J. M., Gardner, K. H., and Carlson, C. H. (2011) 'Examining walkability and social capital as indicators of quality of life at the municipal and neighborhood scales'. *Applied Research in Quality of Life* 6(2): 201–13.

Rose, C. (2010) *How to Win Campaigns: Communications for change*. London: Earthscan.

Rosenthal, A. (2000) 'Spectacle, fear, and protest: a guide to the history of urban public space in Latin America'. *Social Science History* 24(1): 33–73.

Rosenzweig, R., and Blackmar, E. (1992) *The Park and the People*. Ithaca, NY: Cornell University Press.

Rowden, P., Matthews, G., Watson, B., and Biggs, H. (2011) 'The relative impact of work-related stress, life stress and driving environment stress on driving outcomes'. *Accident Analysis and Prevention* 43(4): 1332–40.

Ruggie, J. (2010) 'Report of the Special Representative of the Secretary-General on the issue of human rights and transnational corporations and other business enterprises'. Agenda item 3. United Nations General Assembly Human Rights Council, fourteenth session, 9 April.

— (2011) 'Guiding principles on business and human rights: implementing the United Nations "Protect, Respect and Remedy" framework'. Agenda item 3. United Nations Human Rights Council, seventeenth session, 21 March. Available at: www.business-humanrights.org/media/documents/ruggie/ruggie-guiding-principles-21-mar-2011.pdf [Accessed 30 November 2012]

Rydin, Y., Bleahu, A., Davies, M., Dávila, J. D., et al. (2012) 'Shaping cities for health: complexity and the planning of urban environments in the 21st century'. *Lancet* 379(9831): 2079–108.

Sachs, A. (1995) *Eco-Justice: Linking human rights and the environment*. Worldwatch Paper 127. Washington, DC: Worldwatch Institute.

Saldivar-Tanaka, L., and Krasny, M. E. (2004) 'Culturing community development, neighborhood open space, and civic agriculture: the case of Latino community gardens in New York City'. *Agriculture and Human Values* 21(4): 399–412.

Sanchez, J. (2010) 'An assessment and analysis of issues and patterns associated with the utilization of open spaces by Latino immigrants in an urban neighborhood in Boston'. Unpublished MA thesis. Medford, MA: Department of Urban and Environmental Policy and Planning, Tufts University.

Sandercock, L. (1998) *Towards Cosmopolis: Planning for multi-cultural cities*. Chichester: John Wiley and Sons.

— (2000) 'When strangers become neighbors: managing cities of difference'. *Journal of Planning Theory and Practice* 1(1): 13–20.

— (2003) *Cosmopolis II: Mongrel cities of the 21st century*. London: Continuum.

— and Forsyth, A. (2005) 'A gender agenda: new directions in planning theory'. In: Fainstein, S. S., and Servon, L. J. (eds) *Gender and Planning: A reader*. Piscataway, NJ: Rutgers University Press, pp. 67–85.

Sarkar, S. (2011) *The Crises of Capitalism:*

A different study of political economy. Available at: www.oekosozialismus.net/The+Crises+of+Capitalism.+Saral+Sarkar.+2011.pdf [Accessed 30 November 2012]

Sauter, D., and Huettenmoser, M. (2008) 'Livable streets and social inclusion'. *Urban Design International* 13: 67–79.

Schiff, R. (2007) 'Food policy councils: an examination of organizational structure, process, and contribution to alternative food movements'. Dissertation. Perth: Institution for Sustainability and Technology Policy, Murdoch University.

Schlosberg, D. (1999) *Environmental Justice and the New Pluralism: The challenge of difference for environmentalism*. Oxford: Oxford University Press.

— (2004) 'Reconceiving environmental justice: global movements and political theories'. *Environmental Politics* 13(3): 517–40.

— (2007) *Defining Environmental Justice: Theories, movements, and nature*. Oxford: Oxford University Press.

— and Carruthers, D. (2010) 'Indigenous struggles, environmental justice, and community capabilities'. *Global Environmental Politics* 10(4): 12–35.

Schor, J. (1999a) *The Overspent American: Why we want what we don't need*. New York, NY: Harper Perennial.

— (1999b) 'The new politics of consumption'. *Boston Review*, Summer.

— (2005) 'Sustainable consumption and worktime reduction'. *Journal of Industrial Ecology* 9(1–2): 37–50.

Schwartz, S. H. (2006) 'Les valeurs de base de la personne: théorie, mesures et applications'. [Basic human values: theory, measurement, and applications.] *Revue Française de Sociologie* 47: 929–68.

Schwieterman, J. P. (2011) 'The travel habits of Gen Y'. *Planning*, May/June: 30–3.

Sen, A. (1999) *Development as Freedom*. Oxford: Oxford University Press.

— (2009) *The Idea of Justice*. London: Allen Lane.

Sen, S. (2005) 'Diversity and North American planning curricula: the need for reform'. *Canadian Journal of Urban Research* 14(1): 121–44.

Sennett, R. (1970) *The Uses of Disorder*. New York, NY: Knopf.

— (1990) *The Conscience of the Eye: The design and social life of cities*. New York, NY: Knopf.

— (1994) *Flesh and Stone: The body and the city in Western civilization*. New York, NY: W. W. Norton.

Shaer, M. (2011) 'Not quite Copenhagen: is New York too New York for bike lanes?' *New York Magazine*, 20 March. Available at: http://nymag.com/news/features/bike-wars-2011-3/ [Accessed 30 November 2012]

Shaftoe, H. (2008) *Convivial Urban Spaces: Creating effective public places*. London: Earthscan.

Shareable (2011) 'Are bike lanes expressways to gentrification?' *Shareable: Cities*. Available at: http://shareable.net/blog/are-bike-lanes-an-express way-to-gentrification [Accessed 30 November 2012]

Sharp, J., Pollock, V., and Paddison, R. (2005). 'Just art for a just city: public art and social inclusion in urban regeneration'. *Urban Studies* 42(5/6): 1001–23.

Sherlock, H. (1991) *Cities Are Good for Us*. London: Paladin.

Shinew, K. J., Glover, T. D., and Parry, D. C. (2004) 'Leisure spaces as potential sites for interracial interaction: community gardens in urban areas'. *Journal of Leisure Research* 36(3): 336–55.

Shiva, V. (2002) 'The real reasons for hunger'. *Observer*, 23 June. Available at: www.guardian.co.uk/

world/2002/jun/23/1 [Accessed 30 November 2012]

Shrivastava, P. (2006) 'Sustainable transportation strategies: China'. *Greener Management International* 50: 53–63.

Sinnett, D., Williams, K., Chatterjee, K., and Cavill, N. (2011) *Making the Case for Investment in the Walking Environment: A review of the evidence*. London: Living Streets. Available at: www.livingstreets.org.uk [Accessed 30 November 2012]

Skinner, R. (2004) 'City profile Bogotá'. *Cities* 21(1): 73–81.

Slocum, R. (2006a) 'Whiteness, space and alternative food practice'. *Geoforum* 38(3): 520–33.

— (2006b) 'Anti-racist practice and the work of community food organizations'. *Antipode* 38(2): 327–49.

Smith, A. D. (1981) *The Ethnic Revival in the Modern World*. Cambridge: Cambridge University Press.

Sofoulis, Z., Armstrong, H., Bounds, M., Lopes, A., and Andrews, T. (2008) *Out and About in Penrith: Universal Design and cultural context: Accessibility, diversity and recreational space in Penrith*. Sydney: University of Western Sydney, Centre for Cultural Research.

Sorkin, M. (1992) *Variations on a Theme Park: The new American city and the end of public space*. New York, NY: Hill and Wang.

Southworth, M., and Ben-Joseph, E. (1995) 'Street standards and the shaping of suburbia'. *Journal of the American Planning Association* 61(1): 65–81.

Spangenberg, J. et al. (1995) *Towards Sustainable Europe*. Brussels: Friends of the Earth Europe.

Stamps, S. M., and Stamps, M. B. (1985) 'Race, class, and leisure activities of urban residents'. *Journal of Leisure Research* 17(1): 40–56.

Steinbach, R., Green, J., Datta, J., and Edwards, P. (2011) 'Cycling and the city: a case study of how gendered, ethnic and class identities can shape healthy transport choices'. *Social Science Medicine* 72(7): 1123–30.

Steinberg, F. (2005) 'Strategic urban planning in Latin America: experiences of building and managing the future'. *Habitat International* 29(1): 69–93.

Stiglitz, J. E. (2002) *The Roaring Nineties: Seeds of destruction*. London: Allen Lane.

— Sen, A., and Fitoussi, J. P. (2011) *Report by the Commission on the Measurement of Economic Performance and Social Progress*. Available at: www.stiglitz-sen-fitoussi.fr/documents/rapport_anglais.pdf [Accessed 30 November 2012]

Stoks, F. (1983) 'Assessing urban environments for danger of violent crime: especially rape'. In: Joiner, D., Brimilcombe, G., Daish, J., Gray, J., and Kernohan, D. (eds) *Proceedings of the Conference on People and Physical Environment Research*. Wellington, New Zealand: Ministry of Works and Development.

Street Plans Collaborative (n.d.) 'Tactical urbansim'. Available at: www.scribd.com/doc/51354266/Tactical-Urbanism-Volume-1 [Accessed 30 November 2012]

Sweet, E., and Etienne, H. (2011) 'Commentary: diversity in urban planning education and practice'. *Journal of Planning Education and Research* 31(3): 332–9.

Taleb, N. N. (2007) *The Black Swan: The impact of the highly improbable*. London: Penguin.

Talen, E. (2008) *Design for Diversity: Exploring socially mixed neighborhoods*. Boston, MA: Architectural Press/Elsevier.

Tan, E. (2006) 'The Copenhagen experience: what the pedestrian wants'. *NovaTerra* 6(1): 31–5.

Tapscott, D., and Williams, A. D. (2006) *Wikinomics: How mass collaboration changes everything*. London: Atlantic.

Taylor, D. (2009) *The Environment and the People in American Cities, 1600s–1900s: Disorder, inequality, and social change*. Durham, NC, and London: Duke University Press.

Thomas, J., and Ritzdorf, M. (eds) (1997) *Urban Planning and the African American Community: In the shadows*. Thousand Oaks, CA: Sage.

Thompson, C. (2002) 'Urban open space in the 21st century'. *Landscape and Urban Planning* 60(2): 59–72.

Tides Foundation (2007) *The Right to the City*. San Francisco, CA: Tides Foundation.

Transport and Environment (2011) *Funding for transport infrastructure in the new EU budget*. Brussels: Transport and Environment. Available at: www.transportenvironment.org/publications/funding-transport-infrastructure-new-eu-budget [Accessed 30 November 2012]

Transportation Alternatives (2004) *Streets for People: Your Guide to Winning Safer and Quieter Streets*. New York, NY: Transportation Alternatives. Available at: http://transalt.org/resources/streets4people/ [Accessed 30 November 2012]

— (2009) *I Walk in My Street: A guide to planning successful pedestrian streets in New York City*. New York, NY: Transportation Alternatives. Available at: www.transalt.org/files/newsroom/reports/2009/walk_in_my_street.pdf [Accessed 30 November 2012]

Tuan, Y. (1974) *Topophilia: A study of environmental perception, attitudes, and values*. Englewood Cliffs, NJ: Prentice Hall.

TUC (2008) *A Green and Fair Future: For a just transition to a low carbon economy*. Touchstone pamphlet 3. London: Trades Union Congress. Available at: www.tuc.org.uk/touchstone/justtransition/greenfuture.pdf [Accessed 30 November 2012]

Tully, J. (1995) *Strange Multiplicity*. Cambridge: Cambridge University Press.

Turner, J. C., Hogg, M. A., Oates, P. J., Reicher, S. D., and Wetherell, M. S. (1987) *Rediscovering the Social Group: A self-categorization theory*. Oxford and New York: Basil Blackwell.

Umemoto, K. (2001) 'Walking in another's shoes: epistemological challenges in participatory planning'. *Journal of Planning Education and Research* 21(1): 17–31.

— and Igarashi, H. (2009) 'Deliberative planning in a multicultural milieu'. *Journal of Planning Education and Research* 29(1): 39–53.

USDA Economic Research Service (2009) 'Food Security in the United States: measuring household food security'. Last modified 16 November 2009. Available at: www.ers.usda.gov/topics/food-nutrition-assistance/food-security-in-the-us/measurement.aspx [Accessed 30 November 2012]

Uyesugi, J. L., and Shipley, R. (2005) 'Visioning diversity: planning Vancouver's multicultural communities'. *International Planning Studies* 10(3/4): 305–22.

Valiente-Neighbours, J. M. (2012) 'Mobility, embodiment, and scales: Filipino immigrant perspectives on local food'. *Agriculture and Human Values* 29: 531–41.

van Velden, B., and Reeves, D. (2010) 'Intercultural public spaces.' Presentation at the International Planning Conference, Christchurch, New Zealand, 20–23 April 2010.

Vazquez, L. (2009) 'Cultural competency: a critical skill set for the 21st century planner'. *Planetizen*, 21 December. Available at: www.planetizen.com/node/42164 [Accessed 30 November 2012]

Veenhoven, R. (1996) 'Happy life-expectancy: a comprehensive measure of quality-of-life in nations'. *Social Indicators Research* 39(1): 1–58.

Viney, S. (2011) 'Reuniting Cairo and its residents through better use of public space'. *Egypt Independent*, 23 September. Available at: www.egyptindependent.com/news/reuniting-cairo-and-its-residents-through-better-use-public-space [Accessed 30 November 2012]

von Weizsäcker, E. U., Lovins, A. B., and Lovins, L. H. (1997) *The Factor Four*. London: Earthscan.

Wackernagel, M., and Rees, W. (1996) *Our Ecological Footprint: Reducing human impact on the earth*. Gabriola Island, BC, Canada: New Society Publishers.

Walker, G. (2011) *Environmental Justice: Concepts, evidence and politics*. London: Routledge.

Wallace, M., and Moore Milroy, B. (1999) 'Intersecting claims: possibilities for planning in Canada's multicultural cities'. In: Fenster, T. (ed.) *Gender, Planning and Human Rights*. London: Routledge and Kegan Paul.

Warner, K. (2002) 'Linking local sustainability initiatives with environmental justice'. *Local Environment* 7(1): 35–47.

Washburn, R. F. (1978) 'Black underparticipation in wildland recreation: alternative explanations'. *Leisure Sciences* 1(2): 175–89.

Watson, D. (2009) 'Building bike cities'. *Sierra*, March/April: 40–1.

Weaver, S. (2007) *Creating Great Visitor Experiences: A guide for museums, parks, zoos, gardens and libraries*. Walnut Creek, CA: Left Coast Press.

Westover, T. (1986) 'Park use and perceptions: gender differences'. *Journal of Parks and Recreation* 4(2): 1–8.

White, T. J. (2007) 'Sharing resources: the global distribution of the ecological footprint'. *Ecological Economics* 64(2): 402–10.

Whyte, W. H. (1980) *The Social Life of Small Urban Spaces*. Washington, DC: The Conservation Foundation.

Wightman, A. (2010) *The Poor Had No Lawyers: Who owns Scotland and how they got it*. Edinburgh: Birlinn.

Wilde-Ramsing, J., Oldenziel, J., and Freeman, C. (2011) 'What businesses should know about the OECD guidelines'. *Ethical Corporation*. Available at: www.ethicalcorp.com/governance-regulation/what-business-should-know-about-oecd-guidelines? [Accessed 30 November 2012]

Wilkinson R., and Pickett, K. (2009) *The Spirit Level: Why equality is better for everyone*. London: Allen Lane.

— and De Vogli, R. (2010) 'Equality, sustainability, and quality of life'. *British Medical Journal* 341: 1138–40.

Winne, M. (2008) *Closing the Food Gap: Resetting the table in the land of plenty*. Boston, MA: Beacon Press.

Winson, A. 1993. *The Intimate Commodity*. Toronto, Canada: Garamond Press.

Wood, P., and Landry, C. (2007) *The intercultural city: Planning for diversity advantage*. London: Earthscan.

World Commission on Environment and Development (1987) *Our Common Future*. Oxford: Oxford University Press.

Wright, L., and Montezuma, R. (2004) 'Reclaiming public space: the economic, environmental, and social impacts of Bogota's transformation'. Paper presented to 'Walk 21-V Cities for People', Fifth International Conference on Walking in the 21st Century, Copenhagen, Denmark, 9–11 June.

Wrigley, N. (2002) '"Food deserts" in

British cities: policy context and research Priorities'. *Urban Studies* 39(11): 2029–40.

Wu, F. (2010) 'Gated and packaged suburbia: packaging and branding Chinese suburban residential development'. *Cities* 27(5): 385–96.

WWF (2012) *Living Planet Report: Biodiversity, biocapacity and better choices*. Gland, Switzerland: WWF International.

Yakini, M. (2010) 'Building local power: communities take back their food system'. Presentation at 2010 Community Food Security Conference. Available at: http://vimeo.com/16075527 [Accessed 30 November 2012]

Young, I. (1990) *Justice and the Politics of Difference*. Princeton, NJ: Princeton University Press.

Zidansek, A. (2007) 'Sustainable development and happiness in nations'. *Energy* 32(6): 891–97.

Zukin, S. (2010) *Naked City: The death and life of authentic urban spaces*. New York, NY: Oxford University Press, pp. 125–59.

INDEX

About Zed Books

Zed Books is a critical and dynamic publisher, committed to increasing awareness of important international issues and to promoting diversity, alternative voices and progressive social change. We publish on politics, development, gender, the environment and economics for a global audience of students, academics, activists and general readers. Run as a co-operative, Zed Books aims to operate in an ethical and environmentally sustainable way.

Find out more at:

www.zedbooks.co.uk

For up-to-date news, articles, reviews and events information visit:

http://zed-books.blogspot.com

To subscribe to the monthly Zed Books e-newsletter, send an email headed 'subscribe' to:

marketing@zedbooks.net

We can also be found on **Facebook**, **ZNet**, **Twitter** and **Library Thing**.